Suffragist, Peace Crank, and Preacher

Suffragist, Peace Crank, and Preacher

The Extraordinary Life and Message of Maude Royden

EDITED BY
KERRY WALTERS

☙PICKWICK *Publications* · Eugene, Oregon

SUFFRAGIST, PEACE CRANK, AND PREACHER
The Extraordinary Life and Message of Maude Royden

Copyright © 2025 Kerry Walters. All rights reserved. Except for brief quotations in critical publications or reviews, no part of this book may be reproduced in any manner without prior written permission from the publisher. Write: Permissions, Wipf and Stock Publishers, 199 W. 8th Ave., Suite 3, Eugene, OR 97401.

Pickwick Publications
An Imprint of Wipf and Stock Publishers
199 W. 8th Ave., Suite 3
Eugene, OR 97401

www.wipfandstock.com

PAPERBACK ISBN: 979-8-3852-4106-4
HARDCOVER ISBN: 979-8-3852-4107-1
EBOOK ISBN: 979-8-3852-4108-8

Cataloguing-in-Publication data:

Names: Walters, Kerry [editor]. | Royden, A. Maude (Agnes Maude), 1876–1956 [author].

Title: Suffragist, peace crank, and preacher : the extraordinary life and message of Maude Royden / by Kerry Walters.

Description: Eugene, OR: Pickwick Publications, 2025 | Includes bibliographical references and index.

Identifiers: ISBN 979-8-3852-4106-4 (paperback) | ISBN 979-8-3852-4107-1 (hardcover) | ISBN 979-8-3852-4108-8 (ebook)

Subjects: LCSH: Royden, A. Maude (Agnes Maude), 1876–1956. | Suffragists—Great Britain. | Women in the Anglican Communion—England—History—20th century. | Feminism—Religious aspects—Christianity. | Women in Christianity—History Sources. | Peace—Religious aspects—Christianity.

Classification: BT83.55 W385 2025 (paperback) | BT83.55 (ebook)

11/17/25

Contents

Introduction: The Irreplaceable Maude Royden   1

PART 1. THE "GREAT ADVENTURE" OF PEACE

Obedience to Peace	37
The Great Adventure	45
Poetics of Peace	55
Feminism and Militarism	60
"A Weapon We Haven't Got"	68

PART 2. "WOMEN ARE HUMAN BEINGS"

Women and Work	75
A Motherhood Endowment	81
Marriage and Morality	88
Sacrament of Sexual Love	92
The Church's Untouchables	100
The Anti-Feminist's Last Ditch	108

PART 3. THE CHURCH IS "CHRIST'S SOCIETY"

The Church	121
What Hinders the Reunion of the Churches?	135
Churchmanship and Discipleship	141
The Heart of Worship	147
Must the Church Always Be Last?	152
Church and Politics	154
Sacramentalism	160

PART 4. THEOLOGY "CAN NEVER REST CONTENT"

Orthodoxy's Quest	173
Incarnation	176
Atonement	189
Personal Survival	201
A Soft Theological Revolution	207

PART 5. "CALLED TO THE HIGH ASCENT"

Being Christian	215
What Is Prayer?	221
Christ's Law	225
Divine Personhood	229
God's Non-Coercive Love	234
Two Sides, Same Truth	243
Jesus the Poet	248
A Vice of the Mind	253
Pagan Virtues and Christian Graces	258

PART 6. "FROM THE BEGINNING THERE WERE THREE OF US"

Selections from *A Threefold Cord*	269
For Further Reading	285
Index	287

Introduction:
The Irreplaceable Maude Royden

> She has devoted herself to religious and social, rather than political work, but her activities touch secular affairs and moral issues. She represents as effectually as anyone the conscience and the moral sense of the community, and her piety is charged with a modern spirit and a freedom from cant that are always refreshing and sometimes a little startling.[1]

ON JUNE 28, 2019, a handful of people assembled in front of Frankby Hall, once the palatial home of Liverpool's wealthiest shipbuilder, to dedicate a historical blue plaque to Agnes Maude Royden. Nearly a century earlier, author Frances Parkinson Keyes, never one prone to hyperbole, praised her as "the best-known woman preacher in the world."[2] That was true, but not the whole truth. As the plaque announced, Royden was also a "suffragist, pacifist and first campaigner for the ordination of women."

Royden first gained recognition—and notoriety—shortly before World War I as an ardent campaigner for equal treatment of women under the law and in the marketplace. Women, she insisted, have an "especial contribution to give, not only to the practical affairs of life, but to its thinking and to its idealism."[3]

Once the war erupted, her efforts turned to pacifism, a position that proved even more unpopular with many of her fellow countrymen than the suffrage movement. Royden considered her opposition to war a

---

1. A. G. Gardiner, *Certain People of Importance* (London: Dent & Sons, 1929), 196.
2. Frances Parkinson Keyes, "Torchbearers to Humanity," *Good Housekeeping* 86:1 (Jan. 1928), 90.
3. A. Maude Royden, *Women at the World's Crossroads* (New York: Womans, 1922), 94–95.

natural outgrowth of her advocacy for women's rights. The spirit of militarism, she believed, was antithetical to feminism.

Toward the end of the war, Royden discovered yet a third way to campaign for women's rights, and it proved to be the one most important to her for years. A devout Christian and lifelong Anglican, Royden became convinced that the Church of England's refusal to allow women to participate meaningfully in ecclesial governance, much less to preach or be ordained, was both immoral and contrary to the inclusiveness practiced by Jesus. Subordination based on gender, she argued, was contrary to the spirit of genuine Christianity. Yet the church seemed determined to go its own way.

In the 1920s and early 1930s, Royden preached at two non-Anglican churches, attracting huge congregations in both, lectured throughout North America and Asia, and published a steady stream of articles and books that earned her an international reputation as a popular theologian and champion of women's rights. Her fame only deepened the distaste traditionalists had for her liberalizing and inclusive message.

Royden died nearly forty years before the Church of England finally got around to ordaining women, and by that time she was nearly forgotten by all but a handful of historians. As one of her closest friends remarked, "After her death, it was almost as though no trace remained. She was an irreplaceable personality, you see. She had to be there."[4]

Royden is gone, but it's not true that no trace of her remains. She left behind a body of work that at one and the same time offers insightful thoughts about ethical and religious concerns and gives us at least a feel for the vibrant person she was. Strength, determination, wit, sincerity, and above all a deep respect for women and men are traits that come through clearly in her writing. She was indeed, as another of her admiring contemporaries put it, "born for the pulpit and the spiritual life."[5]

Royden's early championing of women's rights in general and priestly ordination in particular prepared the ground for the reforms she didn't live to see, but her lively writings on feminism, pacifism, and Christianity still speak to us today. In fact, in a time when women's rights are being challenged, war and rumors of war are on the rise, and Christianity in

---

4. Daisy Dobson, quoted in Sheila Fletcher, *Maude Royden: A Life* (Oxford: Basil Blackwell, 1989), 289. Dobson was Royden's private secretary. She compiled the only other anthology of Royden's writing: a calendar book offering an inspirational quotation for every day of the year, entitled *Consider the Days* (New York: Womans, 1942).

5. Gardiner, *Certain People of Importance*, 194.

English-speaking countries is in crisis, her voice is just as relevant now as it was during her lifetime. She is truly irreplaceable.

Early Years

Maude Royden was born on 23 November 1876 into a family that exemplified Victorian success and respectability. Her father, Thomas Royden, was one of the wealthiest shipbuilders in Liverpool. When he died in 1917, he left behind a fortune, a palatial mansion called Frankby Hall, and a history of public service: lord mayor of Liverpool, member of Parliament, and high sheriff of Cheshire. In recognition of his accomplishments, Edward VII raised him to the baronetcy in 1905.

Maude, in short, grew up in a privileged family, surrounded from birth by a small army of servants. Unlike other social reformers of her day, she never had to worry about money. First her father and later her elder brother Thomas, who inherited the baronetcy and became chairman of Cunard Line, were happy to bankroll her.

The youngest of eight children and the sixth daughter, she was always called "Maude," a name she thought ugly, never "Agnes." As the last-born in a large and sometimes hectic household, she felt neglected at times by her exhausted mother and workaholic father. Additionally, she was unable to join many of the rough-and-tumble physical games enjoyed by her siblings. Although the condition wouldn't be definitively diagnosed until X-ray technology became available some years later, Maude was born with dislocated hips. Although easily treatable today, there was no effective remedy at the time for her disability. So she endured discomfort, decreased mobility, and later in life, suffering from arthritis and rheumatism, chronic pain. As an adult she frequently walked with a cane.

Although she rarely spoke of her condition, Royden's disability profoundly affected her view of herself as well as her religious sensibilities. She believed that it made marriage impossible for her: what man would want to marry a woman who limped when she walked? Her condition also provoked religious questions in her from an early age: why would the God of love preached from the pulpit every Sunday inflict a child with disability (not to mention the ugly name of "Maude")? Finally, she suspected that her disability might've encouraged in her a special sensitivity to others marginalized by physical infirmity or other hardships such as economic poverty or prejudice.

But by all accounts, Royden's childhood, despite her infirmity, was a relatively happy one. Her intelligence was recognized and encouraged, and when she asked as a teenager to attend boarding school, her parents readily agreed. It was an unusual request in the contexts of both her class and her family—none of her sisters had any desire for further education. But Maude was an unusual child. It might've also been seen as a convenient way to lessen the mayhem of a household of children. So, in 1893, she was packed off to Gloucestershire's Cheltenham Ladies College, some 140 miles south of Frankby Hall.

Founded in 1854 with eighty-two pupils, the College had a student population of six hundred by the time Royden arrived. Housed in an impressive Victorian mansion with plenty of wooden paneling, arches, and stained glass windows, Cheltenham Ladies College had a distinctly church-like feel to it. This suited Maude. It appealed, she said many years later, to her "sense of beauty," offering her "my first real religious experience."[6] Her three years at the College were happy ones. She proved to be a good student academically, but also enjoyed a lively social life, was active in school theatrics and, despite her disability, was extremely fond of dancing. She was also pretty liberal in sharing with classmates the funds regularly supplied by her father.

From Oxford to Little Luffenham

With her parents' probably somewhat bemused approval, Royden enrolled in 1896 as a history student at Lady Margaret Hall, Oxford. Founded only eighteen years earlier to serve female students, Lady Margaret was, formally, one of the constituent colleges of Oxford University. In practice, however, university women were still treated as second class citizens who enjoyed no formal academic standing in the university. Although allowed to attend lectures and sit final exams to determine their rank upon completion of their studies, they weren't permitted to receive degrees—one of the first instances of gender discrimination to genuinely irk Royden.[7]

While at Oxford, she gained a reputation for loving her social life more than her studies. She threw herself into theatrics, and her talents were evidently admired because she landed leading roles—Romeo and Shylock—in at least two plays. Additionally, her memory was prodigious,

---

6. Margot Oxford (Asquith), ed., *Myself When Young* (London: Muller, 1938), 366.
7. It took another quarter-century before Oxford granted degrees to women.

enabling her to learn lines with ease. She also participated in the Oxford Students' Debating Society, although its back-and-forth exchanges came harder for her than performing on stage in dramatic productions. And she made two lifelong friends, Evelyn Gunter and Kathleen Courtney, both of whom would be active in the women's movement.

Maude finished her education at Lady Margaret Hall in 1899, graduating with the equivalent of a second class degree; she was disappointed but, given her involvement in extracurricular activities, not terribly surprised. Returning home to Liverpool, she found herself at loose ends, particularly since her two best friends had snagged what Royden considered to be fruitful career opportunities. Evelyn Gunter took a post with the Oxford Extension Delegacy, the administrative branch of the university's relatively new program for non-traditional students. Kathleen Courtney took herself to London to work at a settlement house.

The settlement movement, launched in 1884 by Church of England priest Samuel Barnett, aimed to place graduates of Oxford and Cambridge in some of England's worst city slums to live among the poor, teach them life skills, and expose them to the benefits of culture. Barnett's "bridge of personal service" to help the poor elevate themselves was inescapably patronizing, even though the young men and women who served in the settlements were genuinely well-intentioned. Coming from privileged backgrounds, they were also genuinely shocked by the squalor, violence, and despair they witnessed, not to mention the personal antagonism they sometimes encountered.

Students at both Cheltenham College and Lady Margaret Hall were encouraged by their tutors to participate in the settlement movement. Maude certainly wanted to follow Kathleen, partly out of a sincere desire to serve but also from an equally ardent wish to escape the tedium of Frankby Hall. But her mother was unwell—apparently Mrs. Royden suffered from depression—and Maude's older sisters were tired of bearing all the burden of caring for her. So, for now, it was Maude's turn. She was stuck at home.

It was around this time that she began to think seriously about the role of religion in her life. Although the beauty of Cheltenham's architecture had prompted what she called her first religious experience, she no longer enjoyed the easy certainty of her childhood when it came to her beliefs. Like many university students then and now, she went through a period of skepticism while at Oxford, even referring to herself as an agnostic. But at the same time, ritual in the high church tradition moved and attracted her. Beauty as a route to the divine would become a constant theme in her later writing and preaching.⁸ It was also what, in these early years, attracted her to liturgically rich Roman Catholicism. As she later wrote, "It is because of Beauty that, at the worst, I have never disbelieved in God, and it has been the care for beauty in the Roman Catholic Church that has sometimes made me homesick for it."⁹

Oxford, of course, was the home of the Tractarian Movement, which in the 1830s, led by Edward Pusey and John Henry Newman, sought to infuse a Catholic sensibility into Anglican liturgy and theology; several of its luminaries, including most famously Newman, eventually joined the Roman communion. Maude read Newman's *Apologia*, his autobiographical account of his road to Rome, while she was at Oxford—she gushingly wrote in a letter to Kathleen of her "hero worship of this saint of God"—and began worshipping at a church shepherded by the Cowley Brothers, whose Anglo-Catholic services introduced her to plainsong. "I felt as if my soul had been *born* there!" she reported.¹⁰

At Oxford and back home at Frankby Hall, Maude went through something of a religious crisis, seesawing between her cradle Anglicanism and a rather romanticized attraction to Roman Catholicism. Visiting Italy in the spring of 1900 with one of her sisters, she was alternately enchanted by the beauty of Milan's ecclesial art and repulsed by what she saw as rampant superstition in Rome. But despite her mixed responses, her friends Kathleen and Evelyn were convinced—and terribly concerned—that Maude was likely to convert to Catholicism. Although they wanted her to be happy and pledged to support her if she went over to Rome, abandoning the Church of England for Rome simply wasn't the respectable thing for members of Royden's social class to do.

That October, still struggling to get her religious bearings, Maude at last began doing something she considered worthwhile: she commenced working at Liverpool's Victoria Women's settlement house. It wasn't London, but at least it was something. Another concession: unlike many volunteers, she didn't initially reside on site, but instead, at the insistence of her parents, lived at home. It wasn't until nearly a year later that she

---

8. Indeed, she devoted an entire book to it: A. Maude Royden, *Beauty in Religion* (London: Putnam's Sons, 1923).

9. A. Maude Royden (Mrs. Hudson Shaw), *A Threefold Cord* (New York: Macmillan, 1948), 10.

10. Maude to Kathleen Gunter (16 April 1903), quoted in Fletcher, *Maude Royden*, 26, 27.

actually moved into the house, a dreary, cramped place that struggled to find living space for five residents plus a dispensary and basement classroom.

Maude's eighteen months of settlement work were both physically and emotionally grueling, and by the end of them she suffered a breakdown.[11] But she credited her painful yet eye-opening experiences working with impoverished mothers, many of whom were married to abusive husbands, some of whom turned to drink out of sheer despair and weariness (she claimed she'd drink too if she had to live like them), as seedbed for her later involvement in the suffrage movement.

By the summer of 1901, Evelyn Gunter had grown so concerned about Maude's religious indecision, no doubt exacerbated by the grind of her settlement house work, that she arranged for her friend to meet with the Reverend Hudson Shaw, one of the star lecturers in the Oxford University Extension program of adult education. This meeting proved to be one of the most significant in her life, inaugurating a deeply loving platonic relationship that would last until Shaw's death in 1944. At their first meeting, Shaw, seventeen years Maude's senior, patiently listened to her religious concerns and then gently advised her to "let the Eternal Problem rest a while. I can see you are tired of never-ending questionings. After all, God will be with you, whether you remain Anglican or must find rest with Rome."[12]

Shortly before her breakdown, Maude consulted Shaw again, this time about whether she should remain at Victoria House. Sensing that she needed a change of pace, and probably because he was already falling in love with her, Shaw suggested that she join him in his South Luffenham parish in the East Midlands, sharing (on an unsalaried basis) some of his pastoral duties and serving as a companion for his invalid wife Effie. Maude arrived there in early 1902 and stayed for three years.

Effie Shaw's invalidism was psychological rather than physical; she most likely suffered from a form of schizophrenia. Chronically withdrawn, riddled with anxiety, subject to periods of black depression, and

---

11. In *Threefold Cord*, Royden claims that her breakdown was caused by "the fact that my lameness had been diagnosed, by a number of eminent orthopedists, as hysteria and, X-rays not being then in common use, I was told I could walk well if I chose. I couldn't, but naturally I tried, being a little troubled by the fear that I could 'if I chose,' and that I had been making a fuss about nothing" (13). One suspects her orthopedists' cruel counsel was the tipping point, after months of settlement work exhaustion, rather than the source, of her breakdown.

12. Royden, *Threefold Cord*, 10.

repulsed by physical intimacy, her marriage with Hudson was sexless after the birth of their only child,[13] a traumatic event that nearly killed her and put her in an emotional tailspin for the next two years.

Although initially unsettled by Effie's strangeness (notwithstanding her claim a half-century later that she loved her at first sight), Maude soon established a relationship with her that eventually graduated from caregiver to companion and friend. As the emotional attachment between Maude and Shaw grew—she tells us that they finally confessed their love for one another in 1905—Effie gave it her unqualified blessing. At least according to Royden, Effie was incapable of jealousy; in fact, she seemed relieved that Shaw finally received the unqualified (albeit chaste) love she was unable to give him. "She was glad that Hudson should have something at least of what he needed: she was glad that I should. She understood our deepest need and met it without effort, with the perfection that can only come from perfect love."[14] The "threefold cord" that bound Effie, Maude, and Shaw together lasted until Effie's death four decades later.

Maude's time assisting in Shaw's rural parish seems to have helped her resolve her religious indecision. She recommitted herself to the Church of England. But she soon also felt herself stagnating intellectually. "Much as I loved them [Effie and Shaw], I strained at the leash."[15] Shaw, perhaps realizing that he'd lose her if he tried to keep her exclusively at South Luffenham, used his standing with the Oxford University Extension program to get her appointed a traveling lecturer. She was one of the first women so employed, even though the vast majority of the Extension's adult learners were women. Although initially a bit intimidated, especially since Shaw was such a popular lecturer that she doubted she could measure up to him, she soon discovered that people were interested in hearing what she had to say. Soon her English literature courses—"Selected Plays of Shakespeare" and "Shakespeare's Women," among others—were hits, and Maude was traveling north and south to teach them. In 1905 she relocated to Oxford, a more convenient location for her Extension work. But she maintained close contact with the Shaws.

---

13. Their son Bernard, who enlisted at the beginning of World War I, was killed in early 1917.

14. Royden, *Threefold Cord*, 27.

15. Royden, *Threefold Cord*, 25.

Championing Women's Rights

In the decade before the First World War, Royden[16] eased away from her Extension teaching to throw herself into the suffrage movement. From the very start, her fight for women's rights had everything to do with her Christian faith. Christ, she argued, makes no distinction between men and women in the Scriptures. Neither should a nation that calls itself Christian, much less the church. As her biographer notes, "the suffrage fight became for her a passionate revolt against the double moral standard conventional in a 'Christian' society."[17] Her religious commitment distinguished her from many of her fellow suffragists.

Like everyone who championed women's rights, including her friends Kathleen and Evelyn, Royden believed passionately that members of her sex deserved the right to vote. But the movement, and her involvement in it, was about much more than simple enfranchisement. It sought to improve conditions for working women, to redress the societal power imbalance between men and women, to lobby for material support for mothers, and to do away with the double moral standard that turned a blind eye to male promiscuity while censuring the least public expression of sexual desire in women. Along with other feminists of her day, Royden was especially focused on eliminating prostitution and sexual slavery.

She came to the movement rather late, when she was thirty years old. The Women's Social and Political Union (WSPU), founded by Emmeline Pankhurst, had been agitating for women's rights in England for nearly a decade. Its tactics, however, had become increasingly violent. By 1905, the public heckling of unsympathetic politicians by WSPU members was a common practice, and in the five years before the war, confrontations with police as well as property destruction—ripping up golf courses, defacing National Gallery of Art paintings, putting acid in mailboxes, bombings, physical assaults on political figures—were part and parcel of the WSPU's direct action for drawing public attention to its cause. During this period, more than one thousand of its members, including Pankhurst and her daughter Sylvia, were jailed.

Royden was both temperamentally and morally opposed to WSPU tactics. The militants, she said in a 1911 interview, "were throwing away one of the great arguments for the cause of women—that government

---

16. It seems appropriate at this point to cease referring to Royden by her Christian name.

17. Fletcher, *Maude Royden*, 80.

is not based on force."[18] So she chose to align herself with the more law-abiding National Union of Women's Suffrage Societies (NU), founded by Millicent Garrett Fawcett in 1897. It wasn't long before her speaking talents, honed by her work with the Oxford Extension, were recognized by the NU, which then regularly sent her out to address audiences, both sympathetic and unsympathetic, on the struggle for equal rights for women. She also discovered during this period that she could write, and was soon contributing articles to *Common Cause*, the NU's official organ. By 1909 her influence as a speaker and author had grown to such an extent that she was named its editor, remaining so for the next five years. Upon taking the reins, she gave *Common Cause* a new banner: "WOMEN'S SUFFRAGE: THE COMMON CAUSE OF HUMANITY." This reflected her conviction that what the feminist movement was at its very core was the struggle for women "to be classed—finally—with human beings." It was a recommendation and celebration of humanism. In fact, given this goal, she went so far as to claim that the word "feminism" was somewhat misleading.[19]

In 1911, Royden was elected to the NU's executive committee and found herself busier than ever. In addition to crisscrossing England to lecture (more than 250 in 1912 alone!), she embarked on her first speaking tour outside of England: a whirlwind trip to the United States. She lectured in Philadelphia, New York, and Boston on suffragism but also on some of the topics in English literature she'd taught in the Oxford Extension program. Back home, she continued lobbying tirelessly for equal workplace opportunity for women and eagerly collaborated with other suffragists and social reformers to put an end to the economic inequality that forced some women to earn their living as sex workers. Prostitution, she wrote, "is the ultimate instance of exploitation. There is nothing comparable to it in the history of the world."[20] What she found particularly objectionable was the cultural hypocrisy about sexuality that surrounded prostitution. "Respectable" women were taught, perniciously in her view, to dislike or even be repulsed by sex. Men, for their part, publicly extolled the "purity" of "good women" like their wives while secretly

---

18. *New York Evening Post* (27 October 1911), quoted in Fletcher, *Maude Royden*, 91.

19. A. Maude Royden, *Common Cause* (1 June 1911), quoted in Fletcher, *Maude Royden*, 85.

20. A. Maude Royden, *Women and the Sovereign State* (London: Headley Bros., 1917), 53.

visiting prostitutes to satisfy their frustrated sexual urges. One can't help but think that Royden must have had Effie Hudson's aversion to sexual intimacy in the back of her mind when she made this point.

In 1918, toward the end of the War, Royden condemned the British government's establishment of so-called *Maisons Tolerées*, officially sanctioned brothels intended for soldiers serving in France. The goal of this ill-conceived program was to reduce the spread of venereal disease, and it was endorsed, even if reluctantly, by many clergy. Royden was especially indignant when some women, out of what she took to be misplaced patriotism, also supported it. "To any woman who believed the sacrifice to be necessary," she thundered, "I would say that she ought herself to volunteer! The men who urge regulated prostitution on the grounds of national necessity ought to invite their wives and daughters to fill the places left vacant by the women who are worn out!"[21] The *Maisons Tolerées* program was soon discontinued.

Another campaign in which Royden enthusiastically participated was the push for a "national endowment" for mothers. Royden argued that raising children was one of the most important jobs any citizen could undertake. Most of the burden fell upon mothers who sacrificed, out of love as well as a maternal sense of duty, the opportunity to have professions outside the home. Royden recommended that they be paid a stipend by the government for their services. The payment was in no way to be considered welfare or charity. Instead, Royden envisioned it as bona fide wages for a job crucial to society's well-being.

Believing as she did that equality between the sexes was founded on Christ's teaching, Royden helped to found the Church League for Women's Suffrage in 1909. Three years later, in a speech at Queen's Hall before an assembly that included several Church of England bishops, she insisted that the "franchise" she and her fellow Christian suffragists asked for was nothing less than membership in the kingdom of God in which women and men were seen as equals. Her insistence on tying the struggle for women's rights to her faith sat poorly with some of her fellow suffragists and even less so, although for different reasons, with many of her co-religionists. William Temple, future archbishop of Canterbury but serving as a London parish priest in 1915, regretted the formation of the Church League for Women's Suffrage and refused to allow meetings of it

---

21. Quoted by Joseph Fort Newton, "Maude Royden: The Story of a Great Woman's Great Opportunity," *Century Magazine* (Mar. 1928) 566–67.

in his church—this despite the fact that he proclaimed himself a "keen suffragist."

The tension between Royden's religious sensibilities and secular feminism came to a head when England entered the cataclysmic conflict idealistically misnamed at the time as the War to End All Wars. The NU supported the war effort, albeit not as enthusiastically as Pankhurst's WSPU, and Royden, by this time a committed Christian pacifist, found herself increasingly alienated from the organization to which she'd given nearly a decade of her life. Slowly and reluctantly pulling away from her association with it, she became secretary of the newly formed pacifist Fellowship of Reconciliation (FOR) in late 1914. Just a couple of months later she resigned from the NU to throw in her lot with a more compatible organization, the Women's International League for Peace and Freedom, founded like the FOR in response to the outbreak of war. For the next few years, Royden would combine her concern for women's rights with her opposition to war and militarism. So far as she was concerned, they were cut from the same cloth.

Peace Crank

Royden's journey to pacifism, like her one to feminism, took a few years. While at Oxford, the Boer War made little impression on her, even though Kathleen Courtney's brother had been killed in it. Throughout most of her twenties she was perfectly content with the notion that British colonialism was an essential civilizing force in the world. Indeed, as we'll see, she never quite abandoned the conviction. But by late 1914, her study of Scripture had persuaded her that war was antithetical to Christ's teachings and participation in it antithetical to Christian living. Moreover, she knew that war's primary victims were always women and children. In its own way, it was just another form of oppression against women. She kept waiting for better known voices than hers to speak out against the war, but none did. So she believed she had to.

Royden was naively unprepared for the hostile responses she received when she did. Clergymen, including her beloved Cowley Fathers, tried to convince her that the war was an apocalyptic battle between good and evil that Christians were obliged to rally behind. A Church of England bishop gently suggested that in denouncing war, she was trying to rush God's plan. "Even God," he wrote her, "can only get out of each age the morality of which the age is capable."²² Others were more interested in vilifying than persuading her. The *Daily Express* called her a "Peace Crank," insisting that her defense of pacifism was "practically a plea for national suicide" and intimating that she belonged behind bars.²³ The resistance to her position was so intense and so widespread that she asked herself more than once if she could possibly be right and everyone else mistaken. But she drew strength from the Gospels, where Jesus's repudiation of violence is unquestionable—"put away your sword!" (Matt 25:52)—despite the best efforts of churchmen to qualify it.

The proposal of Royden's that especially infuriated the public came from her 1915 pamphlet *The Great Adventure*. England, she wrote, should've disarmed instead of getting sucked into the war. True, such a move might have been viewed as a reprehensible neutrality that refused to come to the aid of smaller nations threatened by the "Hun." But it may also have provided a world-changing example of nonviolence that could've forestalled the war in the first place. Contrary to the *Daily Express*, it wasn't national suicide that Royden was advising, but, as she soberly said, national crucifixion for the sake of peace. Nations have been willing to kill and die for victory in war. Are none, she asked, willing to die for peace? War calls for great courage on the battlefield; it's an adventure that quickens the blood and elicits heroism. But the struggle for peace, said Royden, is an adventure too, the "great adventure," and calls for courageous heroics on the part of its champions.

In the summer of 1915, Royden put her money where her mouth was. She'd already floated the idea of pacifists who would place themselves between opposing sides on battlefields, an uncanny anticipation, as we'll see, of the Peace Army she and Dick Sheppard tried to organize in the early 1930s. Now she collaborated with the FOR to organize a domestic version of it: a peace mission that would travel from the Midlands to London witnessing Christian pacifism along the way. Volunteers from several Christian denominations eagerly joined the mission. They walked the roads from town to town, accompanied by a horse-drawn wagon large enough to hold food supplies and sleeping places for some of the women. Because of her disability, Royden usually rode instead of

---

22. Bishop Arthur Foley Winnington-Ingram to Royden (28 January 1915), quoted in Fletcher, *Maude Royden*, 126. Winnington-Ingram, bishop of London (1901–39), was a prolific author and staunch supporter of World War I. He and Hudson Shaw would later clash over Royden's preaching in Shaw's parish of St. Boltoph's.

23. *Daily Express* (4 August 1915), quoted in Fletcher, *Maude Royden*, 126.

walked. When they neared a town or city, she and her companions would find a spot to camp and then hold a public prayer meeting followed by a lecture explaining the purpose of the mission. They would stay a day or two before moving on.

Initially they were met with curiosity or indifference. But as word about the mission spread, anger grew, especially among people who had sons and fathers at the Front. Moreover, the *Lusitania* had been torpedoed just a couple of months earlier, ratcheting up fury at Germany and renewed support for the war.

The resentment that had been building against the peace mission exploded when Royden and her companions arrived in the market town of Hinckley, located in the center of England. Word began to circulate among the locals that the missioners were all German spies. After a couple of nonviolent but ominous verbal confrontations, a large mob, estimated (and likely exaggerated) by police to be two or three thousand, attacked the mission's campsite. They tore down the tents, tipped over the wagon, and set it and anything else they could lay their hands on ablaze. Several of the rioters made as if to toss a couple of the missioners into the fire but were dissuaded at the last minute. A drunken man actually seized Royden by the throat as she knelt in prayer. The mob only dispersed when the flames began to die down. The traumatized missioners managed to make their way to the local police station where, in the wee hours of the morning, they were quickly and unceremoniously loaded onto an express train to London. They had displayed heroism on their great adventure, but it had ended disastrously and ignominiously.

Royden never forgot that night. Terrifying as it was, she always felt a certain sympathy for the mob—a testimonial to her capacity for compassion—appreciating that it saw the mission's witness for peace as a betrayal of loved ones fighting and dying in France. Nevertheless, she never regretted her opposition to the war nor her participation in the peace mission.

Still, after Hinckley, Royden was shaken. So was Hudson Shaw, who urged her to show more prudence in her defense of pacifism. (Shaw was a supporter of the war effort, even after the battlefield death of his and Effie's son. But he never tried to talk Royden out of her opposition to it.) For the remaining years of the war, she contented herself with writing and speaking against conscription, which commenced in January 1916, taking a nursing course in midwifery (although she never actually practiced) and exploring and writing about the effects of the war on women. Even though it inflicted grave economic and psychological hardship on wives whose soldier husbands were absent from home, Royden argued that it also showed the nation that women, to whom civilian employers turned to fill the gaps left by men, were perfectly capable of fully participating in England's economic life.

Challenging the Church's Caste System

Maude Royden took a line from Ecclesiastes (4:12), "a threefold cord is not quickly broken," to describe the bond of love between herself, Hudson Shaw, and Effie. It can just as easily name the three great commitments of her life: suffragism, pacifism, and women's ordination. All three were inseparably bound together. Her work in any one of them bled naturally into the others, and all three were firmly glued by her Christian commitment. But beginning around 1915, the struggle to break the Church of England's gender-based caste system became her abiding concern.

By then, Royden had been involved with the Church League for Women's Suffrage for seven years. She had served, in fact, as its first chairperson. The League's original goal, as its name suggested, was primarily to lobby for the right of women to vote. Its methods were tame enough, revolving around public prayer and education. Even so, detractors angrily denounced it. The dean of Westminster, for example, grumbled that "the name of the 'Church' has been usurped by militant fanatics!"[24]

Before long, the Church League's efforts broadened to include lobbying for a greater role for women in the church itself. In 1915, it launched a campaign against the Church of England's refusal to allow women to participate in ecclesial councils above the parish level. Women were the mainstays of the church, the League noted, both in the parish and on missions. It was absurd that they had no voice in higher governance, and the usual response from ecclesial authorities, a vague insistence that there were "fundamental reasons" against including them, was infuriatingly patronizing.

Maude had long thought that women deserved greater roles in the church, up to and including ordination. But the tipping point for her, the moment in which she began to devote herself to the cause of women's ordination, was reached in 1916.

---

24. Quoted in Brian Harrison, *Separate Spheres: The Opposition to Women's Suffrage in Britain* (New York: Holmes & Meier, 1978), 184.

In October of that year, the Church of England launched the National Mission of Repentance and Hope, an ambitious revival movement intended to boost the spirits of a war-weary England. Several women, including Royden, were asked to serve on its governing council. She was delighted to accept; it struck her as a step in the right direction. But then things went sour. The original plan had been for the "archbishop's messengers," revivalist speakers who would travel to churches across the land, to include women. But opposition was soon voiced. It wasn't proper for women to preach, critics said; they had no less standing in the church than any other layperson. (Actually, this was quite false; laymen could be readers, altar servers, collection plate stewards, and vestry members. Women could not.) Women were allowed to "lecture," but only at the steps of the chancel, not behind the pulpit; even better, just to be on the safe side, the recommendation was to confine them, if they insisted on lecturing, to church classrooms rather than consecrated sanctuaries. And then the final blow: the decision came down that it would be up to each bishop to decide if he'd allow women messengers to "lecture" in his diocese at all. Most of them wouldn't.

Royden was disgusted by all this, and in a white heat of rage whipped out one of her best pamphlets, *Women and the Church of England*, in which she famously demanded to know if women were "untouchables in the religion of Christ after all." Organized religion, she thundered, "has become profoundly undemocratic," particularly when it comes to women. "We find it intolerable that while the veriest little ragamuffin of a boy may 'serve' at the altar, women whom we revere as leaders, reverence as saints, are excluded."[25]

This rebuke of the church's powers-that-be was insulting enough to traditionalists. But even more offensive to them was the shocking fact that at least some members of the Church League wanted much more than permission for women to lecture; they wanted women actually to be allowed to take Holy Orders! The horrified *Church Times* was confident that "for any sane person, the thing is so absolutely grotesque that he must refuse to discuss it. The monstrous regiment of women in politics would be bad enough, but the monstrous regiment of priestesses would be a thousandfold worse."[26]

---

25. A. Maude Royden, *Women and the Church of England* (London: Allen & Unwin, 1916), 9, 4, 9–10.

26. *Church Times* (24 July 1914), quoted in Fletcher, *Maude Royden*, 143.

City Temple

In March 1917, Royden was invited by City Temple, one of London's most thriving nonconformist churches, to preach at one of its Sunday morning and evening services. Built in 1874, the Temple was known for its liberal religious tendencies. They were on full display in the invitation to Royden.

Temple parishioners were so impressed by her that they invited her back several more times that spring. The press and her fellow Anglicans were less enthusiastic. Newspapers sensationally predicted that pacifist Royden would preach "national suicide" from the pulpit (she didn't). Predictably, many members of the Church of England were alarmed, and some outraged, by the very idea of a woman preaching: hadn't that issue been settled? Others, even many of Royden's friends, thought it improper for an Anglican to participate in nonconformist worship services.

To those who disapproved of women preaching, Royden replied that because the Church of England refused to lead when it came to empowering women who felt called to ministry, someone else—namely herself—had to. To her acquaintances who worried she was turning her back on the Church of England, she insisted that she remained a loyal Anglican: "I am not a member of the City Temple Church. I have not been ordained or 'set apart' as a minister, pastor, or official of any kind; nor is it possible that I should be, seeing I am not a Congregationalist."[27] This was a bit disingenuous, because Royden functioned from the pulpit as if she *were* a church official, even if she wasn't formally one. But the point was that she saw no incompatibility between her cradle allegiance to Anglicanism and ministering to a nonconformist church, an ecumenical fluidity ahead of its time (and, truth to tell, still difficult for many Christians to swallow even today).

When Royden first visited City Temple, the church was between pastors. By the summer of her own appointment, the trustees had called Rev. Fort Newton, a young American Baptist who later became an Episcopal priest, to be their primary minister. Insisting that the workload was too much for a single person, Newton asked that Royden be offered the position of "pulpit assistant" as a condition of his accepting the call. Temple officials agreed and Royden was hired.

---

27. A. Maude Royden, letter to the *Challenge* (5 October 1917), quoted in Fletcher, *Maude Royden*, 174.

The initial description of her duties stipulated that she would officiate at one Sunday and one Thursday service a month. She was also to make herself available to offer pastoral counsel to Temple members, especially young women. Unsurprisingly, she soon began preaching more often and taking on a much heavier schedule of duties. Her relationship with Newton was everything she could've hoped for. Recognizing her talents and being unthreatened by them, he thought of her more as a co-pastor than an assistant. The two of them didn't see eye-to-eye on everything; Newton, for example, disagreed with Royden's pacifism. But they made a good team and the Temple flourished under their stewardship.

Royden was always captivating when she preached. She had the knack of speaking about faith, morality, Scripture, and even current events in terms that were both engaging and easy to follow. Drawing no doubt on her years of teaching for the Oxford Extension, her aim was for her parishioners to learn as well as to be spiritually edified. To that end, she introduced what came to be called the "after meeting" discussion, in which she would step away from the pulpit and invite discussion from the congregation about the day's sermon. It wasn't fair, she told them, for them to have to listen to her without the opportunity to respond. The practice took a bit of getting used to on the parishioners' part. But they soon came to love it for the democratizing and educating strategy it was. Fort Newton praised her pastoral skills in a 1928 article, long after both of them had left City Temple.

> An adept in theology, Miss Royden avoids its vocabulary, and rightly so, knowing that one hot tear on the cheek of God is more mighty to move us than all anemic abstractions. Instead, she deals with the old issues of faith as an educated, spiritually-minded woman in sensitive contact with life, inspired by a lofty faith and guided by a sanctified common sense. There is no "pious pap" in her preaching, no prettified rhetoric decorating a candied Christianity. She casts aside the "muffled Christianity" which [H. G.] Wells once described as the religion of the well-to-do classes, holding resignation to be "a detestable virtue," however canonical, if it means that worship is to be an opiate and the sermon a stick of candy. At once stimulating and provocative—at times provoking—it is no wonder that she shocked many of the staid, respectable folk when she made her advent in the City Temple.

war and a mother who died shortly after the child's birth. The second was a four-year-old Austrian lad, Friedrich Wolfe, whose growth was stunted by the horrible postwar deprivations he endured as a baby and toddler. She spoke of him in one of her Temple sermons.

> There is in my home a little Austrian boy. When he landed in this country a year ago he was 4 years old, and he had never walked. He was so rickety that he could not walk.... That little boy's face was like a little old man's. He had that terrible, anxious, harassed look that is pitiful on any human face, but is heartrending on a child's.... The mark is on his very soul. You cannot be starved for the first four years of your life and be just the same in your soul at the end of it.[31]

By her own admission, Royden wasn't the best of mothers. She was already in her forties and set in her ways when she adopted the two children. She was also extremely busy with a punishing workload, and so didn't devote as much time to them as she could've, a failure she regretted later in life. As a consequence, her relationship with Helen and Friedrich was never as warm as she would've wished.

By 1920, Royden felt it was time to move on from City Temple. She had enjoyed her time there, but was increasingly exhausted and had begun to suffer terrible migraines. Besides, Fort Newton had already left to take a position back in the States. Her intention all along had been to remain at the Temple only for a while. So in March 1920, three years almost to the day after she preached her first guest sermon there, she resigned her post as pulpit assistant. A new chapter, the most fruitful one of her entire life, opened almost immediately afterward.

The Fellowship Guild

Royden had known Anglican priest Percy Dearmer from her earliest days in London. Influenced by the Arts and Crafts Movement's emphasis on cultivating beauty in everyday life, Dearmer was a liturgist who strove in all the parishes he served to express the Christian message in poetical sermons, beautiful music, and appealing architecture. His two best known books, *The Parson's Handbook* (1899) and *The English Hymnal* (1906), aimed at encouraging priests to infuse beauty into their own parishes.

---

31. A. Maude Royden, *Political Christianity* (New York: Putnam's Sons, 1922), 11, 12.

Dearmer left parish ministry when war broke out in 1914 and with his first wife, Mabel White, joined an ambulance corps. The following year was an awful one for him. Mabel died in Serbia of typhus and one of their sons was killed in the Dardanelles campaign. Shocked and unmoored by the double loss, Dearmer drifted for a bit, working a few months with the YMCA in France, spending a year in India, and teaching at a seminary in the United States. Eventually he found himself longing to take up parish work again but wanted to do it his way. So when he heard that Royden had stepped down from City Temple, he contacted her with a proposal: why not start their own fellowship, one in which they would be free to experiment, unburdened by ecclesial restrictions from the Church of England?

Royden jumped at the prospect. She and Dearmer insisted to friends and critics alike that they weren't starting a new church, but instead organizing a faith community that would welcome people of all or no denominational backgrounds. It was to be called the Fellowship Guild.

The Guild's first service was held on Easter Sunday 1920 in a rented space in Kensington Town Hall. But after a modest beginning, the congregation, mushrooming to around one thousand, outgrew the venue. So the following year the Guild relocated to a huge, empty Congregationalist church in Eccleston Square. The place needed some work, but after much scrubbing and painting it was ready for use. It became Royden's pastoral home for the next sixteen years. It was called, appropriately, the Guildhouse.

The services Dearmer and Royden led on Sunday evenings were modifications of Anglican Evensong. There was plenty of Quaker-like silence for meditation and prayer, post-sermon discussions like the ones Royden had inaugurated at City Temple, and fabulous music, supervised by the conductor and hymnist Martin Shaw. Dearmer and Royden shared preaching and teaching duties, often organized around a "Five Quarters" system invented by Dearmer: a service lasting one hour and fifteen minutes divided into five sections devoted to music, readings, message, and so on. Artists, authors, scientists, and statesmen were often guest lecturers in the Five Quarters. Alfred Hitchcock spoke on film, for example, Osbert Sitwell on poetry, and Julian Huxley on birth control. In a typical service, there would be scriptural and non-scriptural selections from poets like Tennyson or playwrights like Euripides. Hudson Shaw was a regular visiting speaker, each time spellbinding his audience with the intrinsic interest of his topics and the skill of his delivery. The goal of

INTRODUCTION: THE IRREPLACEABLE MAUDE ROYDEN   23

the Guild, as one of its 1925 bulletins stated, was to "generate that moral energy and intellectual enthusiasm that will in the end remake the life of the people." The throughline of all Guildhouse services was Christ and his message, but Dearmer and Royden strove to create an atmosphere in which a wide gamut of opinions and ideas was welcome. Their goal, as the bulletin stated, was to be a "clearing-house of thought" in pursuit of "the good, the true, and the beautiful."[32]

People who visited the Guildhouse were struck by the joy displayed by its regular members, many of whom had found themselves either uninspired or unwelcome at more conventional Christian churches. Although there were many well-heeled visitors who visited the Guildhouse out of curiosity, most of the congregants were working folk; others lived on the edge of genteel poverty. As Royden herself said, "I never had a rich congregation."[33] An American visitor in 1928 rather snootily remarked that she found the building "crowded with a heterogeneous gathering, most of its members shabbily or at least plainly dressed."[34] More women than men were regulars at the Guildhouse's religious services, but there were plenty of events and regularly scheduled meetings throughout the entire week to attract both sexes. The Guild hosted a library, a branch of the League of Nations Union, a drama society and music club, and various study groups. It was, intentionally, as much a community center as a place of worship.

Given the wide range of guest speakers at the Guildhouse, it's obvious that political topics were often centerstage. But Royden insisted that Jesus's message—not to mention that of the prophets who came before him—was inevitably political because it was about justice, tolerance, equality, and love. She was also quite convinced that sometimes "good" Christians can be on the wrong side of a moral issue. Merely feeling strongly about a public policy was no guarantee of its truth, she argued, and she referenced support in the past from "good" Christians for practices such as slavery and child labor. The responsible pastor's role was to encourage deep reflection on the part of congregants about the political implications of their faith. But she appreciated that when it came to subjects about which people had strong views, it was unfair to expect a congregation to sit silently through sermons in which their own opinions

32. "Five Quarters" (1925), quoted in Fletcher, *Maude Royden*, 215.
33. Royden, *Threefold Cord*, 78.
34. Keyes, "Torchbearers to Humanity," 31.

couldn't be expressed. So the post-sermon discussions became even more important at the Guildhouse than they were at the Temple.

Royden herself defended the 1926 General Strike from the pulpit and frequently championed the League of Nations. She also interested the congregation in Albert Schweitzer's medical work in Lambarene, Gabon, and regularly collected money for his hospital there. This outreach particularly delighted Hudson Shaw, who considered Schweitzer a close friend and one of the noblest Christians he'd ever met. Royden's congregants were delighted in their turn when Schweitzer, on a visit to England, spoke at the Guildhouse to thank them personally for their generosity.

Royden's reputation throughout the 1920s brought her invitations from a number of different countries to visit and speak. She made a short trip to the United States in 1922 and a much more intensive one the following year, delivering seventy-five speeches to nearly sixty cities in just two months. She lectured in churches, town halls, civic buildings, schools, and even opera houses. Her primary aim was to boost the fledging League of Nations, which the isolationist-minded United States still hadn't (and never would) join, despite (or perhaps because of) ex-President Wilson's support of it. Royden the pacifist was convinced that the League was the best means to avoiding future wars and healing the wounds of the last one. Many of her lectures, sermons, and writings throughout the 1920s focused on helping others recover a sense of spiritual equilibrium upended by the horrible war years.

Percy Dearmer left the Guildhouse in 1924. The circumstances of his leaving are somewhat murky. Probably he did so because he was stretched too thin: his ministry with the Guild competed with his literary labors as well as a teaching position at King's College he'd held since the end of the war. But rumors also circulated that tension had been growing between him and Royden. As one Guild member suggested, both had such large personalities that they were bound to come into conflict.[35] Be that as it may, Royden became the heart and soul of the Guild after Dearmer's departure. She enlisted a number of clergy, including Hudson Shaw, to spell her with occasional assistance.

In addition to her preaching and counseling, Royden took on duties at the Guild, especially after Dearmer left, traditionally performed only by priests. She founded and wrote the rule for a devotional group called the Little Company of Christ that regularly met under her supervision.

---

35. Fletcher, *Maude Royden*, 223.

She served as a spiritual director, officiated at marriages and baptisms, and even heard confessions, especially from women who for one reason or another couldn't bring themselves to confess to a male priest. She had long felt herself called to ordained ministry; at the Guild, she performed every priestly function except consecration. Her inability to officiate at the Eucharist was particularly irksome to her. In a memorandum she wrote to a Church of England committee charged with reporting to the 1930 Lambeth Conference on the question of women's ordination, she gave full throat to her frustration. Referring to retreats practiced by the Little Company of Christ, she wrote: "It seems quite extraordinarily artificial that at such times, we, who are joined together with a very deep and real fellowship, should have to scour the country for some priest [to celebrate Eucharist], who knows nothing whatever about our society and does not in the least want to be fetched." Such a situation was especially absurd, she concluded, "when after all, in a very real sense, I am myself their priest."[36] One can well imagine how Royden's description of herself as "their priest" went over with the clerical committee.

As the decade progressed and a steady stream of her books appeared, Royden's fame spread. She was increasingly called to preach outside of London. Her congregants were proud of her influence and steadily supported her various ministries outside of the Guild, but they also suffered from her absences. Although Royden repeatedly insisted that the Guild didn't depend on her or any other single individual, it was clearly her personal charisma that held the thing together. That would become ever more apparent over the next few years.

A turning point in the Guild's fortunes occurred in 1928, when Royden, accompanied by her personal secretary Daisy Dobson, embarked on an extended world tour. Substitute preachers were lined up to serve in her absence, and Royden promised to keep in touch with the congregation by sending a monthly letter recounting her experiences abroad. But as events proved, her year-long absence from the Guild marked the beginning of its decline.

Royden's first stop was the United States. She lectured and preached there for three months, using the speaker's funds she received to pay for

---

36. "Women and Priesthood"; memorandum submitted by the Anglican Group for Bringing the Subject of the Admission of Women to the Priesthood before the Next Lambeth Conference (1930). Lambeth Palace Archives, LC 168, 32, quoted in Fletcher, *Maude Royden*, 246.

the rest of her journey. From there she and Dobson proceeded to New Zealand, Australia, Japan, China, Ceylon, and India.

Her American audiences were generally huge, although several evangelical churches objected to her presence: they'd learned she was a smoker, and this only cemented their suspicion of her as a "liberal" pseudo-Christian. There were even prayer meetings in Topeka, Kansas, focused on imploring the Lord to prevent her appearance there. (The Lord didn't come through.). She was also popular in Australia and New Zealand, where she lectured mainly on women and equality and, predictably, the League of Nations' importance for securing world peace. Her public speaking in Japan and China was minimal, and she held no public meetings in India at all.

Royden's primary reason for going there was to speak with Gandhi, whom she had met once before on one of his visits to England and esteemed for his commitment to pacifism. But their discussion at his ashram wasn't quite what she expected. Although she says she wanted to talk with him about God, their conversation almost immediately turned to politics, she maintaining that British colonialism had been a great civilizing force, Gandhi responding by calling such an attitude poisonously arrogant. They didn't, of course, fall out because of their disagreement. Both were too irenic in temperament for that. But there was definite tension.

When Royden returned to England in January 1929, she was enthusiastically welcomed home by Guildhouse members. But the speaking tour had clearly worn her out, and throughout the entire year she was often physically or emotionally incapacitated and unable to serve. In early 1930 she suffered a genuine breakdown, generically described at the time as a nervous collapse, that kept her totally away from active ministry for yet another year.

Her state of mind during her invalid year was only further upset when the Lambeth Conference announced its veto of women's ordination but (gratingly, in the mind of Royden) thanked women for their many subordinate contributions to the church. Acknowledging that there was a shortage of priests in the church, one of the arguments Royden and others had offered for the ordination of women, the Conference announced that it would begin raising up bi-vocational clergy, men who already had careers in the secular world. Royden saw this as an outrage. In her eyes, the bishops' decision was a clear proclamation that they privileged men who by necessity would split their energies between jobs and parishes over women who, feeling a call to ministry, were willing to sacrifice everything to serve in that capacity. It was as blatant an example of ecclesial discrimination as one could find. The Church of England, Royden had written six years earlier in her book *The Church and Woman*, was the "last ditch of the anti-feminist."[37] She had hoped that the 1930 Lambeth Conference would put the lie to that accusation. It didn't.

Royden finally returned to the Guildhouse pulpit in 1931, but her more or less continuous three-year absence had inflicted serious damage on its finances. She had always been the main draw; so long as she was present and preaching, attendance was high and contributions steady. But both had been negatively affected by her world tour and her illnesses, and now the Guild was having difficulty meeting its expenses. To make matters worse, the Depression had come to England, even further reducing financial contributions.

In late 1931, Royden entered into what many of her acquaintances, including even her secretary Daisy Dobson, thought of as her most quixotic campaign: the Peace Army. The idea was immediate sparked by the Japanese Manchurian War, a short but shockingly brutal conflict.

Collaborating with Anglican priest Dick Sheppard and Presbyterian minister Herbert Gray, and influenced by Gandhi's example of nonviolent resistance in India, Royden returned to an idea she had first raised in her 1915 pamphlet *The Great Adventure*: pacifists willing to place themselves as human barriers between opposing armies, thus forestalling their attacks on one another. The plan was announced to the world along with a call for volunteers. The public's general response was that it was a risible proposal. Still, one of the first to sign on as a volunteer was an Irish brigadier general, and this raised the trio's hopes that their plan could gain traction. Their spirits were further boosted when the secretary general of the League of Nations spoke favorably of the Peace Army scheme, although it's not clear how much trust he actually had in its practicality. But the hard edge of reality soon set in. All told, only about one thousand volunteers responded, forcing Royden, Sheppard, and Gray to shelve the idea.

Still, the Peace Army project, unsuccessful though it may have been, seemed to focus Royden's attention throughout the 1930s back on the peacemaking of her early days and away from her decades-long campaign for women's ordination. Perhaps it was the 1930 Lambeth Conference's point-blank refusal to countenance the ordination of women that sapped her vitality. Perhaps it was in part her nervous breakdown

---

37. A. Maude Royden, *The Church and Woman* (New York: Doran, 1924), 150.

as well as her increasingly poor physical health, especially her disability, now exacerbated by rheumatism, and her gradual loss of hearing. But Royden reached the point where she claimed she no longer yearned for Holy Orders herself, either in the Church of England or in any other denomination. In the first place, she had grown too unorthodox, she said, to subscribe to the Thirty-Nine Articles. In the second, she now too identified with people who were outside of any established church to tie herself to a particular sect. Her sense of ministry, in other words, had broadened. She had reached the point where she no longer needed her call to be recognized by ecclesial authority. She no longer needed to be officially recognized as a "priest." As she wrote in the 1930 memorandum, she already was, "in a very real sense," one.

Honors came to her in quick succession in the first half of the decade. She was made a Companion of Honor in 1930, a recognition that delighted Hudson Shaw to no end. Glasgow University named her a doctor of divinity the following year and the University of Liverpool awarded her an LL.D in 1935. This last recognition, coming as it did from her hometown, was especially pleasing. Although her literary output was slowing down, her books were still selling well. But despite this, her time at the Guildhouse was drawing to a close. As much as it grieved her, Royden resigned from its ministry in 1936. She told its members that trying to juggle her ministerial duties to them and her outside peace work was beyond her strength, and there's probably some truth in that. But it might also be the case that she suffered from a certain degree of burnout, familiar to many pastors who have worked long and diligently in a parish. At any rate, leaving the Guild, although painful, was also surely something of a relief for Royden. For the first time in twenty years, first at City Temple and then the Guild, she was free of formal pastoral responsibilities.

The Final Two Decades

Many Guild members felt abandoned after her departure and drifted away. But the Fellowship stumbled on for another two decades, although in different physical locations, the Guildhouse proving too expensive for the dwindling congregation to retain. For her part, Royden embarked in 1937 on yet another trip to the United States. She went there at the invitation of pacifists who, alarmed at the European geopolitical situation, had organized the Emergency Peace Campaign. Royden had already begun to express doubts about the practicability of absolute pacifism, a move that greatly saddened Dick Sheppard without rupturing their close friendship, and it cannot have escaped her notice that the Emergency Peace Campaign was motived at least as much by isolationism as by a principled stand for peace. Nonetheless, she thought it essential to do anything possible to prevent the new war she and many others sensed was coming.

In the months leading up to war between England and Germany, it was obvious, however, that Royden was increasingly torn between her dedication to peacemaking and her growing fear that pacifism simply had no practical response to offer to Hitler. In 1938, in a near desperate attempt to remain loyal to the ideal of nonviolence, she joined and wrote for the Peace Pledge Union, the pacifist organization, founded by her friend Dick Sheppard (who had died months earlier), in which members pledged not to support England's war effort. "We say no!" was their shared motto. But within a year, feeling that she could no longer support absolute pacifism in the current situation, she resigned. And in the early summer of 1940, after the calamitous defeat of English forces in France and the heroic rescue at Dunkirk, Royden publicly declared her support of the war. "I believe now," she wrote, "that Nazism is worse than war. It is more hideously cruel, more blind, more evil—and more important." She insisted that she was still a pacifist at heart because she believed that "spiritual power is the right weapon." The problem was that most humans, presuming that spiritual power was identical to "doing nothing," had never really given it a try.[38]

Predictably, Royden's position shocked, saddened, and even angered many pacifists with whom she'd collaborated during the Great War and into the 1920s. Years later, one of them, Constance Coleman, was still bitter: "Then in 1939, bang went her pacifism! Some people felt, 'What's the use of that woman'?"[39]

In late 1941, Royden returned to the United States, perhaps in part to get away from the criticism she was receiving for her volte-face on war but certainly to explain to Americans why she'd changed her position. It was a perilous time to travel; the London Blitz was in full operation—both City Temple and the Guildhouse were destroyed—and crossing the Atlantic risked running into German U-boats. Nevertheless, she arrived

38. "I Was a Pacifist," London *Sunday Dispatch* (16 June 1940), quoted in Fletcher, *Maude Royden*, 274.

39. Quoted in Fletcher, *Maude Royden*, 274.

safely and spent four months there. She was in the States when the Japanese bombed Pearl Harbor, propelling the nation into the war, and she quickly moved to reassure her shocked audiences that despite the horror of a world fallen into conflict, it was important to keep the spirit of peace alive.

Some of Royden's friends, aware of the dangers of wartime travel, had urged her not to go to the States. Hudson Shaw, whose counsel Royden most trusted, urged her to go, for which she expressed gratitude to several of her acquaintances.

After twenty-three years at St. Boltoph's, Shaw had finally retired from active ministry in 1935. He and Effie left London and settled into a fourteenth-century cottage in Kent—a "little paradise," according to Royden. Somewhat to the surprise of those who knew him, Shaw took to rural retirement. He delighted in his garden and the beauty of the countryside and seemed not to miss the busyness of active ministry at all. As Royden dryly observed, "Hudson, like many retired parsons of my acquaintance, showed a marked distaste for church-going. I suppose they feel they have had enough of it!"[40]

Royden was fortunate enough to find a place for let just next door to the Shaws and was in daily contact with them after her return from the United States. But their time would be short. Hudson had suffered from heart disease for years, and by 1942 he was in his eighties and terribly infirm. There came a point when he couldn't even traverse the short distance between their two houses. Effie, younger than Hudson, seemed healthy enough. But quite unexpectedly, she took ill and died in February 1944. Both Hudson and Royden were shocked; everyone, including Effie, had supposed that he would be the first thread of the threefold cord to come undone.

After the grief began to subside a bit, Hudson pressed Royden to marry him. Initially, she declared herself content to let things remain between them as they'd been for forty-three years, but she eventually agreed. The bishop of Rochester joined them in wedlock at the beginning of October 1944. Even the brief and private ceremony proved too much for the frail Hudson; he nearly died from it. He managed to pull through, but only just. Two months later he was dead. Now only one thread in the cord remained.

---

40. Royden, *Threefold Cord*, 92.

The final decade of Royden's life was a quiet one, partly because of her sense of loss at the deaths of Hudson and Effie, but also because her own health diminished her activities. During her final trip to America her disability and pain forced her to use two canes and, at times, a wheelchair. After she returned to England, she had to give up driving, something she very much enjoyed. She continued to write a few articles, sit for the occasional interview, and in the early 1950s made a few well-received radio broadcasts for the BBC. She also officiated at an occasional baptism or wedding. But her active life of ministry and public reform was, for the most part, over.

She still had one more book in her, however. In 1948, now in her seventies, she published *A Threefold Cord*, a memoir and loving tribute to her relationship with Effie and Hudson Shaw. Some of her closest friends, including Daisy Dobson, advised her not to publish it when she showed them the manuscript. They thought it too sentimental and feared that it would raise suspicions about just how chaste a forty-three year love affair could've possibly been, despite Royden's insistence in the book that it was.[41] They feared it would ruin or at least sully her reputation.

But Royden believed she owed this public acknowledgment of a long-hidden love to Effie and Hudson, and she published the book. Some readers were, indeed, shocked by it. But most applauded both her candor and the tenderness with which she tells the story. Some (I count myself among them) even considered it the single best piece of writing to come from her pen.

Toward the end of her life, Royden left Kent and returned to London. At times she felt as if her life had been for naught: her pacifism hadn't ended war, her crusade for women's ordination was still unsuccessful, her years at the City Temple and Guildhouse long over, the love of her life dead and gone. Her growing physical infirmities depressed her. She was bewildered that a God of love would allow humans to be so afflicted. And she was tormented by the suspicion that her years of active service had actually been strategies for deviously avoiding the soul-searching necessary

---

41. "What seems to me really inexplicable is the assumption that we—Hudson and I—could have had an illicit love and continued with the work that we were doing. We both called ourselves Christians. We were not only committed to a Christian way of life but we took it upon ourselves to teach others. Hudson was a priest and I, though I was refused ordination the priesthood of the Church of England on account of my sex, preached in the name of Christ. . . . How could we do this if we didn't believe in it? . . . To what depths of insincerity were we supposed to have sunk?" Royden, *Threefold Cord*, 121–22.

to establish intimacy with God. This is, of course, a doubt that assails many ministers after long and busy careers. Royden was no exception.

Agnes Maude Royden died on 30 July 1956, four months shy of her eightieth birthday. Thirty-eight years later, the Church of England finally ordained women to the priesthood. And a quarter-century after that, the blue memorial plaque commemorating "the best-known woman preacher in the world," as Francis Parkinson Keyes described her in 1928, was affixed to Frankby Hall, the home in which she was born and raised so many years earlier.

Royden's Continuing Relevance

The fact that Royden was one of the most influential women in the English-speaking world between the two World Wars is alone enough to make familiarity with her life and work worthwhile. She also more than deserves recognition for her pioneering struggle for women's rights, especially when it comes to ordination. But what makes her refreshingly relevant—"irreplaceable"—is that so much of what she wrote remains helpful for Christians trying to navigate their way through today's troubled political, moral, and religious waters.

Christians continue to find themselves torn between Caesar and Christ. As citizens, we have a responsibility to the state. But what do we do when the state solicits our assent or collaboration with policies and courses of action that run counter to our faith? War is perhaps the most obvious point of tension, one that Royden spent decades of her life worrying over. Her reflections on the strengths and weaknesses of Christian pacifism offer us today a sobering but still hopeful assessment of nonviolent resistance as a response to armed conflict. As she insisted, peacemaking is as much an adventure as going into battle and calls for as much, and perhaps even more, courage.

The first set of selections in this anthology, "The 'Great Adventure' of Peace," offers representative samples of her reflections on Christian pacifism, as well as her eventual ambivalence about it in the face of Nazi aggression.

Royden also speaks to us today in her refusal either to accept or despair over the stale and even oppressive resistance to change that can overtake ecclesial institutions. Churches in our time, just as in hers, too often defend policies that seem to fly in the face of the Lord's life and message. They sometimes enthusiastically support war; they fixate in a pharisaic way on propriety and appearance rather than service and inwardness; they discourage free enquiry and ill tolerate dissent; and they encourage a caste system in their own ranks that too often privileges clergy over laypersons and, frequently, men over women.

Royden was a cradle Anglican and always remained a loyal member of the Church of England, even during her years serving at City Temple and the Guild. But she believed that it had become too self-satisfied, too monolithic, too deafened to the promptings of the Spirit, and that it was her duty to help awaken it, especially when it came to its treatment of women. It's striking, and disturbing, that many of the same arguments heard today from churches that deny women ordination were current in her own time. Royden skewers them all with her unique insight—rare in her own day and still not particularly fashionable in ours—that Christianity, properly understood, should be a wholehearted embrace of feminism. One can be a churchman, she argued, or a disciple. The first choice ensures that the church will always "be last" when it comes to defending equality and freedom. The second has the potential to transform our entire understanding of what "church" can be.

The second and third sets of selections, "Women Are Human Beings" and "The Church Is 'Christ's Society,'" offer examples of Royden's writings on women's rights and the need for ecclesial reform.

Her City Temple collaborator Fort Newton, a seminary-trained clergyman, praised Royden's grasp of theological concepts, even though she had no formal seminary schooling, as well as her ability to express them in listener-friendly ways in her sermons, writing, and personal counseling. Her general theological approach may best be described as liberal. She never denied central Christian doctrines such as the Incarnation or the Atonement, but she explored them in unconventional ways that breathed new life into them. She was suspicious of "orthodoxy," thinking it all too often designated a frozen-in-time approach to faith. For her, the only absolute foundation of orthodoxy was the claim that God is love. As she wrote, "The heart of religion that Christ taught and the nature of the God he revealed are the same. They are love."[42] This meant that she utterly rejected any understanding of the Atonement as an act of penal substitution as well as belief in eternal damnation of the wicked. In a particularly intriguing argument, she suggests that the personalities of

---

42. A. Maude Royden, *I Believe in God* (New York: Harper & Brothers, 1927), 113.

wicked individuals simply cease to be at their physical deaths while their spirit, the image of the divine with which they were stamped at birth, returns to its Source. Postmortem survival of the self is, then, conditional.

The fourth set of representative selections, "Theology 'Can Never Rest Content,'" offers some of her most sophisticated work on Christian doctrine.

Over her twenty years at City Temple and the Guild, Royden became a skilled spiritual director, counseling parishioners and others troubled by moral uncertainty, religious skepticism, doubts about their identities as Christians, feelings of hopelessness and despair, and curiosity about alternative faiths. Her talent for down-to-earth but insightfully wise and frequently pity spiritual counseling is demonstrated in the anthology's fifth set of selections, "Called to the High Ascent."

Finally, the sixth and final set, "From the Beginning There Were Three of Us," offers samples from *A Threefold Cord*, her touching memoir of the forty-three-year-long relationship with Hudson Shaw and his wife Effie that served as her emotional center of gravity. In her description of their lives together, Royden lays bare the beauty, and occasional pain, of their shared love.

Much time has passed since Royden ministered, wrote, and struggled to build a more inclusive and peaceful culture both within and outside of the church. But her ideas and sensibilities still speak to us today. They carry with them timeless truth—or as she might've said, a hint of eternity—that may from time to time be forgotten but, when remembered, ever refreshes. At the conclusion of one of her books, she beautifully reminds us, in writing specifically about the passing of the seasons, that truth travels across the ages, past generations passing it on to future ones. It's a fitting passage on which to end.

> The passing of time, the marking of the passage of time which we call the Old Year and the New, brings us into the presence of eternity. It is a strange paradox that these conventional periods and dates should bring us to eternity, but they do. We see things for a moment against the background of our own immortality. We realize, if only for an hour, that we must awake out of sleep and cast from us the works of darkness, and put upon us the armor of light. Here and now we set out; let us set out for something nobler, braver, freer than we have been in the past. The cynics tell us that the way to hell is paved with good resolutions; they forget that the way to heaven has a precisely similar pavement.[43]

43. A. Maude Royden, *Life's Little Pitfalls* (New York: Putnam's Sons, 1925), 153.

Part 1.

The "Great Adventure" of Peace

Selections from Royden's writings on war and peace

Obedience to Peace

ROYDEN ACKNOWLEDGES IN THIS lecture, originally delivered at a Cambridge Fellowship of Reconciliation conference in December 1914, that Christians struggle with divided loyalties in times of war. On the one hand, as citizens, they feel the urge to show patriotic solidarity with their fellow countrymen. On the other, as Christians, they feel called to follow Jesus's teaching and renounce violence. Many Christians chose to support the outbreak of hostilities in 1914 thinking that doing so was a lesser evil than neutrality. But Royden argues that there was a third choice that avoided both war and neutrality: modeling Jesus's example of peaceful resistance to violence. Embracing this choice wouldn't have been easy. But obedience to the Lord shouldn't be withheld or compromised "till the world is ready for it."

In seeking the right path for Christian people to walk in, when war broke out at the beginning of August 1914, it was assumed by many of us that we had before us only a choice of evils. In the glare of the conflagration we looked back and saw, with sudden and terrible clearness, all the steps that had brought us where we were. And as we are all members of the nation, responsible each in our degree for the national temper, acquiescent—most of us—in a state of affairs which, though we had called it "peace" was in fact war in its jealous fear of other nations, we began to think of the war rather as a punishment than as a crime, and to believe that it was the lesser of two evils to accept our part in it. The nation, some of us thought, would do worse to remain neutral than to go to war, and to go to war—owing to a past for which we were all together responsible—was the only way in which to fulfill our obligations. With heavy hearts we assented to the belief that we had only a choice of evils. It is this belief that lies at the heart of the difference between those who still preach peace and those who uphold the war as not good in itself, but better than the only alternative that was open to us—neutrality. And those that are for peace must realize that so much of the view that they dissent from is true, that there is a real difference between a "just" and an "unjust" war. There is an eternal difference between an aggressive war against a little nation, and a war of self-defense, or a war in defense of the weak. There is an element of greatness which will never fail to move the human spirit in such a war as the American war against slavery, the wars of Holland for religious freedom, the wars of the Italian Risorgimento. And inasmuch as many have thrown themselves into the present war because they would not stand aside and see Belgium trampled upon,[1] there is greatness in this war also. For a pagan country, it may be said that there was no better course open than the one we took, and that the choice was truly one of evils. But for Christians the decision is a harder one, and its difficulty arises from the fact that when we turn to our Lord for guidance we find a paradox in His teaching on conflicting claims. We have a divided loyalty between our duty as citizens and our duty as Christians, and this division is reflected in the divided counsels of Christian people today. Some think that we should do as the nation does, and if we do so at peril to our souls, we must incur that danger. It is our business to help each other to do the best we can, and at this time our nation in doing the best it can has risen to its utmost capacity of idealism—in fighting for Belgium and France. We therefore must help it to do this, disregarding ourselves, hoping for a better future, and realizing with penitence our own share in the guilt which makes that "better" not possible now.

Such a position has much that is Christ-like in it. None can fail to be impressed with the emphasis laid on human love and service and sharing, by Christ. No religion is so human as His religion. None inculcates a greater forgetfulness of oneself, one's soul, one's life, or more insistently proclaims that our Father finds that love alone to be real which expresses itself in human service. Not those who believed, or preached or prayed well are in Christ's parable found fit for the Kingdom; but those who in corporal works of mercy served their fellowmen. Not those guilty of gross sins—as we conceive them—bore the weight of His denunciation; but those Pharisees who held themselves apart and thought themselves better than other men. And greatest of all His words of love is that saying—"He that seeketh to save his life shall lose it" (Matt 16:25; Mark

---

1. In order to avoid fortifications along the Germany-France border, German armies invaded neutral Belgium at the beginning of August 1914. This brought England into the war. (KW)

8:35; Luke 17:33). On the other side stands the absolute claim of Jesus Christ, "Whosoever loveth his father and mother more than Me, is not worthy of Me ..." (Matt 10:37). "If a man *hate not* his father and mother, yea, and his own life also" (and his nation?) "he cannot be My disciple" (Luke 14:26). There is the tremendous nature of His claim for Himself: "Whither I go ye know, and the way ye know. Thomas saith unto Him, Lord, we know not whither Thou goest; and how can we know the way? Jesus saith unto him, I am the Way ..." (John 14:5). There is something to those outside the Christian faith, terrible, almost repulsive, in such claims as these. "Other religious teachers," says a critic, "point their disciples to God. But Jesus of Nazareth, with a colossal egoism, points to Himself—'I am the Way.'" How is it that no Christian finds this egoism in Christ? And how do we reconcile the paradox of His insistence on the reality of that love only which shows itself in human service and sharing, with this other insistence "If any man hate not his father and mother ... he cannot be My disciple"?

If the paradox were indeed a contradiction, we should be forced, if we thought honestly and clearly, to give up one or the other. We do not, because we know that though Truth is very often only to be expressed in a paradox, it never involves a real contradiction. Both of these teachings are true and both to be obeyed. But how?

First, it is clear that our Lord, in His own life, rejected the view that the nation's claim is absolute. And His refusal to take the "national" position, and become the leader of a national revolt against oppression, is the more significant that—by our own standards—it was not an unjust cause that He was desired to lead. The Roman rule over Palestine was a cruel and a tyrannous oppression. Resistance to it was as noble a task as the resistance to Austria of Garibaldi and Mazzini. And it is certain that the Jewish peoples hoped that Christ would lead an armed rebellion against their rulers—that He would follow in the footsteps of the Maccabees, and, at last, set His people free. Our Lord refused. It was His refusal that turned the people against Him. When they cried "Crucify Him!" they expressed their hatred of the man who might have helped his people, and who would not.

The impression left upon His disciples was that they must follow His example. They offered no resistance to persecution. Their women and their children suffered, and themselves; but it did not occur to them that they had a right to resist, or that the example given to them by their

Master could be for any reason set aside. They seemed to have felt, with Tertullian, that when He disarmed St. Peter, Christ disarmed them all.

We are accustomed to say that the blood of the martyrs is the seed of the Church. And we are right. For no man is converted by a preacher who does not in his life prove that he believes what he teaches: and everyone who does so is a preacher whether he speaks in pulpits or not. There is no missionary force like a life, and we who still speak of the "ages of faith" with a great longing, could have them back today, if we would give our lives for them. But we have first to realize how singularly unimpressive to the non-Christian is our attitude toward our own faith. Briefly, our doctrine of compromise with the world is summed up in the text—"Give not your pearls unto swine" (Matt 7:6). The world, we say, is not yet ready for the Kingdom as we see it: it cannot reach the standard we shall some day set before it. We therefore will read the Sermon on the Mount aloud in our churches, to remind us of the vision we have to strive after. But when the nation relies not on love, but on torpedoes and machine-guns, we will commend what is good in its action, and be silent on what is bad.

Is this really the meaning Christ put on His own words? That they should be preached and made known, but with the proviso that we are not expected to put them into practice at present? It is hard to believe it. The world, wholly unconscious of any superiority over the average Christian in swine-like qualities, is moved indeed by the Christ-life lived, to an effort, however pathetically weak and unsuccessful, to follow after; it is moved by the spectacle of Christians preaching a gospel to be practiced in the future, to nothing but a conviction that the preachers do not believe in their own doctrine. Christ came to a world not ready for Him—so unready that it crucified Him. He taught His disciples that they must not be overcome with evil, but must overcome it with good; and by "good" He does not seem to have meant swords and other arms but love and patience and kindness and meekness. He rebuked a disciple who imagined that he might defend his Master with the sword (Matt 26:52), and those others who desired to punish a village which rejected Him (Luke 9:54–55). He did not wait to come until the world was sufficiently advanced at least not to crucify Him and torture His disciples. He did not tell them that some day, when good was stronger and men better than now, it would be their duty to rely wholly on love and put aside earthly weapons of defense. He told them to overcome evil with good *now*, and in this command there was surely contained a promise—the promise that good is really stronger than evil; not to be stronger some day, but stronger *now*. They were, they believed, to stake everything on this promise, and to go on believing it, even if it resulted in their death. For Christ, believing in the triumph of love, was crucified, and so they knew that the most frightful risks and the most abject (apparent) failure were to be accepted with unshaken confidence in His promise. They were to "be perfect" not at some future time when other people also were better, and they no longer tied and bound with the chain of their own sins; but *now*. And again the command implies a promise. For the pagan world there may only be a choice of evils, but for the Christian, the command is, "Be ye perfect" (Matt 5:48). This surely is the liberty of Christ.

We are reminded that Christ also said—"I have yet many things to say unto you, but ye cannot bear them now" (John 16:12). In the light of the command "Be ye perfect," we are hardly free to interpret this as permission to put off the hour of complete obedience to a future time. It is surely part of the same truth that "He that doeth the will shall know of the doctrine" (John 7:17). Christ, laying down His guiding principles for us, knew that His followers could not see at once how such principles would work out in life. He knew also that as each sought to apply and live them, he would find the way. But He surely never meant that we were free not to apply them, as they revealed themselves! When once we see that the sacredness of human personality forbids (for example) slavery; or the sacredness of the body, prostitution; we are not then free to assent to these things. The moment of seeing is the moment for action. There are many things, doubtless, that we cannot yet "bear," which are therefore not revealed to us. But when they are revealed, we must move forward. It cannot be that we should sin against the light. Nor can it be that we should withhold from others the light that comes to us. "Heaven doth with us as we with torches do—not light them for themselves."[2] And progress comes by no automatic revelation, but by the blood and sweat of those who see and cannot forget or turn away. Each seeks the truth after his fashion, but if he sees it and does not struggle after it, it will not reveal itself in spite of him. He must strive after it, until he falls, and another takes his place and sees further and strives better. And so the world follows after, and at last all see. But the world does not follow a light of which a man says, "I see it, but you cannot, and so I shall not try to reach it yet." The world only believes from this that he does not really see the light at all, and turns to

---

2. Shakespeare, *Measure for Measure*, 1.1. (KW)

other prophets who at least believe what they say. Perhaps it stones them; but it believes them in the end, and it will not believe any other.

If then we believe in Christianity in the sense that we believe it to be the redemptive force of the world, we must live it. There is no other missionary force. And here the heart of our paradox appears. It is true that Christ's claim upon us is absolute, supreme, immediate. But there is no such conflict of loyalties as we feared, for only by perfect loyalty to Him can we be loyal to our fellow men. Imperfect as we are, it is only in perfection that we recognize the true type of humanity—Ecce Homo! Behold the Man! It was not for nothing that the only Man altogether without sin called Himself "Son of Man" as well as God. Our sins and imperfections divide us: there is no such thing as a bond of hatred or a communion of sin. Sin always divides and destroys. But in a perfect Man, we imperfect ones realize our real humanity: in Christ we are one. The nearer we come to Him, the more truly we live His life, the more loyal are we to all our obligations to our fellow men. We may seem apart and alone, as did our Lord upon the Cross. But the separation is seeming, the loyalty is real.

Everything that is sin disunites, and everything that is less than ideal is less than perfect loyalty. Could anything be more "separatist" in fact than this belief that we must wait, we Christians, to insist on perfect obedience to our Lord, till the world is ready for it? The world is much better than we think. We dare not say to it, "Be ye perfect," because we believe that though we are ready others are not ready. But Christ said it, and though they crucified Him, He conquered. Was He, when He refused to lead a national revolt, when He foresaw and wept over the destruction of Jerusalem, yet assented to it, more or less true to His own people, because He was true to an ideal first? If we had followed Him without compromise, as did His first disciples, we should have been accused, as they were, of being "bad citizens," disloyal to the State; but we should by now have made war impossible, and saved the world from evils unspeakable, and hatred and disunity. If we had accepted in August 1914 His teaching in its glorious idealism, we should even then perhaps have saved Belgium and the world from a devastating conflict. If now we did so, not because the sacrifices of war are too great, but because we see that peace is better, and love a greater force than war, what then would happen? Still it would be true that loyalty to Christ would include all other loyalties, and only loyalty to Christ can perfectly do so. This is what is meant by "believing on Christ." Sometimes we clearly see it, and see how it is so; sometimes we cannot see how, and we still believe and set out on our way. Christ did not answer (in one sense) St. Thomas's question—"Lord, we know not whither Thou goest, and how can we know the way?" (John 14:5). But He said, "I am the Way" (John 14:6). There is no time at which our Savior ceases to be the Way.

There is no time at which good is less strong or evil stronger than before. We plead that now is not the time, and point to our own sins as ground and excuse for putting off the hour of the ideal. "We make a god of our own weakness and bow down to it" (cf. 2 Cor 12:9). And it is true that every succeeding sin has made it harder to turn to Christ, but it is not true that any sin has absolved us from doing so. It is true that in putting off so long our attempt to make the will of God prevail "in earth as it is in heaven" (Matt 6:10), we have made a world very unlike heaven; but it is not true that at any time we are justified in putting it off a little longer, until it is a little easier. It will never be easier. If we do not believe in the Sermon on the Mount in such sense that we consent to live by it when it is dangerous, we shall not find the world ready to listen to it when it is safe. The world is not so false as that. It would not give to any human leader the half-hearted obedience that we Christians call loyalty to Christ. Let us at least choose whom it is that we follow, and if we cannot follow Him now, let us take another name and leave the name of "Christian" to those who perhaps some day will be able to do so. We are not worthy of it. "From that time many of His disciples went back and walked no more with Him. Then said Jesus unto the twelve, Will ye also go away?" (John 6:66–67). If they had gone, they might well have said it was the best that they could do. Certainly the Jews were not ready for Christ; but they were ready, perhaps, to make great sacrifices in a noble cause. They were ready to rise against a mighty tyrant, and sweep away, even at the cost of their lives, a horrible oppression. This was the best that they could do, and it was great. A man could wish no nobler cause, and surely no Jew could, at such a time, do less.

But if they had gone away, these few, these ignorant, materially minded, ambitious, faithless few, always misunderstanding their Master's teaching, persistently disputing which should be the greatest and what their reward—if they had gone away? There must have been better men in Israel, surely, than some of these disciples of Jesus of Nazareth, with their incredible failures and selfishness and fears. But only these accepted the leadership of Christ at any risk and without reserve. Were they more or less true to their fellow men in being so true to Him? Doubtless those who were already suffering in the national cause held them false, and called them traitors. The conscience of the world has reversed that judgment now.

Source

A. Maude Royden, "The Nature of the Christian Obedience," in *Christ and Peace*, ed. Joan Mary Frye (London: Headley Brothers, 1915), 34–44.

The Great Adventure

WRITTEN A YEAR AFTER her lecture on war and Christian obedience, The Great Adventure, *although covering a bit of the same ground, offered a more sophisticated case for the moral and religious superiority of pacifism over militarism. Given the destructiveness of war, argued Royden, the countries invaded by Germany wouldn't have been any the worse off had England adopted a policy of disarmament and negotiation. Many nations are prepared to die for freedom. England could've offered an inspiring counterexample by not killing for peace. At any rate, Christians have no choice but to embark on the "great adventure" of peacemaking, an enterprise that calls for all the heroism, and perhaps more, demanded by war. Jesus's ideal of nonviolence, which isn't at all a passively neutral position, can't be sacrificed even for national necessity.*

What is the way of the Christian in War time? Can War ever be right? To ask these questions—and we have all been asking them—is perhaps to make too large an assumption. It is to assume that, in itself, war is not a good thing; and there are people who argue that it is good, absolutely good, good in itself. But the number of these people in our own country is, I believe, small, and of that small number fewer still are found who have so truly the courage of their opinion as to propose the making of war for its own sake, and to refrain from satisfaction because at the beginning of August, 1914, Sir Edward Grey exhausted every means open to him to secure peace.[1] I shall not, therefore, discuss here the view that war is an absolute good, though it is a perfectly logical and comprehensible view. It is more to the purpose in addressing Christian people to ask whether war

---

1. Edward Grey (1862–1933), England's foreign secretary at the outbreak of World War I, tried unsuccessfully to prevent the outbreak of hostilities between Austria-Hungary and Serbia after the July 1914 assassination of Archduke Franz Ferdinand in Sarajevo. (KW)

may not sometimes be a necessary evil, or even in comparison with some other alternative, relatively good.

The alternative must certainly be a terrible one; for war, even within the rules of warfare, means the shattering of human bodies, the torturing of human nerves. It means bombarded cities, wrecked industries, and devastated countryside. It means unmeasured and immeasurable loss to the race in child-life, as well as the lives of the strongest and bravest of its grown men. There is a good deal of rather glib talk at present about the negligible quality of material losses; but to Christians conscious of the intense sensitiveness of their Master to human suffering, and the readiness with which He gave Himself to its alleviation, such pain as war inflicts can never be a little thing. There is further the inevitable anger, hatred, and desire for revenge, which the infliction of suffering and the attempt to coerce evokes.

War then is evil. In the words of a soldier, "war is hell."[2] And many Christian people look for the time, however far distant, when we shall make no more wars, and when we shall have found other and less disastrous methods for settling international disputes. After all, we have found other means for settling our private quarrels than the duel. It is not too much to hope that war may die a like death, at last. But it will not be without sacrifice and struggle that such an end will come, and it should surely be the hope of every Christian that to the end desired his own country may be ready to sacrifice something. [. . .]

Nevertheless, there are still those who hold that war is always wrong—for Christians. It is for them that I try to speak.

We were bound indeed to defend Belgium by every means in our power. And I think we were bound, as Christians, to defend her, and to defend France also, when they were threatened, even had we not been further bound by treaties or understandings. To defend the weak is always our duty, when defense is any way possible. And I for one agree that to have remained neutral last August would have been worse than to go to war. To stand out, to seek our own safety, to remain spectators only of the agony of Belgium, would have been the basest of all betrayals.

War was better than neutrality, if these were the only alternatives. But is it not tragic that, nineteen hundred years after the Crucifixion, we Christians should still conceive of peace in terms of neutrality? Was Christ, then, "neutral" on the Cross? Or was His life one long act of

---

2. William Tecumseh Sherman (1820–91), American Civil War general. (KW)

"non-resistance"? Was it not rather a perpetual resistance to evil, and in spite of apparent failure, a triumphant resistance? Christ was not neutral between God and man, but neither did He make war. He chose another alternative—He made peace.

What then could we have done? How could we have made peace? [. . .]

We could have called, not on our allies only, but on the world to support us in our demand for peace. We could have called on every neutral nation to refuse aid of any kind to the war maker, and on our allies to make no preparation for war, leaving to the first aggressor the appalling responsibility of marching against an absolutely non-resistant people. We could have called forth the peace lovers in the world to fling themselves—if need be—in front of the troop trains.[3] If millions of men will go out to offer their lives up in war, surely there are those who would die for peace! And if not men we could have called out women! It would not be for the first time, nor would they have been slow to respond. There are those who are as ready to die for peace as any of the millions who with such generous courage go to war. And had they been organized and ready, there would have been no war.

I am aware as I write it that the proposal to disarm, and appeal to the love and pity of humanity, sounds strange today.

Yet not stranger surely than the Sermon on the Mount, still read aloud in our churches, by apparently serious priests, to seemingly receptive congregations. And as certainly as I believe that if we lived after the pattern there set forth, we should realize the kingdom of Heaven on earth, so certain am I that if we had disarmed in the first week of last August—not by an arbitrary decision of the Foreign Office, but on a demand from the people—there would have been no war. So great a moral miracle would have had its effect. The world would have been changed. No nation would have rushed into war "in self-defense." There would have been no war.

In this way only, could we really have saved Belgium. For who, looking at that unhappy country now, will claim that with all our efforts and all our sacrifices, we have "saved" her? "At least we have done our best," says one; "at least we are not dishonored." I contend that we did not do our best, and that we are dishonored. Look at Belgium now.

---

3. Royden's first mention of her idea of a Peace Army. In October 1931, reacting to Japan's invasion of Manchuria, Royden collaborated with Christian pacifist Dick Sheppard in a call for recruits to an army that would devote itself to peacemaking. (KW)

When we have driven her violators out, what a country shall we hand back to her people? Can we give back her sons and daughters, or build again her ruined industries? No indemnity we can exact or pay can restore the shattered beauty of her cities, and an industry wrecked takes decades to recover—perhaps it will not recover again. Nor does the case of Belgium stand alone. We great nations stand around the little nations of Europe—Poland, Finland, Denmark, Belgium, the Balkan States—and behold the best that we have done for them! And now, isolating a single glaring iniquity, we point at Germany, and, like a lot of schoolboys in disgrace, cry "He began it!" Began it? Who began it? Which of us is free of blame? What country among us all has broken no treaty and oppressed no weaker member? Every sin against public right has its effect in corrupting public morals, and not one of us has hands that are clean. The best we have done is bad. Indeed, there is no safety for the little nations but in peace. Ask them if they would rather have us all armed for their protection, or all disarmed. There would not be a dissident voice raised on behalf of this sinister protection. The little nations know too well that where force is conceived the only possible basis of international relations, the weak are never safe.

It seems to me that we are dishonored, for, though we did not do the worst thing, neither did we do the best. It is true that disarmament meant taking a great risk, for though I believe it would have prevented war, I must also admit that it might have failed. This admitted risk seems a conclusive argument against it to some who ignore the risks of war. But war also is a great adventure. Those who go to war risk defeat, and they rightly glory in their willingness to take that risk in a good cause. When people advocate neutrality, they are met with the boast that England was prepared to risk something in defense of her word, and surely they are answered? I, too, would have risked something—everything indeed—to win, not a devastated and a ruined Belgium, but Belgium unscathed, untouched. How do we stand as things are? It is actually possible—God forbid that it should happen, but it is possible—that we might be unable to drive the German forces out of Belgium. Suppose the French and Russian armies were crushed, it would be a physical impossibility for ours alone to recover Belgium. Yet we might ourselves remain safe, behind the mighty protection of our fleet! Had we disarmed, we should have at least saved Belgium intact, or suffered with her. Is this a dishonoring alternative? Or can this be called a failure to redeem our pledges? To me it seems the only way in which we could indeed redeem them, and my complaint is not that we risked too much for that end, but that we risked too little.

Nor can it be said that a nation has no right to risk its own destruction. Nations have always claimed that right, and we have applauded them for it. Nations again and again have risked all for freedom. They have been ready to be exterminated rather than yield. The Netherlands in the sixteenth century—Belgium today—have earned the admiration of the world, because they dared everything for freedom and for honor. Will no nation be found ready to die for peace? Or is peace too small a thing to die for? Truly if the nations do not desire peace, none will be found to die for it; only do not let us deceive ourselves by pretending that a nation must not dare all for an ideal, when only today we pay our homage to the heroism of little Belgium. Had we been willing for the peace of the world, to risk all, and had we suffered for it, our suffering would, like the Crucifixion, have been redemptive, and outward failure truest victory. For such a nation could not die, though for nations as for individuals, it is true that they must sometimes lose their lives to save them.

Here, however, we come to a new problem. Behind the question of our pledge to Belgium comes the threat of Germany. Thousands of our soldiers have gone out to give up their lives in order to destroy a false ideal—militarism. For militarism is an ideal. It is not armies and navies, but the worship of armies and navies—the belief that might is right, and that the strongest nation has the right to force its government and its ideals on the less powerful. Against this idea we are now fighting, and I also desire to fight.

But is it not time that we abandoned the hope of exterminating heresies by killing heretics? The history of the Christian Church is stained with blood shed in this belief. And it is true that, though very rarely, "heresies" have sometimes been for a time crushed out in blood. But to do this is to fall into a worse heresy—it is to believe that such cruelty is justifiable. We no longer torture those who disagree with us theologically; but we seek to put a nation to the torture still. For war is nothing less than this. It is not a matter only of those who fight, though that is bad enough. It is a matter also of economic pressure, of slow exhaustion, of the inconspicuous unheroic deaths of those who never come near the field of battle. It is children unborn, and babies who die because their mothers are pressed to death with anxiety and fear and overwork. The infant death rate in Great Britain has gone up with a leap since the war began. What it is in Germany we do not know. But it makes our rules for the protection of non-combatants seem farcical when we face the fact that the desired exhaustion of Germany means—and must inevitably mean—the deaths of women and children. "The economic pressure on Germany," said Mr. Lloyd George[4] in the House of Commons, "is developing satisfactorily." And the applause broke out at once. Economic pressure! It is a graceful phrase for torture; and thinking of the women I know in England whose babies are born dead, from "economic pressure" on their mothers, I ask myself if these are indeed the means by which we shall convert the German people from a false idea.

After all, if and when we have succeeded to the limit of our hopes, when we have Germany beaten, what shall we have proved? That we were stronger than Germany! That we have larger armies and more powerful navies, and greater financial resources! Is that the way to persuade anyone that armies and navies are not above all desirable and necessary things? Lord Haldane[5] counts up the population of Germany and her allies; of England and hers; and points triumphantly to our greater numbers. Mr. Lloyd George reckons up our revenues, and boasts that we can go on raising another hundred million when Germany is drained. And when we have done it, shall we have proved that we are right? By no means; only that we are more numerous and more rich.

It is arguable, I admit, that the failure of Prussia may have its effect in weakening the trust of Germany in Prussian ideals. They may conceivably realize that the same desire to domineer which has created the marvelous mechanism of their army has brought against it almost a world in arms. I do not expect it, for it seems to me almost more clear-sightedness than one can expect of broken and humiliated nations. It seems to me far more likely that a defeated country will merely wish it had sacrificed yet more to a still mightier army, or blame its diplomatists (rather than its soldiers) for their stupidity in trying to fight everybody at once. Still, defeat is sometimes—if it is not a vindictive or shameful defeat—good for a nation, and it may conceivably be good for Germany. But while this remains a very disputable point, it is at least equally questionable whether victory may not establish the heresy of militarism in the heart of our own country. I have not, I confess, observed much growth of pacifism in

---

4. David Lloyd George (1863–1945), minister of munitions at the time Royden wrote this, succeeded H. H. Asquith as prime minister at year's end, 1916. (KW)

5. Richard Burdon Haldane (1856–1928), lord chancellor of England at the beginning of World War I. Previously serving as secretary of state for war, Haldane acted as an unofficial advisor to the War Ministry during the early stages of the conflict. (KW)

Germany, but I have seen much growth of militarism at home. Once more we seek to destroy a heresy by violence, and we enthrone that very heresy in our own hearts. The determination to crush the enemy altogether, the hatred of individual "alien enemies," the belief that war is after all a good thing, as well as an inevitable thing—all this, which is the very opposite of Christianity, is openly professed by people who are quite unaware that they are not Christians. We seek to convert the Prussian from his heresy, but we ourselves know not what spirit we are of.

There is only one way to kill a wrong idea. It is to set forth a right idea. You cannot kill hatred and violence by violence and hatred. You cannot make men out of love with war by making more effective war. Satan will not cast out Satan, though he will certainly seek to persuade us that he will, since of all his devices this has been throughout the ages the most successful. To make war in order to make peace! How beguiling an idea! To make Germans peaceable by killing them with torpedoes and machine guns—that does not sound quite so well. Yet this is what we set out to do when we "fight German militarism" with the weapons of militarism.

You cannot kill a wrong idea except with a right idea. This warfare is the most heroic of all, and heroism will always move mankind. It is the heroism of war, not its cruelty, that leads all the world after it. Whose heart is not stirred, whose breath does not come faster, when the soldiers pass us in the street? Look at their faces, and realize how much they are prepared to sacrifice. Every one of them faces death, and there are things worse than death, and they go gaily to face all these things. Is it not heroic? Well, I tell you that there is a mightier heroism still—the heroism not of the battle, but the cross; the adventure not of war, but of peace. For which is the braver man when all is said—the man who believes in armaments, or the man who stakes everything on an idea? Who is the great adventurer—he who goes against the enemy with swords and guns, or he who goes with naked hands? Who is the mighty hunter—he who seeks the quarry with stones and slings, or he who, with St. Francis, goes to tame a wolf with nothing but the gospel? We peace people have made of peace a dull, drab, sordid, selfish thing. We have made it that ambiguous, dreary thing—"neutrality." But Peace is the great adventure, the glorious romance. And only when the world conceives it so, will the world be drawn after it again. "I, when I am lifted up, will draw all men unto Me" (John 12:32).

But after all, our nation is now at war. And for this we are all responsible. The temper which makes war possible is created by us all, and no one can say he had no part in it. Now, therefore, it seems, we should be silent about peace. To speak against the war we all have made seems a kind of disclaimer of responsibility, a treachery to those who are fighting and dying in France. We ought—so think many of the best and truest of my fellow Christians—now, for very shame, to "stand in with the nation," and to help them do the best they can. "If we are to be damned for this war," said one disputant to me, "let us all suffer together. I am not going to stand out, and try to save my own soul."

There is a noble recklessness in this attitude which makes an almost irresistible appeal. For in all the teaching of Christ this glorious recklessness is present, and no quality is more truly Christian than the willingness to lose even one's soul for others. The New Testament itself could not, in a sense, rise higher than the Old, which said: "Blot me, I pray Thee, out of the Book of Life" (Exod 32:32). [. . .]

If it is true that Christian ethics can never rise higher than the level once reached in the Old Testament, it is also true that in the light of Christ's life we can see further into the truth. No teacher ever set so great a value on the love and loyalty of man to man, or more sternly rebuked those who sought to stand apart from humanity. Those who in Christ's parable are found fit for the Kingdom are not those who believed rightly or prayed well, or kept themselves without blame, but those who, in corporal works of mercy, served their fellow men. "If a man love not his brother whom he hath seen, how shall he love God, Whom he hath not seen?" (1 John 4:20). There is no evading such a challenge.

And yet beside it stands that other tremendous claim of Christ. "Whosoever loveth his father or mother more than Me, he is not worthy of Me. . . . If a man hate not his father and mother, yea, and his own life also, he cannot be My disciple" (Luke 14:26). Can we evade this challenge either? Or how shall we be true to both?

I think we shall be true to men when we are true to Christ, and that by no conceivable tragedy shall we ever find that to do less than the best we can see, is the best that we can do for our fellow men. Not less strange, if we realized it, than the paradox of Christ's teaching is the paradox of Christ Himself. For is it not a paradox that He, who alone among men was sinless, should be to us the eternal type of humanity itself? "Ecce Homo"—Behold the Man! The Son of Man, no less than Son of God, because so do we crave after perfection that only in a perfect man do we, imperfect, sin-stained beings, find the human type we recognize. In this paradox lies the solution of our problem of conflicting loyalties. Evil is always disloyalty to man, as well as God; and less than the best that we can do and see of the ideal is less than perfect loyalty to both. If war is wrong, we shall do well to preach this doctrine even now, when every nerve thrills with the desire to be "one with the nation," and every past sin and error of our own cries out against our raising such a standard. How often when we are most alone, are we indeed most loyal to our race! How often, when we seem most at one with the world, do we indeed betray it!

There comes a moment, perhaps, when one who is speaking achieves a great sympathy with his audience; when he knows that with a word, a phrase, he can strike out the laughter or applause which makes electric his touch upon them. Perhaps even as he says it, he betrays them, and would, that word left unsaid, have been more true. This thrill of sympathy the peacemaker today foregoes; nor will he count it a great thing to bear if he is reproached with treachery. For we who seek peace know best how often we have in our own souls made war, and we shall not find the world's judgment on us too harsh. But neither will we *now* betray what has been too often betrayed, or keep silent on what we believe to be the truth. Truth does not come to men in easy ways, nor will it ever come by those who see a vision, and put it by as a thing too fair for the present hour, to be realized some day. It will be realized, but only when those who see it, however dimly, live up to all they see at any cost. It will come by no automatic process of revelation, but by the blood and sweat of those who see it now. "He that doeth the will shall know of the doctrine" (John 7:17), and through him the world. This is loyalty both to Christ and to "our brother whom we have seen."

And here I seem to find a proof of this; for it is noticeable that many agree that peace is better than war, but hold the world not ready yet for such teaching. I cannot so separate myself from the world, and to me the separation involved in preaching that *here* and *now* war is wrong, when so many think it right, is less real than the separation implied in the belief that I can see a vision others cannot. I am convinced that what I can see others can see, and nothing will persuade me that the world is not "ready" for an ideal for which I am ready. To us who plead for peace, the idea that we stand apart from other men in our capacity for idealism, would be grotesque, if it were not tragic. We are certain that we can serve only by giving the best we have and see; not by withholding any part of it because we judge "the world" not ready yet.

For the truth, as they see it, men are laying down their lives today in Belgium and France. And we who see another truth—shall we be less true to it than they? Not so does the world go forward. "We are all trying to see," said one to me the other day; "if you think you see something we do not, tell it us. *Truth is more to us than Victory.*" Let us, also, believe this. We cannot sacrifice the Christian ideal even to a national necessity. Truth is more than victory. Christ indeed consecrated patriotism, as He consecrated every earthly love. He taught us that love is all one, and all divine, because it is love. But in spite of His own love for the Jewish race, His anguish as He foresaw the destruction of Jerusalem, He would not sanction war. He might have led a revolt against the cruel tyranny of Roman rule in Palestine, and—whether in success or failure—have added another name to the long list of patriot-heroes who shed their blood for their country. Yet He refused. Was He more or less true to humanity by that refusal?

Truth is more than victory. We cannot tell whether defeat or triumph is best for a nation, or whose success upon the battlefield is better for the world. But we know that only he who is ready to die for an ideal can truly be said to be loyal to that ideal, and this hard saying is true of nations as of men. What is the Christian ideal? Submission to evil? Resignation to the sufferings of others? No—"Be not overcome with evil—*but overcome evil with good*" (Rom 12:21).

Source

A. Maude Royden, *The Great Adventure: The Way to Peace* (London: Headley Brothers, 1915).

Poetics of Peace

IN THIS FOREWORD SHE wrote for William King Baker's Penn the Statesman and Gulielma: A Quaker Idyll—*a long and not very good poem about the early days of Quakerism—Royden argues that abstract pacifist arguments influence very few people. What's needed, she believes, is a narrative full of poetry and heroism that is able to stir the imagination and reason as ably as war stories of battlefield courage and sacrifice do. Royden finds William Penn's "holy experiment" in Pennsylvania, the theme of Baker's book, to be exactly the sort of inspiring tale to set hearts and minds ablaze with a desire to consecrate national ideals to the cause of peace. It's this kind of conversion, elicited by skillful poets, and not martial victory over a foe, that has the potential to end all wars.*

Many who have been interested in the ideals of the Society of Friends since the outbreak of the great war have regretted that they have not been enshrined in some more striking and dramatic form than has generally been the case. Pacifism has suffered more than its advocates realize from the drab unmoving character of its presentment. The world is athirst for heroism, and its appeal needs only to be high enough and hard enough to move men who had seemed to be deaf to any appeal but that of selfish interest. The war has taught us that. Terrible as it is, none of us can ever forget the glorious willingness to die which has transformed it and made it a great spiritual adventure to men from whom their country had asked so little before—and for whom, in many cases, it had done still less. But we must not stop here. We must go on to a yet higher appeal, and ask of all who have sacrificed so much, that they should be willing, when the war is over, to fight one more battle for the founding of that better world for which war, after all, can do no more—at the best—than clear the ground.

And if that better world is to find some better way than these appalling conflicts, of removing injustice, recognizing change, and settling international disputes, it must not be built upon the mere substitution of one kind of antagonism for another. Class hatred or sex hatred are just as truly "war" as military war. The spirit of war is not destroyed by the announcement of a new enemy more terrible than the last; but by the refusal to admit enmity at all which caused Christ to speak to Judas Iscariot as "Friend." Such a "war against *all* war" as that must have more than the heroism of war as we know it, and I think that only the man who can *feel* the heroism of the soldier and love it—who can share the (often inarticulate) devotion to national ideals which is so profound an instinct of the heart, and who desires not to abolish it but to consecrate it, can really help the world today. Only he who realizes with passionate sympathy the glory of war can lead us to a yet more glorious peace.

This will sound to some pacifists a contradiction in terms. I believe it to be not a contradiction but a paradox, and truth which is paradoxical can perhaps only be perfectly expressed in a life, or a poem. Truth is more than merely intellectual; hence the element of paradox in every great teacher. Christ's words are as full of it as they are of poetry. The attempt to reduce His teaching to a formula is hopeless. It has been undertaken too often, and pacifists are not the least eager in the attempt. For this reason, their argument seems too academic and separative to appeal as the argument of war appeals.

But in the early history of the Society of Friends there is all the appeal of heroism and romance, all the beauty of peace with the courage of war. The sense of power, the passion for humanity, which make of Christ the most moving figure in the world's history, are here. It is not an academic argument that is given us in the history of Fox and Penn and the rest, but the very romance of peace. Men may disagree with these early Friends in their theology and their politics; they cannot deny them the sympathy and reverence which are a necessary preliminary to understanding.

I therefore have some quarrel with the Society, that its annals have been given to the world for the most part in so plain a dress. Doubtless the absence of pomp and boast is of the essence of Quakerism. But surely there is an appeal to be made to human sympathy and to a noble imagination. The world is adventurous: be it so. Show us then the adventure of peace, and we will follow it!

The "holy experiment" in government made by the Friends in Pennsylvania is one of the most amazing of all romances. It shows us a "pacifist" State in being, and shows that peace cannot, in actual practice, be divorced from the rest of life or sought as a separate thing.

Transparent honesty in all its dealings, loyalty to all its pledges, justice and honor were the foundations on which the relations of Pennsylvania with other races rested. Penn was the—

> Famous builder of the great new world,
> Who with no oath but word of truth to Indian bands,
> Compelled acknowledgment e'en of infidel Voltaire—
> *The only treaty made without an oath—the only treaty kept!*[1]

Yet how little the world knows of this sublime adventure. Most who have heard of it know only that it failed. That its failure was due not to the breakdown of the principles on which it was undertaken, but to their abandonment, hardly any outside the Society of Friends have heard at all. "Very wonderful," the world says of the Holy Experiment: "but after all they had to give it up!" They did give it up indeed; but—"had to"?—

> If they who followed soon forgot,
> It is the old tale told again,
> When one wept o'er Jerusalem,
> I would have gathered—ye would not![2]

The world does not love war, least of all modern war with all its almost inconceivable sacrifice: only the world sees no other way. And therefore it happens that the appeal of war is often most irresistible to those who are nearest to the love of Christ. Those who go into it hating it most—perhaps even believing it to be altogether wrong—surely come into the term of the great paradox—"Whosoever will save his life shall lose it, and whosoever will lose his life for my sake shall find it" (Matt 16:25). To such as these, a "peace-making" that was constructive, adventurous, humane, would make an appeal they would never wish to resist.

Perhaps the great paradox of peace-making needs a poet even more than a prophet. It is in poetry that the highest and the deepest truths find expression. The paradox which, reduced to prose, becomes an unconvincing contradiction, in poetry is recognized for truth against which there is no appeal. We speak despondently of the ugly truth, the sordid truth, the brutal truth: but Keats tells us in triumph—

> Beauty is Truth, Truth Beauty,[3]

---

1. William King Baker, *Penn the Statesman and Gulielma: A Quaker Idyll* (Edinburgh: Oliphants, 1926), 10. (KW)

2. Baker, *Penn the Statesman*, 186. (KW)

3. John Keats, "Ode to a Grecian Urn." (KW)

and we know that it is true. The world is full of hatred and suspicion, of darkness and cruel habitations. Shelley (who knew much of the world's hatred) affirms a greater truth: —

> Common as light is Love,
> And its familiar voice wearies not ever.

Is that not true? The very Truth itself? And do we not not only assent but even dimly *recognize* its certainty? There is some poet in us all, and with that divine faculty we know what these greater, more articulate poets express for us. Somewhere, somewhen, we knew it all, and Shelley, Keats, Wordsworth, Shakespeare himself but reminds us of a thing we knew before. Beneath the contradiction of facts, and the superficial logic of the brain, is a truth to which the prophet and the poet alike appeal, and do not appeal in vain. For such great affirmations are not based on reason only, nor do they evoke a solely intellectual assent. They are addressed to the whole human being (not leaving out but including his intelligence), and are easily dissected and derided by anyone who meets them on a lower plane. The derision leaves them untouched. The poet stands in the midst and cries—"He that hath ears to hear, let him hear" (Matt 11:15).

Poetry, therefore, should be read in wartime, and not least then. For its sublime audacity, its tremendous faith is needed more now than ever before. Now, when men know that reason is not everything, that there are mighty instincts and great passions which are only partly influenced by reason and can never be perfectly controlled by it, now it is fatally easy to throw reason overboard and give passion the reins. And when this happens it is not the noblest passions that rule. For men have reason as well as instinct, and the whole human being is needed for the service of the world. It is the poet's glory that he appeals to the whole. No man is too intellectual for Shakespeare or Wordsworth. Yet Shakespeare is never merely an intellect. His work is penetrated with emotion also, and with that "transcendental element" which makes it the heritage of every man that has a human spirit. None of us is without it. All of us at times know those "obstinate questionings"—

> Of sense and outward things,
> Fallings from us, vanishings;
> Blank misgivings of a Creature
> Moving about in worlds not realized;
> High instincts before which our mortal nature
> Doth tremble like a guilty thing surprised.[4]

---

4. William Wordsworth, "Ode: Intimations of Immortality from Recollections of Early Childhood." (KW)

That world not realized he realizes for us, and teaches us to know it for our spiritual home. We believe it and take courage. Surely courage was never needed more than now.

It is then with joy that I welcome the affirming of yet another great truth in poetry.

> Those are truly great
> Who, as the centuries slowly pass,
> Are found by each succeeding race
> Near to the heart of human love.[5]

Is that true? Has it ceased to be true because the world today seems full of hate? A thousand times No! The conquerors of the world are still found among those who are "near to the heart of human love," whether they be soldiers or Quakers. Indeed, these great lovers must always in a sense be both. The adventurous spirit, the eagerness to risk all, the light holding of one's own life in comparison with another's, these are the qualities of God's lovers throughout the world's history; and it is the lover, not the separatist, who will save us.

Such a lover was William Penn. No doctrinaire, but a gallant spirit taking on the whole armor of Christ—His love and pity, tenderness and freedom, His great might and courage also, and His wide compassion for every perplexed and struggling human aim. Such are no more gone from us when they die, than is their Master Christ. Penn's name is still a beacon and his faith a call to every heroic adventurer of the soul: —

> He fell, but never knew defeat,
> Whose soul was set to victory;
> His name brings glow of triumph still,
> A buoyant note, like bugle call
> That rings out o'er the battlements
> Of each entrenched and ancient wrong.[6]

Source

A. Maude Royden, Foreword to *Penn the Statesman and Gulielma: A Quaker Idyll*, by William King Baker (Edinburgh: Oliphants, 1926), 4–8.

---

5. Baker, *Penn the Statesman*, 299. (KW)
6. Baker, *Penn the Statesman*, 300. (KW)

Feminism and Militarism

IN THIS CONTRIBUTION TO a pacifist anthology published in the second year of the Great War, Royden argues that militarism and imperialism—vehicles propelled by physical force—are contrary to the woman's movement's embrace of moral force, which "is not nobler only but stronger than coercion." When a spirit of coercion infects a nation, it breeds "bitterness and hostility" among those who are victimized and "brutality and moral stupidity" on the part of those who victimize; when nations go to war, a parallel dynamic between victors and losers occurs. Because the woman's movement rests on the assumption that consent is more powerful than coercion, it offers a creative and life-affirming alternative to war.

Among the influences making for international understanding, the Woman's Movement has been reckoned by its supporters to be one of the strongest. [. . .]

Conviction was deepened by the great chapter on "Women and War" appearing in Olive Schreiner's *Woman and Labor*.[1] Expressing with a noble idealism the right attitude of women toward war, Olive Schreiner gave to an emotion its philosophy. Women, she said, were not only the worst sufferers from war: they were by nature the guardians of life. Conservers of the race, mothers of its children, war must be to them the worst of all catastrophes. As a sculptor would cast into the breach any stone rather than that which he had wrought into a statue, so women, when the gulf opens between the nations, would cast in anything rather than the men they have made. "No woman who is a woman," writes Mrs. Schreiner, "says of a human body, 'It is nothing.'"[2] This phrase, like the whole chapter in which it appears, became a classic of the Woman's Movement.

---

1. Olive Schreiner, "Women and War," in *Woman and Labor* (New York: Stokes, 1911), 157–86. (KW)

2. Schreiner, "Women and War," 175–76. (KW)

It was believed to express the true, the inevitable attitude of women as a sex, whether in or outside the progressive ranks. It was assumed to be so "natural" to them, that to put power into their hands was to forge a weapon against war. It was not denied that they might feel that war might in some cases still be a national duty; but it was believed with conviction that women, from their very nature, would approach the question with an unspeakable reluctance, that war would appear to them in all its naked horror, shorn of glory, that they would be free from the "war fever" to which men so easily fall victims.

In support of this view, it is to be borne in mind that women's internationalism has on the whole broken down less conspicuously than men's, two international congresses having been held since the war began, and both representing women. It is probably also true that among working people the desire for peace is still stronger among the women than the men. On the other hand, the belief that women are innately more pacific than men has been severely shaken, if not altogether destroyed. It is now very evident that they can be as virulently militarist, as blindly partisan, not as the soldier, for in him such qualities are generally absent, but as the male non-combatant, for whom the same cannot always be said. Among women, as among men, there are extremists for war and for peace; pacifists and militarists; women who are as passionately convinced as Bernhardi that war is a good thing,[3] women who accept it as a terrible necessity, women who repudiate it altogether. All these views they share with men. There appears to be no cleavage of opinion along sex lines. Nor perhaps should we have expected it. History shows no war averted by the influence of women; none against which women, as women, have worked, or organized, or offered more than here and there a sporadic protest. Queens have been no more reluctant than kings to look on the dead bodies of men and say, "It is nothing." The fact that war brings to women personally no glory, but only suffering, is empty of significance; they are well accustomed to vicarious glory and well accustomed to suffering. The appeal to their loyalty comes with irresistible force. "We cannot fight," they say; "let us at least be willing to suffer."

Not what is noble only, but what is ignoble in women, is enlisted easily in the service of war. The importance of fear as a factor in warmaking cannot be overlooked, and can hardly be overestimated. Any politician can play on panic when he wishes to stampede a people into

3. Friedrich von Bernhardi (1849–1930), Prussian general and author who promoted and glorified war. (KW)

war. The fear of being attacked enables him to blind them, and makes them an easy tool for a war which is really one of aggression. And in the creation of panic a sex trained to timidity is hardly likely to play a restraining part. Personal courage is the one quality held indispensable in a man: it has not been extraordinarily admired in women, and since fear is the mother of cruelty, it should not surprise any of us if those who have never been expected to be brave should sometimes outdo the men in vindictiveness. That so many women remain untainted by fear should rather give us hope. Nevertheless, it is reasonable to remember that so long as fear plays a part in the making of wars, women are hardly likely as a sex to be more uncompromising in their desire for peace than men.

It should, therefore, have surprised no one (though, in fact, it surprised many of us) that women throughout Europe have accepted war as an inevitable evil, or even, in the earnestness of their loyalty, as a spiritual good. Nor does their attitude toward war in general, or this war in particular, prove those wrong who have believed that the Woman's Movement is one of the great influences making for peace. It is true that its effect will not be so direct or so obvious as had been supposed. The mistake has been rather about the nature of its influence than about its ultimate effect. Women may, when they have the power, no more "vote against war" than men; it remains a fact that every woman who is working for the advance of the Woman's Movement is, however martial she is herself, however profoundly she may mistake the meaning and the foundation of her work, working against militarism. She is forever asserting a principle of which war is a perpetual denial. One principle must, in the end, destroy the other.

The Woman's Movement in all its aspects, but especially, of course, in its political one, is an assertion of moral force as the supreme governing force in the world. If its adherents are wrong, and it is physical force which is "the ultimate appeal," then the militarist is right, and the physically weaker sex, like the little and weak nation, has no claim that may not be set aside. The weak have no rights in a world governed by brute force; they have only privileges, which may be granted, revoked, or withheld. It has been the fundamental principle of the Woman's Movement that it claims rights and duties, but never privileges. By what right, however, do those who are inferior in physical force ask to share, equally with their superiors, in government, if government rests on physical force? Such a claim could not be entertained. And women, recognizing this, have rightly based their demand on the great principle that government rests upon consent, and that the use of physical force is not "the ultimate appeal," but a confession of failure.

Argument has raged round this vital question, and in consequence the women's position and that of the opposition to it has been again and again defined. The "physical force argument" has been put forward with great effect and with an enthusiasm no Bernhardi could exceed by notable Anti-Suffragists.[4] In their writings and speeches the conviction that women could have no right to self-government while they lacked physical strength to enforce it has been expounded in terms which almost grotesquely resemble the expositions of "Prussianism" and the treatment of "little nations" which have burned themselves with such horror into our memories to-day. "The State is Power," says Treitschke; "there is something laughable in the idea of a small State."[5] What power? Certainly not moral power, for there may be a greater moral power in a little State than a big one. But physical power, in which the big State must be superior. "There is something laughable" in the idea that a little State, a people wanting in sheer force of numbers and arms, should dream of independence, of freedom, of developing along its own lines its own civilization. "Something laughable"! There is also something obscene in such laughter—something unimaginably brutal. The same brutality (though we had not learned to call it "Prussianism") found something laughable in the idea that women, who are inferior to men in muscle, should claim as "rights" what could (if allowed at all) never be more than privileges in a world ruled by brute force. Certainly if the world is so ruled the claim does become laughable. Herein lay the weakness of the militant movement, which appealed to a principle which the whole Woman's Movement was concerned to deny. But even here, regardless of logic—or perhaps conscious of a deeper logic than their policy suggested—the women who resorted to violence frequently argued that they did so only to prove the utter failure of violence used against themselves. Nor can any misunderstanding on the part of Suffragists of their own position destroy

---

4. See especially "The Physical Force Argument against Woman's Suffrage," by A. McCallum Scott. (MR)

5. Heinrich von Treitschke (1834–96), German historian and nationalist. This appears to be a paraphrase of a passage from Treitschke's *Politics*, trans. Blanche Dugdale and Torben de Ville (New York: Macmillan, 1916), 1:34: "On close examination then, it becomes clear that if the State is power, only that State which has power realizes its own idea, and this accounts for the undeniably ridiculous element which we discern in the existence of a small State. Weakness is not itself ridiculous, except when masquerading as strength." (KW)

the fact that it rests upon a principle which militarism denies. The strife between the two is internecine. Militarism and the Woman's Movement cannot exist together. Take a militarist religion like that of Islam, and you see women reduced to the lowest level of degradation; a militarist legal code like the Code Napoleon, and you have women without human rights and only sex functions—breeders of potential soldiers merely; a militarist civilization like that of Prussia, and again women without rights, almost without privileges, women lagging behind their sisters in other civilizations otherwise near akin to them. "You do not know what it is like to be a woman," said a prominent German Suffragist, "in a country which has built its whole existence on a successful war."

As militarism waxes or wanes so, in inverse ratio, does the Woman's Movement. In Russia—a race essentially pacific, whatever criticisms may be brought against its government—women hold a much higher position than in Germany. In France, a country once "militarist" to the core, but now no longer so, the Code Napoleon remains, the legacy of the arch-militarist, Napoleon; but the higher level of civilization reached today reflects itself in the improved actual (as distinct from the legal) position of French women. In Norway and Sweden, countries so earnest in their desire for peace that their division into two kingdoms under separate sovereigns was actually effected (though with some soreness and jealousy) without a war, women have in one case actually achieved political freedom and in the other are upon the verge of it. In America women hold a high position, and are constantly improving it. In Great Britain both the friends and the foes of their movement illustrate the same truth.

There has been—perhaps still is—a section of public opinion in this country which believes that the British Empire is held together by the sword. It has even been stated that India is "held at the point of the bayonet." The fact that for a long time our mighty Empire was seldom without its "little wars" somewhere along its vast frontiers gave color to a belief which otherwise seems actually grotesque. And it is significant that the opponents of Women's Suffrage were largely drawn from the ranks of this school of imperialist thought. Their argument was developed along two lines: one, that women could take no part in the business of holding the Empire by the sword, the other that they could not "think imperially." The latter argument was frequently put forward by women so obviously capable of performing the duty whose possibility (to other women?) they earnestly denied, as to remove its sting and its effect. The former was the real line of defense, and as long as this jingo school of imperialism remains so long inevitably must there be an irreconcilable party of opposition to the Woman's Movement in this country. Its wane and the rising of a nobler conception of Empire has coincided with the gathering strength and power of that movement. Both spring from the same root: the belief that government, whether of a nation or an Empire, must rest upon consent, or confess its failure; that moral force is not nobler only but stronger than coercion; that an Empire "held at the point of the bayonet" must fall to pieces at the first shock of danger, while one in which there is freedom for the least as well as the greatest of its members stands "whole as the marble, founded as the rock."[6] We do not imagine today that New Zealand, with its population of two or three millions, has less right to the free development of its own type of civilization than we with our fifty millions. We do not call that right a "privilege," or find "something laughable in the idea of a small State." We do not assume that there are no rights where there is not power to enforce them. On the contrary, we know that such rights can never be violated except at fearful cost to the violator. Not only does the act of injustice brutalize his conscience, but it vindicates again the principle which must at last react against him. Nations have assumed the right to act solely in their own immediate interests so far as they have the power to do so; but no nation can always be the strongest, and the time will come when another stronger arises, or many strong ones find their common interest against the violator, and then the old insistence that might is right destroys what it had set up.

In a deeper sense also the strong stand to lose by a violation of the rights of the weak. Mr. Lloyd George, in one of the noblest passages of a great speech at the beginning of the war, spoke of the debt owed by humanity to the little nations, who brought to its lips some of the "choicest wines."[7] And we would add that even those little nations who have no specially glorious history, no radiant names, have yet enriched the civilization of the world by their difference and variety of type. To crush out all

---

6. Shakespeare, *Macbeth*, 3.4. (KW)

7. On 21 September 1914, five weeks after Britain entered World War I, Lloyd George, then chancellor of the exchequer, delivered a speech in London in which he referred to Serbia and Belgium as choicest wines: "God has chosen little nations as the vessels by which He carries His choicest wines to the lips of humanity, to rejoice their hearts, to exalt their vision, to stimulate and strengthen their faith; and if we had stood by when two little nations were being crushed and broken by the brutal hands of barbarism, our shame would have rung down the everlasting ages." (KW)

those who have the right to exist but not the power to enforce that right is to commend to one's own lips, not the "choice wine" of humanity but

> The bitter dregs of woe
> Which ever from the oppressed to the oppressor flow.[8]

The spirit which disregards this danger and despises this loss to civilization is "militarism"; and those who assert that rights remain rights even when they cannot be enforced, and that the moral law violated by physical violence vindicates itself in the end by the destruction of the destroyer, are fighting against militarism, whether they desire it or not. The Woman's Movement is based on belief in the moral law. It is concerned to assert the supremacy of moral force, and it can show that wherever the rights of the weak are set aside there enters into the State an element of bitterness and hostility on the one side, of brutality and moral stupidity on the other, which lowers its standard of strength and effectiveness as well as of moral nobility.

It is true that although the principles of militarism and feminism are fundamentally opposed many people do not know it, and—since we are not a peculiarly logical race—many Englishmen and women who are genuinely shocked at Prussianism as expounded by Bernhardi and applied to Belgium, have themselves expatiated eloquently in the same vein when the question was of classes or sexes instead of nations. There are militarists who believe themselves feminist, and feminists who are undoubtedly militarist. And, after all, since we are most of us perfectly aware that "logic is not a science but a dodge,"[9] we must beware of dismissing a paradox merely because it involves an *apparent* contradiction. When, however, the contradiction is real—when the opposition between two principles is fundamental—the human mind cannot forever hold them both. One must drive out and destroy the other. Those feminists who had most closely thought out their position had already grasped the issue. When war broke out, and ordinary political activities were necessarily suspended, it seemed to them as inevitable that they should take up the task of combating the real enemy of women (and of civilization)—militarism—as it was that they should take their share in the relief of the physical miseries and

---

8. Percy Bysshe Shelley, "The Revolt of Islam," canto 8. (KW)

9. Often attributed to Benjamin Jowett (1817–93), theologian, translator of Plato, and master of Balliol College. Known for both his vast learning and mordant humor, Oxford undergraduates immortalized him in this bit of doggerel: "I am the master of Balliol College; and what I don't know is not knowledge." (KW)

material burdens of war. There was no question of opposition to the war itself within the great Suffrage organizations, since the vast majority of their members believed that war had been forced upon us and was, on our part, a battle against a militarist ideal. But there was a deep consciousness that the spirit of militarism is very hardly separated from the fact of war, and that this spirit is immovably opposed to the feminism which rests its whole claim on the supremacy of spiritual force. War, indeed, has its spiritual passion; but the fact that this must find its expression in the crudest forms of violence tends to exalt the latter at the expense of the former. Women can do no greater service to the world than to increase the healthy skepticism of violence as a method of imposing ideals which the history of religious persecution has already created.

War may claim for itself the power to destroy and to clear the ground. It can never construct or create. It is not the means by which ideals are imposed. There is ultimately no way of combating a wrong idea but the setting forth of a right one. Whether they are right who believe that moral force is "the ultimate appeal" against which coercion is vain and violence merely a counsel of despair, or they who see in physical force the real basis of government, let time show. One thing at least is certain—that as the Woman's Movement embodies the one creed and "militarism" the other, so these two must be in eternal opposition. The victory of one is the defeat of the other. Women, whatever other claim may be made for them, are not equal to men in their capacity to use force or their willingness to believe in it. For them, therefore, to ask for equal rights with men in a world governed by such force is frivolous. Their claim would not be granted, and if granted would not be valid. Like the negro vote in America, it would be a cheat and a delusion. But if moral power be the true basis of human relationship, then the Woman's Movement is on a sure foundation and moves to its inevitable triumph. Its victory will be an element in the making of permanent peace, not because women are less liable to "war fever" than men, or more reluctant to pay the great price of war, but because their claim and its fulfillment involves the assertion of that which war perpetually denies.

Source

A. Maude Royden, "War and the Woman's Movement," in *Towards a Lasting Settlement*, ed. Charles Roden Buxton (New York: Macmillan, 1916), 133, 134–46.

"A Weapon We Haven't Got"

ROYDEN REMAINED PERSUADED HER entire adult life that physical violence was contrary to the teaching and message of Jesus. But in the 1930s, she came to the conclusion, albeit reluctantly, that pacifism simply couldn't prevent modern warfare. In this essay written shortly after Mohandas Gandhi's assassination, she recalls that the Peace Army she, Dick Sheppard, and Herbert Gray tried to organize failed to enlist many recruits. Moreover, by the time World War II erupted, the dream of a coterie of pacifists standing between opposing armies to prevent battle seemed particularly unrealistic. So Royden, like many other longstanding pacifists (Bertrand Russell, for example), felt she had no choice but to support the armed struggle against Nazi aggression. Nevertheless, she regretted that after nineteen centuries, the Christian West had still not absorbed Jesus's message of peace.

In those years I was, or believed myself to be, as absolute a Pacifist as the Mahatma himself. I had been so since the first World War broke out in 1914, and held the faith until the second came in 1939. A few weeks after this overwhelming catastrophe I gave up and admitted publicly that I felt we were bound, in all the circumstances, to fight.

Gandhi heard of this and in an article in *Harijan* he reasoned with and gently rebuked me. Miss Agatha Harrison[1] asked me if I would like to reply but I had no heart to do so, and no right. I felt all the justice of his rebuke. Spiritual power was indeed the best—the only perfect—weapon with which to meet material force. I have never hesitated in my conviction of that. My rejection of the Pacifism in which I had believed implied no doubt. But circumstances forced me to realize that it was a weapon that neither I as an individual nor we British as a nation could use. As a friend of mine said, "You Pacifists are trying to use a weapon you haven't got."

1. Agatha Harrison (1885–1954), English pacifist and collaborator with Mohandas Gandhi. (KW)

In 1932, when Japan attacked China, Dr. H. R. L. Sheppard, an English parson, Dr. Herbert Gray, a Scotch minister, and I proposed to call together an army of Pacifists who should offer themselves to the League of Nations as the "shock troops" of peace.[2] We were presented with a unique opportunity, unlikely ever to come again in the history of mankind. I need not go into all the circumstances but will only say that, in modern warfare, the interposition of an unarmed body of civilians of both sexes between two opposing armies will practically always be an impossibility. At that moment it was not impossible. China and Japan were fighting across the streets of Shanghai and Shanghai is on the sea. If the League of Nations could have gathered a Peace Army, transported it to Shanghai and landed it on the Bund or quay which was then under international control, we soldiers of peace would have been but a few hundred yards from the battle.

We launched our appeal. Because of its dramatic character it immediately received an enormous publicity. Sir Eric Drummond[3] then Secretary-General to the League of Nations, himself handed our letter to the press of the world whose representatives were gathered in Geneva. In response to our entreaty that he should not regard our plan as "fantastic," he replied that he did not at all think it so, and advised us to take the necessary steps to get it brought before the Assembly of the League at that time in session.

Meanwhile the proposal to form a Peace Army was received everywhere with tremendous interest and leading articles appeared in the newspapers of countries so widely different as the United States of America and Sierra Leone. Comment, even when skeptical, was friendly. We could not say that the world was ignorant of our offer.

Our first volunteer was an Irish Brigadier General; our second an engineer; our third a Chinese Christian, Mr. T. Z. Koo.[4]

And after that? From the worldwide publicity we received, how many recruits? Just—only just—over a thousand.

---

2. For more on the proposed Peace Army, see my introduction to H. R. L. Sheppard's *We Say No! The Plain Man's Guide to Pacifism* (Eugene, OR: Cascade, 2013). (KW)

3. Eric Drummond, seventh Earl of Pembroke (1876–1951), the first secretary general of the League of Nations. (KW)

4. Ta Zung "T. Z." Koo (1887–1971), Chinese Christian, pacifist, and professor, who for many years worked with the WMCA and the SCM. (KW)

We approached several governments represented at the Assembly of the League of Nations with our plan, but with such a following what could we expect? Courteous refusals or silence. That is what we got, and no wonder.

Perhaps we should have sought to go alone. Perhaps three Pacifists being killed in a manner so much in the spirit of Mahatma Gandhi might have worked a miracle. How can we tell? While we were writing to Prime Ministers and Foreign Secretaries and awaiting replies, the golden opportunity was lost. Fighting speed over a vast front. Our project became impracticable. It seems in the highest degree unlikely that it will ever be practicable again.

But, though at the time I did not realize it, I see how this failure shook my faith in Pacifism. I had believed that Pacifists were only longing for a chance of dying in the cause of peace as soldiers in the cause of war. There were and are some, but how few! For some years I still believed myself to be a Pacifist. Then the war of 1939–45 came and, after some weeks of agonized indecision, I knew that I had no faith at all in the ability of any European or American nation to use the weapon of spiritual power. We had no practice in it, no discipline, and no real faith in it. The only alternative to fighting with material weapons was to do nothing. To do nothing could not, in my judgment, be the right answer to a world in agony.

I know there were men and women who found ways of service. There were Quakers and others who gave their lives in Red Cross work, as stretcher-bearers or in ambulance units, and gave them gladly. But there was nothing resembling the Satyagraha[5] of Gandhi's disciples; no concerted, trained, and disciplined soldiers of the spiritual Power of God.

I could not help feeling that those who recognized this dreadful truth and went out to fight evil with the weapons they could use, had been trained and disciplined to use, were in the right.

But I recognized that this facing of facts was, as I have said, a dreadful thing. After nearly two thousand years of Christianity we were still unable to do better than rely on the frightful instruments of material force. There lay the sting of Mahatma Gandhi's rebuke to me and there the reason why I had no answer to make. To believe that in AD 1939 we Christians could not wield the spiritual power our Master did was to be worthy of rebuke indeed. In common with all Christians who felt forced to fight, I felt the horrible disgrace, the tragic failure, that war is to us. The

---

5. Satyagraha, literally "truth force," the name by which Gandhi's nonviolent resistance became known. (KW)

best Christian in the world and the man most like Christ was a Hindu. He was Mahatma Gandhi.

Source

A. Maude Royden, "Master Christian?" in *Gandhi Memorial*, ed. Kshitis Roy, special issue, *The Visva Bharati Quarterly* (2 October 1949), 132–43.

Part 2.

"Women Are Human Beings"

Selections from Royden's writings on women's rights

Women and Work

IN THIS 1917 ESSAY, Royden argues that an unintended but happy consequence of the war is that it raised awareness that "women are human beings." Traditionally relegated by the "handicap of their sex" to tasks a masculine society saw as relatively unimportant, women proved by their contributions to the war effort—producing food, manufacturing munitions, and serving as medical personnel—that they were perfectly capable of performing traditional male roles. But Royden had no wish to deny differences in dispositions and skill sets between men and women, nor to substitute a "mulier-centric" culture for a "virocentric" one. She argues that the work for which women are especially suited ought not to be seen as signs of female inferiority. Motherhood, for example, is a "job" exclusively reserved for women, and should be valued—and compensated—as legitimate labor.

War, and the atmosphere engendered by war, are the inveterate foes of feminism; but this, and perhaps all future wars, have an element in them which is on the side of the women. The new factor in the case is, of course, the discovery that war itself can no longer, under modern conditions, be carried on successfully without their help. When Sir Douglas Haig[1] called for and expressed the gratitude of the Army to "their comrades in the factories," he put on record the distance traversed by civilization in its estimate of the value of women in wartime since Aristotle compared the women of Sparta with other women so unfavorably, on the grounds that they (the Spartans) were a positive hindrance instead of being merely, "like the women in other states, wholly useless."[2]

If this discovery of the powers of women has its due weight it will go far to counteract the reactionary influences engendered by war. We may

---

1. Douglas Haig (1861–1928), commander of the British Expeditionary Force on the Western Front from 1915 to 1918. Nicknamed "Butcher Haig" by his critics. (KW)

2. *Politics* 2.9. (MR)

then look to see the Woman's Movement developing rapidly and along rather different lines from those on which it has proceeded up to the present. The leaders of the movement in its earlier stages, some forty or fifty years ago, emphasized above all the common humanity of women and men, and in doing so laid the foundations of all future building well and truly. But since men have always assumed that they were the norm, and alone really and wholly human, women have been obliged to seek to prove that they were not only equal to men, but so exactly like them as to be able to do their best work and develop their best capacities under like conditions. Perhaps the genuine and deep admiration of men for themselves a little overclouded the judgment of the women. Certainly it strikes one as a naïve assumption that women should ask to share the educational privileges of men on the ground that in doing so they would certainly secure "the best." One can hardly read the statement today without a gasp, reflecting on the extreme conservatism, the snobbishness, and the inefficiency which characterizes many of the great educational institutions founded for and by men. But Stuart and Hanoverian civilization had to a paralyzing degree over-emphasized femininity of women, had denied them intellectual power, courage, public spirit, wisdom, and independence; and in doing this had only carried on and strengthened a tradition almost as old as what is called "civilization." It was right and inevitable that the Woman's Movement, when it came, should be a movement toward a greater emphasis on the humanity of women, and that in claiming a share in the liberty of men they should seem at least to be "aping" them. It was an easy gibe. It had this amount of truth in it—that no one was concerned to prove the obvious, that women were different from men; every progressive desired and *needed* to show that they were very like them.

But now all this may be taken as proved. Woman, who could prove nothing by showing that she could do her own very necessary work, has convinced even the vanity of man by showing that she can do his. A woman who bore a child or many children, ran a household, and brought up a family fit and virtuous, was still only "arrested man," and a perpetual minor; but a woman who can clip tickets on a tramcar is recognized at once as a Superwoman—in other words, a man.[3] She has been a nurse for many years: this only qualified her for the status of angel. Now she is a doctor in a military hospital and takes an officer's salute, and, whether

---

3. See "The War and Its Effect upon Women" (H. M. Swanwick). (MR)

to rise an angel or not, is buried with military honors. It is the fact that this astonishing discovery has been in the supreme and crucial instance of war which has so foreshortened the long effort to prove the equality of women with men. All the bearing and suffering in the world has not availed to convince the skeptical male as has the anguish of waiting for munitions at the front—the knowledge that women are working night and day to turn them out at home. In modern warfare courage, endurance, even generalship, are useless without munitions. The gradual heaping up of shells, the increasing and now almost perfect accuracy of the guns, are the result of the work of men who have actually in some cases had to be taken out of the trenches for the more urgent need of the factories—and of women.

Today the cry arises for women on the land. We can no more do without food than munitions. It is a war of guns on the front, a war of starvation—blockade and worse blockade—at the rear. Which can hold out longest? We can. But we must produce food, and agriculture has been starved of men. "Women! Your country needs you!"

It has been a tragic lesson, but it is useless to repine that it has been set us. The future is in our hands, and the Woman's Movement of the future is one of its most important factors. It has been, I believe, transformed by the war, and its opportunity is great. A considerable number of people outside the Woman's Movement are now convinced that women are human beings, having a human value outside sex. Enough, indeed, have grasped this fact to make its apprehension probable, in course of time, by that large and slowly moving mass of people who are not in the habit of reasoning out their convictions, but of letting them gradually soak in from outside. It has become necessary, therefore, now to consider the points at which women differ from men, and differ not through artificial circumstances, which may be altered, but in fundamentals, and to demand the conditions which shall enable them to do their best work. It is not necessary to show that they can do men's work under men's conditions. It is necessary to find out what is the work they can do *best*, and which are the best conditions for doing it. The round peg, if sufficiently indiarubbery in composition, can fit more or less a square hole. But it would be more useful and more comfortable in a round one—unless it is ashamed of its roundness.

This is, of course, the crux. The assumption that man was the norm inclined women to show that they could be as square as he. Any difference was assumed by men to be an inferiority, and by some women at least was slurred over and minimized as far as possible. But it remains a fact that women are different from men in certain respects, and, neither minimizing nor maximizing this difference, should simply take it into account, and demand conditions which suit them. If men and women are working together and conditions cannot be made ideal for both, there should be a compromise. At present the "compromise" is apt to consist in the convenience of men being considered, and the inconvenience of women endured in silence as due to an "inferiority" in their natures.

It is, for instance, possible that women "naturally" work faster and take more out of themselves than men. If this is so they should work shorter hours for the same pay. To suppose that this is a sign of inferiority is merely comic. Again, in some cases it has been found that women can work equally long hours, but require them more frequently broken by intervals of rest. Shorter shifts should be the rule for them. It used to be stated that occupations in which women need to stand a great deal were unsuitable for them. I used to believe this myself until, on taking on a certain amount of my own domestic work, I found that most women never sit down at all, and have almost forgotten that chairs were made for anything but for men to sit down on them. Nevertheless, standing is often a most unnecessary expenditure of energy, and if women can win an improvement here it will be all to the good for both sexes.[4] Everywhere they should be working for conditions which suit them, that it may be found (1) what work is really best done by men and what by women, (2) how far a compromise must be effected when men and women work together, (3) in what respects radical changes are necessary in order to get the best service of women wherever it is given.

This, it will be said, may involve an almost revolutionary change in some cases. Certainly, if it is necessary. Why not? The world must cease to be "virocentric" without becoming "mulier-centric."[5] It must cease to suppose that the way in which men work is necessarily the "right" way in a sense which makes any other way the "wrong" way. It must cease to regard physical or psychological differences between men and women as mere instances of inferiority on the part of the women. "The handicap

---

4. Some of the London omnibuses now have seats for conductors, and during many parts of the day these are used without any inconvenience whatever to the public. It would be a good thing if the same consideration were given to the nurses in our hospitals. (MR)

5. Royden means that the world must cease to be "male-centric" without becoming "female-centric." (KW)

of sex" is an expression which could only find its vogue in a virocentric world, or, to revert to my simile, a world made for square pegs and full of pity or contempt for round ones. It is true that, on the whole, the world is organized for the convenience of the square peg only. It is precisely this that must be changed, and will be changed, now that women are not afraid or ashamed of their difference from men. "You do not speak like a man," said a man pityingly to one of our ablest public speakers. "I have no wish to," was the reply. "I speak like a woman." "Dr. Shaw,"[6] said a chairman in America, "is a woman with the brains of a man." "Before I know whether that is a compliment or an insult," was the crisp reply, "I want to see the man whose brains I have got."

It will surely be found that there is a "sex handicap" somewhere and sometimes. Men do not seem to have much capacity for sick nursing or the care of young children. Women no doubt have disabilities, physical or other, for certain walks in life. But at present "the handicap of sex" means nothing more nor less than the difference between men and women. So true is this that it is applied to the women even when it is obviously true of the men. Men have, for example, sometimes greater sexual desire and often less self-control than women. It is consequently sometimes difficult for them to work undisturbed with or near women. The suggested remedy of the anti-feminist is that the women should be shut up, secluded, kept away. Their seclusion in Eastern countries, their exclusion from certain professions in Western countries, is actually justified on ground that some men are thus handicapped by sex. The absurdity of speaking of "sex handicap" as though it were (in this case) the woman's is glaring. But, in fact, this "handicap" (except where artificially created) is an indication only of those differences which fit one sex rather than the other for certain duties. The duties themselves are equal in importance and interest.

The supreme instance of the "sex handicap" is, of course, generally announced to be motherhood. Certainly hitherto it has been made so. But how amazing that this sacred and essential duty should be spoken of in such a phrase! It is true that motherhood takes a great toll of vitality, time, and strength. It is absorbing, and not easily combined with other occupations. The same is true of any creative work—the artist, poet, musician, scientist, are equally "handicapped." But though the fate of artists is often hard, it is in a virocentric world indeed that motherhood should have been made (as it is) a "handicap" in the race of life. Here are citizens

6. Anna Howard Shaw (1847–1919), American physician, suffragist, and Methodist minister. (KW)

able to perform a duty absolutely essential to the existence of the race. Without them it could not continue. And this essential and unique capacity is described by those who but for it would never have existed as a handicap! Not only so, but—so is our world organized—it actually *is* a handicap. A childless woman is underpaid because she is supposed to have no dependents. But a woman with children is immeasurably worse off. She must either part with them into some charitable or poor law institution or starve herself and them to "keep her home together." While her husband is alive she must generally sacrifice all hope of economic independence in order to bear and rear children; for it is not supposed for a moment that work should be paid or can have any economic value that is solely done by women and could never in any circumstances be done by men. Yet economic independence becomes dearer and dearer to women. Those (and they are many) who have tasted it during the war are in no hurry to give it up. Neither, indeed, do they wish to neglect their children. How is the problem to be solved?

By some it is suggested that motherhood need not really be so great or absorbing an affair. Crêches, nurseries, and schools, combined with better hygiene and a State medical service, will set the average woman free to earn outside. By others it is felt that the economic inferiority of women is, and must remain, an accepted fact. I do not believe the Woman's Movement of the future will take these lines. It cannot really be argued that citizens who perform an essential service (which they can withhold if they choose) are economically valueless because that service takes all or most of their strength. As well say that a workman cannot earn his living because his work takes all his strength. Our object will not be to enable mothers to earn their living, but to ensure that, *since they have earned it,* they should get it. I cannot see any way but State endowment of motherhood. The one really fundamental difference between men and women is (again) a "difference," it is certainly not an inferiority. For women to try to reduce it to a trifle when it is really so great a thing is an acceptance of masculine standards too dishonoring and too artificial to endure.

Source

A. Maude Royden, "The Future of the Women's Movement," in *The Making of Women: Oxford Essays in Feminism*, ed. Victor Gollancz (London: Allen & Unwin, 1917), 128–39.

A Motherhood Endowment

AT THE END OF *the previous selection, Royden broached the possibility of paying mothers for their child-rearing labor. In this 1919 piece, she makes the case for a nationally subsidized motherhood salary or endowment similar to the pensions granted war widows. The project was dear to Royden's heart, and she defended and campaigned for the proposal for years. She saw it was an acknowledgment that domestic labor "is truly of national importance"—an appraisal that the war made more obvious than ever—and hence worthy of remuneration.*

The war, with its terrible toll of young life, has taught us the value of babies. They used to be called "encumbrances"; now we are beginning to reckon them up as jewels. But while we dwell on the need for more young citizens to build up the new world, scold their mothers for not bearing and rearing a larger number, and hold "Baby Weeks" in order to give louder expression to our changed views as to the value of babies, we have as yet done little to lighten the burden of those who have families to support, or to create the conditions in which mothers can give the best service they are capable of, to work which is truly "of national importance."

Something is being done by the provision of schools for mothers, baby centers, district nurses, the registration of midwives, and other reforms. But the fact remains that the heads of families are still heavily penalized compared with those who have no such responsibilities; the burden on the shoulders of the working class mother remains as heavy as ever; and the children suffer as a result.

This state of affairs ought not to be allowed to go on. The changes made in our social organization to meet the needs of a nation at war have accustomed our minds to the idea of reform and readjustment on a large scale. Some of these vast changes, at least, have been justified by reason and have proved themselves sound. We ought to be ready in this case to make them permanent if they are seen to meet, not the needs of war only, but a permanent need, which war has perhaps brought sharply into notice but not created.

Such a reform has undoubtedly been the recognition of the nation's debt to the mother and of the first-class importance of her work and her children. Provision has been made for those whose husbands have joined His Majesty's Forces, and this provision has not been adjusted to the earnings of the husband and father, but to the needs of his wife and family. Separation allowances have been made on a scale varying with the number of non-wage-earning children, just as rations have been distributed, not equally to all households—as though each household were the same size!—but in accordance with the number of persons in the household. No one has been foolish enough to suggest that the Food Controller should apportion to a woman living alone the rations which must suffice for her neighbor with ten children; nor has it occurred to anyone that separation allowances should be fixed in the same way. And on the whole the schemes have worked well, in spite of all the difficulties created by wartime conditions. Homes have been kept together and mothers enabled to stay with their children, instead of "boarding them out" with someone else.

It is worthwhile to ask whether a scheme which has on the whole worked so well that no one, however they may criticize it in detail, thinks of abandoning it so long as the war lasts, might not advantageously be retained, and even expanded, in time of peace. For the work of the mother is just as important in peacetime as in war, and the need for assuring good conditions for young children just as great. We cannot afford to disregard these claims now, but perhaps we can afford it still less when the war ends, for then other problems, which have for the moment been thrust into the background, will press upon us for solution. There will be the vexed question of "equal pay for equal work," the peculiarly helpless position of the widow with young children—always the prey of the exploiter—and the fact that there will no longer be a shortage of labor, but perhaps a shortage of employment.

To these vexed questions there can be no single solution. The one that comes nearest to an answer to them all is the National Endowment of Motherhood.

What exactly does this answer mean? It means that the State shall make a grant to every mother of children, plus an allowance for each child up to the age when it goes to school.

To such a scheme there is no hint of pauperism or philanthropy. It is a recognition of the inestimable services rendered to the State by mothers, and so long ignored. It should therefore be given not to "necessitous" mothers only, as though it were a kind of charity, but to all. It should be paid by some authority other than the Poor Law[1] Guardians and the relieving officer. It should be wholly outside the Poor Law, for it would be in no sense "relief"; it would be well earned, we know, and those who earn should not be treated as though they were objects of charity or paupers.

It will be said, "But you cannot pay mothers for what they do for their children." Of course you cannot. You cannot buy with all the money in the world love and devotion and the willingness to risk life itself to bring life into the world. The mother is perhaps, in one sense, like the soldier. You cannot pay a soldier for what he does. You cannot pay a man to be patriotic; you cannot pay him to die; you cannot pay him to give what no money can ever restore or make good to him.

But you do not, therefore, argue that he should have nothing at all. You do not say to him, "Your service is so sacred and noble that we do not dream of offering you any money. If you should happen to want any, no doubt your commanding officer will give you what he thinks proper." No; the soldier does not get much, but at least we do not leave him without anything in return for all he does for us.

Why, then, should mothers be treated so? Why should we say to them, "Your work is so honorable and sacred that you cannot possibly want any money, and if you should wish to give your husband a Christmas present, you will have to ask him to give you the money for it!" That, surely, is putting those whom we claim to reverence more than any other persons in the community—our mothers—in a worse position than any other member of it; for all others, if they work, secure some sort of economic independence; but the mother, who works hardest of all, is by that very fact deprived of all possibility of economic freedom. A working class mother—and the working class is from three-quarters to four-fifths of the community—is committed, while her children are young, to a life of great arduousness. In a book written with studious

---

1. Originating in the Tudor era, poor laws assessed taxes to care for indigents. Originally organized and funded at the parish level, by the mid-nineteenth century they had become centralized. One of the products of the poor laws was the institution of the workhouse system harshly criticized by Charles Dickens and other Victorian reformers. (KW)

moderation and ripe knowledge, *At the Works*, Lady Bell[2] describes the lives of the women who are the wives of her husband's employees, and her verdict is that, for the average woman, the burden she must carry while her children are quite young, is too heavy. Those who have exceptional ability or exceptional physical strength can lift and bear it; the average woman cannot. Something must go: health, vitality, nerves, or the order and beauty of the home. And this verdict is passed upon women who are of the aristocracy of the workers, women whose husbands are highly skilled workmen, whose work is regular and whose wages are comparatively high. How much more true is it, then, of the wives of unskilled or semi-skilled workers, in casual or seasonal employment, with low rates of pay? Such women, when they become mothers, must toil day and night, and yet their work is never done. Health and strength fail in the struggle, vitality is drained away; yet the mother remains absolutely dependent on the earnings of another. She may be an ideal mother, leaving no duty undone, but if her husband loses his work she is left without resources. Her family, and with it her work, may increase, but she must housekeep on the same income, for, though her work is more, her husband's work and wages remain the same. If he is a good husband he gives her all he can spare; but then where is she to look for extra provision for extra children? If he is a bad husband he may give her very little. She has no remedy except, in cases of actual starvation, the Poor Law. What worker, doing her duty to the utmost of her ability, do we threaten first with starvation and afterward with pauperism? No one is so treated except those about whom there is most sentimental talk, the mothers.

It is surely time to be less sentimental and more practical, for the sake both of the mothers and the children.

Let us admit that the desire to have a little money of one's own, well earned, is not a wicked, but a perfectly legitimate and just one. Let us admit that, if mothers were to be endowed by the State, the money they received would be earned, and not lightly earned. In honesty, we must admit the economic value of the mother's work, for if she does not do it someone else must be paid to take her place. Many a mother is nurse, cook, governess, general servant, and housekeeper all in one. In any one of these capacities she could go out and earn money if she chose. Why, because she chooses to stay at home and look after her own children, is

---

2. Lady Florence Eveleen Bell, *At the Works: A Study of a Manufacturing Town* (1907). Bell's book is an exposé of the "needy and unhappy" lot of Yorkshire ironworkers. (KW)

she to be treated as if she did nothing? Every member of her household gains in importance and feels himself of value in the world as he (or she) begins to earn even a little money. Only the mother's work receives from the world no recognition but a flood of empty talk. And if her husband dies she is left absolutely unprovided for, and expected to put her children into some charitable institution and go out to work. Someone, of course, must be paid to run the institutions and look after the children—to make, in fact, an artificial home for them. Would it not be better in every way to leave them in their real home and hand over the money they cost to the real mother to keep it up with? Enable her to do her work as she would like to do it, free from the intolerable strain of anxiety about ways and means. Let her know that, whether her husband is out of work for a while or not, incapacitated by illness or not, even if he deserts her or death bereaves her, she will still be able to keep her children with her and her home together—not indeed in such comfort as when her husband's earnings were in partnership with hers, but at least without the fear of destitution before her eyes.

Such an arrangement would make of the home a real partnership, the mother bringing her share both of work and wages, the father his, to the support and care of the children. It is sometimes said that, in such a partnership, the father would do nothing, but would proceed to give up work and live on his wife's endowment. This is a deplorable view of human nature, and one which seems to be based on a good deal of class prejudice. There are, no doubt, some men in the richer classes who are content to live on their wives, but they are exceedingly few. Most men are rather morbidly afraid of owing everything to a rich wife. And doubtless, among the poorer classes, there are some who would do anything rather than work—even live on their wives. There are some men who do it now, without waiting for the endowment of motherhood. But the vast majority are quite as reluctant as their richer brothers to do anything of the sort. In Lancashire and Yorkshire great numbers of married women go out to work and, in Lancashire especially, earn exceedingly good wages. But Lancashire men are not more prone than others to live on their wives; indeed, many people (not only in Lancashire!) think them among the best workmen in the country. We ought not to deprive all women of the justly earned reward of their labor because here and there one has married a lazy husband, any more than we should refuse the 30s. maternity benefit, given under the Insurance Act,[3] because here and there a man is found brutal enough to take the money from his wife and spend it. Very few husbands would do that, and very few wives are so lacking in spirit as to let them. Most men who are bad husbands, like most mothers who are bad mothers, are so because they have had bad conditions to live in. Mr. Judge Neil, whose devoted labors in America have won for widows with young children dependent on them pensions such as those advocated here for all mothers of children, tells us that many a "bad" mother has developed into a "good" one when, for perhaps the first time in her life, she was set free from overstrain, overwork, and continual anxiety, to do her work and bring up her children, not in riches indeed, but in security. Very few are those mothers who do not respond to the better environment, the new opportunity. And men are just as good as women! If a working woman's health and strength are overtaxed in the years of child-bearing and child-rearing, it is not only she who suffers. Toil as she may, she cannot make her home all she would wish it, and her own nerves are apt to get frayed in the struggle. A husband sometimes becomes a "bad" husband because he finds no peace or order in a home where the mother is always overdriven. For one here and there who would "live on his wife," there are many who would like their homes all the better for the added income which meant a little relaxation of the strain on the wife; and everything the husband earned would go to make the home a better home and give the children a better start in life than he and his wife had. It is much too readily supposed by the rich that they are the only people who cannot be demoralized by having a little more money; and so we hear a great deal of the wicked munitioners who spend their high wages on fur coats and pianos, but very little of those who use them to give their children a better education than their parents had. [. . .]

The endowment of motherhood seems therefore to have all the qualities of a really great constructive reform. The idea is as yet in its infancy: it will have to be discussed and modified by criticism and by experience till the best possible scheme is found to embody it. But we have already, in our system of separation allowances, made a beginning, and found it works well. When the war is over, will the devotion and labor of mothers be worth less to the nation than now? Or the life of a child born the day after the terms of peace are signed be of less value than that of the

3. The National Insurance Act of 1911 created insurance for England's industrial workers. Its primary architect was David Lloyd George in his capacity as chancellor of the exchequer. (KW)

child born today? If the answer to these questions is "No," let us begin at once to work for a system under which the devotion of all mothers, the lives of all little children, shall at least be safeguarded from the worst kind of privation.

Source

A. Maude Royden, *National Endowment of Motherhood* (London: Hodgson & Son, 1919), 3–8, 15. Pamphlet.

Marriage and Morality

MARRIAGE WAS AN IMPORTANT *topic for Royden from both a personal and a moral perspective. Personally, she was drawn to the subject because of her long extra-wedlock intimacy with Hudson Shaw. Morally, she was horrified by the many women she knew who were trapped in marital unions that were, as she says in this excerpt from her 1922 book* Sex and Common-Sense, *"selfish, cruel, and mercenary." Such marriages degraded both women and the institution. Royden believed that a happy marriage benefits all of society because it is a public acknowledgment of the power of love. But she had little patience with the claim that such love can be validated only by a marriage license. Morality is a matter of character, trust, and responsibility, not a legal formality.*

People ask: "What real difference can a mere [marriage] ceremony make?" It does not make any difference to the morality of your relationships with your fellow men and women. Nothing that is immoral becomes moral because it has been done under a legal contract, or consecrated by a rite. There, I think, is where the world has gone so wrong. The idea that a relation that is selfish, cruel, mercenary, becomes moral because someone has said some words over you, and you have signed a register—what a farcical idea! How on earth does that change anything at all? The morality of all civil or religious ceremony lies, I think, in this—that by accepting and going through it, you accept the fact that your love does concern others besides yourself; it will concern your children; and beyond that, it concerns the world. You are right when you ask your friends to come and rejoice with you at your wedding. It is the concern of all the world when people love each other, and it is the failure of love that concerns them when marriage is a failure. Such failure chills the atmosphere; it shakes our faith in love as the supreme power in the universe; it makes us all waver in our allegiance to constancy and love when love fails. It is a joyful thing when people love. "All the world loves a lover." It is an old saying, but what a true one! It is our concern when people nobly and loyally love each other, it is the concern of the community, and those who take upon themselves these public vows seem to me to have a more truly moral conception of love than those who say: "This is our affair only; it is not the affair of the State or the affair of the Church." But the actual ceremony must be the expression of a moral feeling such as that. It cannot in itself make moral what is immoral! The old idea that if a woman was seduced by a man she was "made honest" by the man marrying her is essentially immoral. Very likely all that she knew about the man was that she could not trust him, and to suppose that we can set right what is wrong by tying them together for the rest of their lives is to imagine an absurdity and to establish a lie.

Or take the case from another point of view. I have two in my mind at this moment, who for some reason (a reason not very far to seek if you read our English marriage laws) came to the conclusion that it is not right to place oneself in such a position as a married woman is in under English law. I am not discussing whether they were right or wrong; I say that quite sincere and moral people do come to that conclusion sometimes, and so did these two. They lived together, therefore, without being legally married. They were absolutely faithful to each other; their love was as responsible, as dignified, as true as any such relation could be. It lacked to my mind one thing—the sense of a wider responsibility—but then it had very much that many legal marriages have not. Those two people are put outside society; it is made almost impossible for them to earn their living; and at last in despair they go to the registry office, and sign their names in a book. What difference has been made in their relation to each other? Absolutely none. They are no more convinced of the right and duty of the community to be concerned with marriage than they were before. They have yielded to coercion. Their moral standard, good or bad, is precisely what it was; their relation to each other wholly unchanged. But in the eyes of the world they have become respectable, they are "moral," they can be received back into the bosom of society. And why? Because they have gone through a ceremony in which they do not believe!

Every marriage in the world probably lacks something of perfection. There are no perfect human beings, and, therefore, hardly, perhaps, a perfect marriage; and to my mind those who do not admit the concern of the community in their marriage do lack something. But to suppose that those people are immoral, when others who live together, legally licensed to do so, in selfishness, in infidelity, for financial reasons, or for social reasons, are moral is fundamentally dishonest. When a woman sells her body for money, do you think that it makes it moral that she does it in a church or in a registry office? Is there one whit of difference, morally, between the prostitution that has no legal recognition and the prostitution that has? Is it anything but prostitution to sell yourself for money, whether you are a man or a woman? Do you imagine that because you have a contract to protect you while you do it, you are doing what is moral? If you marry for any reason but love—for experience, to "complete your nature"—without much regard to the man or woman you marry, or to the children you bring into the world, are you not exploiting human nature just as certainly, though not so brutally, as a man who buys a woman in the street? It is not so base a form of exploitation, God knows; that I admit; but when there is any element of exploitation in the bargain it is not made more truly moral because it happens to be blessed in a church or registered in an office. The legal ceremony must be the outcome of a morality which makes you realize that what you do affects other people, that what you do most profoundly affects the children that you hope to have, and that the community has both an interest and a responsibility in all this. That is "moral." But if the relationship thus to be legalized is not moral, it is dishonest to pretend that it can be made so by any ceremony which those concerned may undergo.

But, you will say, we cannot peer into other people's lives and judge them in this kind of way. How are we to know? How are we, who have many friends, many neighbors, on whom our standards must react, to judge their lives? We can tell who has gone through a legal ceremony and who refuses to do so. That is a nice convenient rule by which we can judge and condemn such people. But we cannot go poking into people's lives and studying their motives and judging their fundamental moral standards! No, you cannot. Why should you? This little set of iron rules makes it very easy to judge, does it not? But why do you desire it to be easy to judge? You and I know how infinite are the gradations between the most noble kind of chastity and the most ignoble kind of immorality; but which of us is to create a rigid standard and measure our friends and acquaintances against it? We do not do it with the other virtues: why do we desire to do it with this one? Take such a virtue as truth. Conceive the crystalline sincerity of some truth-loving minds, realize that some have such a devotion to truth that the faintest shadow of insincerity—not a lie, but the merest shadow of insincerity in the depths of their hearts—is abhorrent to them. Consider the infinite gradations between that mind and the mind which takes a lie for truth, a mind that is rotten with corruption, that does not know how to think straight, let alone care to speak straight. You do not draw up your little set of rules and say: "I do not call on that person because he does not speak the truth; and I won't have anything to do with that one—such persons are outside the social pale altogether because their conception of truth is different from mine!"

No, you keep your admiration for the truth-loving and the sincere. You recognize that people have different standards about what is truth. One person will never tell a lie under any circumstances: another will reckon himself free to tell a lie to save a third, or to preserve a confidence; will you judge which is the more honorable of the two? Where is your little set of rules? You cannot have one. You shrink from the person who is morally dishonest and corrupt; you worship the person who loves truth as Darwin loved it.[1] But between those two extremes what an infinite variety of attainment! Who can say: "These people are moral because they are married, and those are immoral, they are not married?" It is not true, it is not honest, to make these rules our measure. They do not meet the realities of human nature, and I contend that we, who have known souls so chaste and lovely that they make us in love with virtue, do far more to raise the moral standard of humanity by seeking to imitate such people than by setting up our little codes of rules and condemning or justifying all men by them. Let us treat this virtue as we do every other virtue, not fitting it to a set of rules which everyone knows do not fit the realities, but taking our courage in our hands and judging human beings (if we must judge them) by their real sincerity, their real unselfishness, their real unwillingness to exploit others—the measure of the chastity of their souls.

Source

A. Maude Royden, "The True Basis of Morality," in *Sex and Common-Sense* (New York: Putnam's Sons, 1928), 83–91.

---

1. Royden was a great admirer of Darwin, speaking and writing of him frequently. See, for example, her "A Modern Prophet: Charles Darwin," in *The Friendship of God* (New York: Putnam's Sons, 1924), 42–57. (KW)

Sacrament of Sexual Love

IN THIS SELECTION FROM Royden's 1917 essay "Modern Love," she condemns older cultural norms about sexuality which persuaded women that sex, even in happy marriages, is an unpleasant marital duty to be endured, and turned a blind eye to men seeking sexual satisfaction outside of marriage. For women, the norm encouraged frigidity and guilt; for men, sexual frustration and guilt; for both, the erroneous assumption that sex is "degraded or base or impure." Royden argues that what's needed to correct the situation is an awareness, fostered by education and a recalibration of the domination of men and subordination of women in marriage, that sexual passion is neither "alien or base." She also objects to the church's strict policy in her day against divorce.

No one of the problems raised by the feminist movement is more difficult to solve or more urgent of solution than that of love and marriage. It carries with it questions of economic, social, and religious importance. It is concerned with the wages of married women in the labor market, and their right to be there: with the rights of children, including their right to be born with the rights of men as well as the rights of women: with the whole character of sexual relations, which means really our estimate of the physical in life. Yet these complex and vital problems cannot be discussed with much freedom even now, and the heart of them cannot be discussed at all yet—in books accessible to the general public. Something, however, may even now be said.

  Mr. Bertrand Russell writes[1] rather despondently of the difficulty of transition from the old ideal underlying marriage to the new. The old ideal, which assumed that marriage made of a man and woman one person, and that one, the husband, had, as he reminds us, a certain dignity

---

1. "Principles of Social Reconstruction," ch. 6. (MR)

and beauty when it was sincerely accepted by both wife and husband as both natural and right. It has now, however, like the feudal system of which the same may be said, become impossible to us to accept it, and we stand uncertain how to proceed. But the race does not wait for our solution, and men and women marry without the old assumptions, which were so simple, and seemed so immutable; and the jarring relationship that sometimes follows is held to be typical and set down as a failure. Those who still secretly or openly adhere to the older view attribute the failure to its abandonment, and not obscurely hint that a woman who married young and had a baby every year, would have no time to think of her rights—which is probably true. The more modern teacher recognizes the futility of a return to medievalism, but seems to admit the failure of modern love no less. To Mr. Bertrand Russell, as to George Meredith,[2] the sense of strain and jar is poignantly present and infinitely depressing.

But to the young themselves this is not so. There is a buoyant hope, and looking forward among them, which is untouched by the depressing spectacle of contemporary failures. Marriage, they will admit, is a much more complicated affair than formerly, but incomparably more interesting, exciting, and worthwhile. And as for failure, it is at least an open question whether the modern marriage, which permits a woman time to discover that she does not like her husband, is really in essentials more dismal or only less tragic than the old one, which gave her no time for anything but bearing children and burying them. In either case, such failures are not—or are equally—to be considered typical. And the young hopefully believe that we are on the threshold of a nobler conception of marriage altogether, for since we already set a higher value, in sexual relationships, on sincerity and knowledge than we did, it is certain we must be moving to a higher plane.

It is, of course, the last relationship in which sincerity and frankness become possible, and this is responsible for much of the jar and fret between married people today. All love between human beings has a physical element in it, and in sex-love the physical and spiritual are more equally balanced than in other loves. But about sex-love, the horrifying superstition has been held, that "physical" means degraded, or base, or impure; that a woman, at least, should love without physical desire, and

---

2. George Meredith (1828–1909), British novelist whose unhappy first marriage with Mary Ellen Nicolls served as the background for his "scandalous" 1859 novel *The Ordeal of Richard Feverel*. His later *The Egoist* (1879) and *Diana of the Crossways* (1885) also dealt with the subject of failed marriages. (KW)

that a really refined and civilized woman should not only be indifferent to, but perhaps actually repelled by, the physical side of marriage. Before marriage, she should even, by preference, be unconscious that a physical side exists.

Such detestable ideas have had their disastrous consequences. Women who are sexually cold have believed themselves to be ideally pure, and it has never even occurred to them—it could not—that they were really subject to a defect which should give them pause before they considered marriage at all. "Why do such women marry?" is the question bitterly asked by men. Well, for many reasons: for position, for freedom, for a living, or because they have nothing else to do. And since they know of the physical side of marriage either nothing at all, or only that they ought to know nothing, it is grotesque to blame them for marrying. Nevertheless, the consequences are often tragic. Indeed, it is difficult to imagine anything more certain to destroy both love and joy than the discovery by any man that that which is to him the very sacrament of love, for whose sake he has kept his body as a temple amid a thousand temptations, is to the woman he loves at worst a horror, at best a "concession to his lower nature." Such barbarous suffering to both can only be avoided by a much better understanding of each other, and hope lies in the fact that some have already attained, and others are attaining, this understanding .

The old view was, apparently, that a "good" woman should be physically unconscious of sex, or if at all conscious, ashamed of it; that "falling in love" should not awaken passion until marriage was actually reached; and thereafter there existed a difference of opinion, men generally holding that marriage should awaken passion, but women on the whole maintaining the unworthy fiction that passion was only to be endured with resignation by the really virtuous wife. I have heard the happy wives of devoted husbands talk with a contempt of marriage which I can only describe as brutal. I have heard them assert that if only women knew what marriage meant, they would never marry. I have been remonstrated with by wives and mothers when I have urged them to tell their children beautifully, what others, if they do not, will tell them unbeautifully. "It isn't beautiful," they say; "why should we put such ideas into their heads?" And this is not the talk of women embittered by the brutality of degraded men, but of women who are beyond contradiction happily married. If marriage were only a "sisterly sweet hand in hand," no one could be happier than they, for in every other respect their husbands are all that they could wish.

Of course there is another side to this; but we speak of the normal—the marriage which has apparently every chance of being happy, where there is real congeniality of taste and character, and where (let us go further, and take the ideal at once) both bridegroom and bride have kept themselves unspotted from the world. But before they essay together the great adventure of marriage, society has already interposed between them an almost insurmountable barrier of misunderstanding on the nature of marriage itself. The girl has been taught, partly by a shocked silence, partly by vague hints and veiled suggestions, that there is something disgusting to a pure-minded woman in certain desires and functions of the body, and the more undeveloped she herself is in this respect, the "purer" she may reckon herself. Perhaps she is in fact undeveloped and ignorant, the mighty prohibition of society compelling and enabling her actually to inhibit her own natural development and arrest her growth: if so, she goes to marriage without the least knowledge of what it is, and prepared only, if prepared at all, for something rather horrible. Her husband, often equally ignorant of her nature, takes it for granted that the passion which was prohibited till the register was signed, will awake at the right moment; and by acting on this assumption convinces her that the physical side of marriage is indeed a concession to the lower nature of her partner.

Or perhaps the horror of being in some unexplained sense not "pure" has not availed to arrest the growing womanhood in a girl. Her case has been perhaps in the past the worst of all, because she has been burdened with a sense of guilt from which her nature forbade her escape. Can we even today measure the suffering of such a woman? If she was unprotected, she probably "went wrong"; if she belonged to the protected class, she became a hypocrite, perpetually pretending, even to herself, a sexlessness she could not feel, and afraid to show herself a generous lover even to her husband.

Perhaps in this she was wise or prudent at least. For with the old lax standard, which took for granted the sowing of wild oats by men, men have often preferred, even after marriage, a certain degree of coldness in their wives. Generous and joyful giving they associated with the courtesan, and shared the strange dishonoring delusion that purity in a woman implied coldness. But (if she was not thus lacking) what a perpetual repression and deceit this meant for her! Never to give all—always to hold back—to flee like Milton's Eve from what she loved—is that a basis on which to build the marriage of true minds?[3] Or is it a wonder that women have been insincere—with such a necessity for falseness laid upon them?

The young lovers of today are changing all this. The modern woman may, or may not, be passionate: that is a matter of individual temperament. But she does not elevate a defect into a quality, or think of sex as something alien and base. Nor does the modern man so easily assume his right to give the rein to his own passions before marriage, and so learn to associate sex with impurity. To both alike the highest purity is passionate, and the candor and courage of both makes real understanding possible before marriage. The man no longer dreams that courtship ends on the wedding night, but knows that love can never *take* what must always be *given*—or destroyed. The woman knows that mere patient giving is not enough—there must be joy in giving or the gift is nothing. There must be equality in passion, or one is shamed.

This clearer knowledge comes of a change in our whole attitude toward the physical. To the modern, "physical" does not mean base, and to say that the love of sex is "partly physical" is not to say that it is "partly vile," but rather that it is very whole and sane. We live in bodies, and find in them the temple of the spirit. We know more and more the meaning of them, and that "soul is form, and doth the body make."[4]

The horror of physical disease, the love of health, which has even given rise to a new religion, is only another side of the same feeling. Whatever one may think of the philosophy of Christian Science, the sense that disease is as hateful to God as sin is surely a great and vital truth. And this truth is lifting us to a nobler sexual love. In modern marriage the body is equally honored with the spirit, and nothing but a love which embraces all is truly marriage. There is a desire for union so complete that sex becomes the outward and visible sign of an inward and spiritual grace, and to take the sacrament without the grace is really "sin." The old "double standard" was only possible so long as a man despised his body so much that he could give it to one woman—or to many women—while reserving a purer love for another; while he could expect the physical expression of love from a courtesan, and give her no more—and (in a natural reaction) prefer a woman more or less passionless for his wife. This divorce is not possible to modern lovers. A man cannot explain to the woman he loves that he gave only physical passion to those others, and that she has no

---

3. Royden is probably referring here to book 9 in *Paradise Lost* when Adam and Eve, after eating the forbidden fruit, are ashamed of their nakedness. (KW)

4. Edmund Spenser (1552/53–99), "A Hymn in Honor of Beauty." (KW)

need to complain, since this did not and could not touch his (quite different) love for her; for she desires a whole love for herself. Neither can he wish for an undeveloped prude for his wife; he respects the physical too much, and asks as whole a love as she.

Some, therefore, advocate "experimental marriages,"[5] that men and women may know each other more completely before they are allowed to pledge themselves for life. There is, of course, nothing "modern" in this in a sense. At least, experimental marriage outside the law is sufficiently common in our own country among those who still regard children as, in the long run, an asset rather than a debt.[6] What is new in the suggestion is its insistence on the need for perfect understanding between married people. But I think it to be a wrong line of development.

A young couple who lived together as friends only, for some time after marriage, regarding the legal ceremony as the door through which they might enter upon a common life, and learn to know each other with such a perfect understanding as to make the consummation of marriage indeed a sacrament of unity, were surely in a better way. But it is curious that before marriage understanding and knowledge should be made so hard. Why not give greater liberty, that the two may be much more sure than in most cases they can be now? Though it is true much must always remain to be known after marriage, this seems no sufficient reason for making it so hard to arrive at the most perfect possible understanding before. We admit this half-heartedly when we condemn the custom of those countries in which young lovers are never left alone together, or perhaps do not even see each other's faces until they are married. But we are very nervous about it still, and still half expect that any greater liberty than that to which we are already accustomed cannot be good. There is a constant expectation that boys and girls, if much together, will do each other harm. What wonder if they do, surrounded by this murky atmosphere with which all things connected with sex have been surrounded?

---

5. I do not mean by "experimental marriage" the Meredithian proposal of marriage for ten years, which is not in the true sense "experimental" at all, and seems to have nothing to commend it; but license for a man and woman to live as though they were married until they have made up their minds whether they wish to enter into a binding contract or not. (MR)

6. Among the poor, especially in the North of England, children are sometimes regarded as an "insurance against old age." It is not considered immoral for a man to "keep company" with a woman until they see whether the union is likely to be fruitful. If it is, public opinion expects them to marry; if not, there is no obligation. This is, in the strict sense, "experimental marriage." (MR)

The modern lovers, who begin with a much more decent regard for each other before they are lovers, turn it into reverence when love comes. With such a reverence freedom is safe and noble.

It may perhaps be urged that freedom—which many think already stretched too far—may sometimes, by putting too great a strain on passionate youth, provoke disaster. I would reply that it is our suggestive ignorances and hints, our grimy expectation of indecency, that has made sex an obsession, and created disaster, and that to expect from youth a noble reverence for a great mystery and force, is to go far toward creating victory—or rather letting conquer a purity which is native, and which we have done our best to destroy. But I would add that, though "disasters" will be much less frequent where there is greater confidence and trust, no system can be devised whereby human beings can be infallibly saved from their own weaknesses and mistakes. Such weakness should not be regarded as a trifling or even amusing matter in the boy, nor should it be regarded as irrevocable damnation to the girl. In both, in either, it is a sin in proportion to the greatness of the ideal sinned against; a wrong haste, which suggests a lack of reverence, and might perhaps suggest further that these two are not yet fit for marriage. But it is no more an irrevocable disaster than it is a reason for rushing into marriage on the assumption that all that was wrong will then be as though it had not been.

On the other hand, though "experimental marriage" be condemned, future legislators may be inclined to return to that more humane and lofty conception of marriage which, on the whole, characterized the old canon law, than to adhere to the caricature of it that is put forward by some ecclesiastical interpreters today. Canon law knew no cause for divorce, and held marriage to be indissoluble for any cause. But since this position was based largely on the text "that which God has joined together, let no man put asunder," canonists did not assume that any and every marriage was made in heaven, or that God had joined together all whom Church and State had bound. Such binding might have been a mistake, and the marriage no marriage at all. The reasons for declaring medieval unions invalid seem sometimes ridiculous in our eyes, sometimes they were obviously invented for political reasons, sometimes casuistical in the worst sense. It remains a fact that the belief in legal marriage as monogamous and indissoluble, but only when and where it is the record and sanction of a true marriage "made in heaven," suggests an attitude of mind far more humane and idealistic than that of the defenders of a stricter marriage law today. Marriage in the future, then, will be based on a much better understanding than in the past. This is good.

Source

A. Maude Royden, "Modern Love," in *The Making of Women: Oxford Essays in Feminism*, ed. Victor Gollancz (London: Allen & Unwin, 1917), 37–48.

The Church's Untouchables

IN HER 1916 PAMPHLET Women and the Church of England, *reprinted in full here, Royden blasts the church for what she sees as oppression and exploitation of women. Both administratively and liturgically, women are treated as if they're untouchables, unqualified—indeed, unfit by virtue of their gender—to hold governing positions or holy orders. When women protest that they are precisely the members who are keeping parishes alive and demand to know why they can't have roles equal to those of men, they're either patronizingly told that they wouldn't understand the explanations or they're referred to cherry-picked verses from Scripture that disparage women. Royden's broadside against the church and her call for women to be treated as equals is one of the angriest pieces she ever wrote. It's also one of her best.*

It is claimed by all the Christian Churches that Christianity has had a great influence in raising the position of women. No one who looks East and West can doubt the truth of the claim. Under the influence of the five or six great religions of the world the position of women varies, and varies not only as religion but as races and civilizations vary. It is difficult to estimate how far each factor controls the result, and it is easy, by a careful selection of examples, to show that women even under Islam are better off than we in the West might suppose. Nevertheless there is no doubt in the mind of most of us that it is in Christian countries that the subjection of women has been most frequently and most successfully challenged.

This is natural. The teaching of Christ is in nothing clearer or more insistent than in the sense it gives of the value of the individual soul. Not Our Lord's words only but His whole life—and His death—bring home to us the sacredness of personality. And such teaching, however far we fall below it, leaves no room for the outcast or the "untouchable." Whatever may be the faults of Christians, no one can read the Gospels as a whole and based upon them a claim to cast out any, either because they belong to an unclean race, a despised class, or an inferior sex. In the religion of Christ there is no room for our mean contempts, our unworthy prides. We are all the children of Our Father in heaven, and having been called to so supreme an honor, we must not stop to measure our infinitesimal differences.

This quality in our religion, though it is a hard saying indeed to most of us, has perhaps influenced our thought and molded our civilization more than any other part of the teaching of Christ. There are many things in which the East compares favorably, or not unfavorably, with the West; there are many in which we resemble one another. But on this point—democracy—how fundamental is the difference! We, at least with our lips, admit the equality of all souls before God; and that our admission is more than mere lip service is proved when slavery goes, when class is found instead of caste, and there are no "untouchables"; when neither women nor children are *merely* chattels, when the deep prejudices of class and sex and race are cut across by the great admission that in Christ there is neither Jew nor Greek, male nor female, bond nor free.

And yet today there are insurgents in the Churches—and notably in the Church of England—who complain that "organized religion" has become profoundly undemocratic, and that this tendency is most strikingly shewn in that very matter of the position of women in which it has been claimed that Christianity leads the world.

In an inspired moment the Rev. William Temple[1] asserted of the Labor Movement that the cause of unrest was not so much due to the desire of the working man for shorter hours, higher pay, or any other administrative or legislative reform, as to his resentment against an attitude on the part of society which was "a perpetual insult to his personality." Nothing could be more true, and it is as true of women as a sex as of the workers as a class. And here again it must be said that this insult is nowhere more perpetually or more intolerably felt than in the Church of England.

While in nearly all secular spheres of work the services of women are asked and given on terms nearer and nearer to equality with men, in the Church women are continually made to feel that they are not wanted. Everywhere there is an extreme anxiety to "get men," coupled with

---

1. William Temple (1881–1944), future archbishop of Canterbury (1942–44). In 1916, when Royden wrote her pamphlet, Temple was a parish priest in London and a canon of Westminster Abbey. (KW)

expressions of contempt for those unfortunate clergy who are obliged to rely on the services of women. Everywhere it is assumed that responsible positions and important work belong by nature to men—even the least capable of them—and not to women, even the most efficient.

The councils of the Church—Convocation, the Representative Church Council, Diocesan and Ruridecanal Conferences, the governing bodies of Missions—all are filled, and *nearly* all exclusively filled, with men. Only the lowest and least of councils finds a place for women; and though they are now as electors to the Representative Council able to vote on an equality with men, they will not easily forget that in the first instance they might only vote if they were *ratepayers as well as communicants*. Before this astounding instance of male ecclesiastical statesmanship most of us stood in silent awe. Only one[2] had breath enough left to point out that under its ingenious provisions the widow who thoughtlessly "cast in all that she had" would immediately have been deprived of her vote; while more prudent Sapphira, who kept back a portion of her goods, would have been welcomed on to the register (Acts 5:1–11).

As with the Church at home, so with the Church abroad. "That the bulk of the work of missions as done at home is in the hands of women goes without saying" writes a lady[3] whose devoted service to the Church is as well known as her lack of sympathy with the advanced wing of the Women's Movement. Yet her pamphlet, which is a plea for the greater share of women in the framing of policy and the administration of missions, is to the outsider, in spite of its studied moderation and courtesy, a damning indictment of the way in which they have been hitherto excluded. "In the Church's work, as exemplified by her missionary boards," writes Miss Gollock, the opportunity for women "to express the result of their knowledge and experience" is "except in rare instances denied." The decisions of the committees at headquarters "for the race are arrived at without recourse to one of its most important constituent elements." Yet it is not claimed—on the contrary, it is explicitly denied—that women take less interest in missionary work, give less time or money, do less work, or gather less experience. Only they are women, and so their help in positions of authority is not desired. The work suffers in consequence, and the women of the last generations excused their rulers: "'They do not

---

2. Mrs. Paget. (MR) [Lady Louise Leila Paget (1884–1958), British humanitarian especially noted for her relief work in Serbia before and during World War I.]

3. Miss M. C. Gollock, "Women in the Administration of Missions." (MR) [Gollock was one of the secretaries of the Church of England's National Mission Council.]

understand,' was the comment accepted by women for many years . . . *Somehow this comment does not now satisfy.*"4

As with the Councils, so with the offices of the Church. From top to bottom it is officered by men, and—incredible to relate—it is not even permitted us to ask why! The mere question, "Why should not women be admitted to holy orders?" causes some Churchmen to cry out and cut themselves with knives, while others, more reasonable, assure us that there are indeed reasons, but of a character so "fundamental" as to prohibit their being put into words. With this it is expected that women— women of the twentieth century—will be content! But, alas! "Somehow this comment does not now satisfy." We desire reasons, and it seems to us nothing but a comedy to suggest that this desire is monstrous, and that no such question should be so much as discussed by the people whom it most intimately concerns. Where, then, have these gentlemen who deny us lived? In what little island of thought have they been segregated from the contagion and movements of modern life, that they honestly believe they can by loud shouting and abusive language silence the demand for reasons when any great monopoly is on its defense? It is possible that women have not the vocation for the priesthood; but it is not possible to persuade them that they commit a crime when they raise the question and ask for an answer. Nor will they consider their doing so as a "conspiracy."5

The exclusion of women from all ranks of the priesthood is paralleled by their exclusion from nearly all other offices. Deacons, choristers, churchwardens, acolytes, servers, and thurifers, even the takers-up of the collection, are almost invariably men. If at any time not one male person can be found to collect, the priest does it himself, or, after a long and anxious pause, some woman, more unsexed than the rest, steps forward to perform this office. In one church, I am told, it was the custom for collectors to take the collection up to the sanctuary rails, till the war compelled women to take the place of men, when they were directed to wait at the chancel steps. In another it was proposed to elect a woman churchwarden, when the Vicar vehemently protested on the ground that this would be "a slur on the parish."6 In another, the impossibility of getting any male youth to ring the sanctus bell induced a lady to offer her

4. "Women in the Administration of Missions," 8. The italics are mine. (MR)

5. See the *Church Times*, July 28, 1916: Mr. Athelstan Riley. (MR)

6. The lady who was, notwithstanding, elected is now popularly known among friends and acquaintances as "the slur." (MR)

services. After anxious thought the priest accepted her offer "because the rope hung down behind a curtain, so no one would see her." The propriety of women conducting the simplest of services or delivering an address from any part of the church excites in the mind of a section of the Church, not so much disapproval as hysterics. While everywhere women are gathering others together in halls, in drawing rooms, in cottages, to join in intercession for their country, their Church, their friends, it is still in almost every diocese impossible for them to meet in the house of God. While every platform in the country is open to them, and every cause welcomes their service as speakers, in the churches only men must be heard. The pilgrims who go out on a pilgrimage of prayer, which should begin and end in the church of every parish visited, must give their messages in the schoolroom instead, where a grown-up congregation accommodates itself as well as it can to the uneasy desks and chairs of children. Conventions are held, but as they are held in cathedrals and churches, no woman, though she be an "Archbishop's messenger"—no woman, though she be indeed inspired by God—can take a part. If a reason is sought, it is conveyed in the answer, "The church is a consecrated place." The modern woman does not find in this statement a reason. She finds in it an insult, perhaps the most comprehensive that could be offered to a human being.

In the same spirit a correspondent in a recent correspondence in the *Guardian* quotes with approval the rule that, at Mass, women are "not allowed near the altar." Are there, then, "untouchables" in the religion of Christ after all? Were we wrong in supposing that in Him there is "neither Jew nor Greek, Male nor female, bond nor free"?

There were women standing near the Cross when Our Lord was crucified. Is the Cross less sacred than the altar? Or the Crucifixion less sacred than the Mass? Or will our brothers in the Church of England give us some reason for this "perpetual insult to our personality" other than the assurance that we are unthinkably wicked to resent it, and that it rests on grounds too good to be put into words? We do resent it. We find it intolerable that while the veriest little ragamuffin of a boy may "serve" at the altar, women whom we revere as leaders, reverence as saints, are excluded. We find it a scandal that the most ignorant of young men may get up and admonish us out of the depth of his inexperience and unwisdom in the pulpit, while women at whose feet the world is willing to sit are treated as though it were a thing impossible that they should have a message from God or know the inspiration of the Holy Spirit. We know they have such a message, and like the rest of the world, we go where we may hear it. Why are the churches empty? Is it because they have too great an abundance of inspired speakers?

Our contention cannot now be answered by a quotation from St. Paul; for we know that that great apostle, if in one place he directed the Corinthians not to allow women to speak, in another, with equal clearness, told them what the women were to wear when they did speak (1 Cor 14:34; 1 Cor 11:5). We know also that the quoter himself sets aside the authority he invokes whenever it seems reasonable to do so. The women of his church come unveiled, in spite of St. Paul (1 Cor 11:5). They wear gold and silver and braid their hair, in spite of St. Peter (1 Pet 3:3). They sit teaching in the Sunday School, in spite of the author of the Epistle to St. Timothy (1 Tim 2:12). They form public opinion on public platforms—even on church platforms—while bishops take the chair for them and priests sit in the audience. Is it not, then, a little comic—or shall I say a little late—to demand that women should yield a literal obedience to an authority so lightly set aside by their critics?

Or is it seriously contended that the literalism which we are assured is a grave error when applied to the Sermon on the Mount, becomes a duty when the speaker is one of incomparably less authority? Let us speak boldly. The great work of scholarship has set us all free from the bondage of the letter, and it seems to us an act of hypocrisy, conscious or unconscious, that men should seek to scare us, like children, with its ancient terrors. Do they suppose that women read no biblical criticism? Do they suppose that women, alone in an indifferent world, "abstain from things strangled and from blood," as directed not by one apostle but by all of them together, blind to the fact that their brothers have "scrapped" these regulations long ago? Do they dream that we can worship this god whom they set up for us—a god who witnesses with complacency the "prophesying" of women in halls and schoolrooms, but is provoked to wrath if they prophesy in a church? Or who meticulously observes whether a chapel is "consecrated" (when a woman may say "There is none other that fighteth for us, but only Thou, O God," but not "Give peace in our time, O Lord") or merely "licensed" (when she may say either or both without scandal)? Or who is seriously concerned whether she enters the church with a hat or a veil or a bow or a wig or only her own hair on her head? This a god to worship? We cannot even respect him. We were not baptized into this religion of rules and of the letter, nor into Paul, nor Apollos, but into Christ (1 Cor 3:4–6). To this supreme Authority we appeal.

We find in the teaching of Jesus no suggestion of inequality between the sexes. On the only occasion on which He was challenged directly on this subject He is reported to have replied by demanding an equal standard from men and women. Elsewhere He appears to have ignored the traditional Jewish attitude toward women, by treating them just as He treated men (Matt 12:49–50). It is not possible to isolate any words of His from their context and to decide from their character or their tone whether they were addressed to women or to men. There is no trace of intellectual condescension in His words to women. There is no hint that a woman's ideal must be different from a man's, or her work, or her sphere. The parable of the talents is unaccompanied by any warning that if a woman has a talent for public speech, or the gift of leadership, or a genius for teaching, she will do well to bury it in a napkin. "His disciples marveled that He was speaking with a woman" (John 4:27), but He talked to her of the deepest religious truths, as He might have spoken to St. John. He shrank from the touch of none, He received all who truly desired to follow Him, His eye fell without reproach on those who at the last stood by Him on the Cross. What a world of difference between all this and the close and stuffy intellectual atmosphere of our churches! Between the Christ who appeared first to a woman on His rising from the tomb, and the Churchmen who forbid a woman to be "near the altar"!

And with this sense of difference in our minds, we women of the twentieth century appeal to the leaders of our Church to go forward. At first a leader in this as in other movements toward real democracy, the Church now has fallen behind and handed the torch to others. In public life, in the State and the municipality, in movements for social reform, in the Labor Movement as well as in their own movement, in non-Christian organizations often, women find a more generous recognition of their value, a greater readiness to work side by side with them, than they find in the Church. Is it wonderful that they choose to give themselves where they can do so most freely, and work where their work is least hampered by petty restrictions and insulting prohibitions? There was a time when religious work was almost the only avenue for a woman's energies, but now the world is all before her where to choose. Are we wrong—we who are Churchwomen—in regretting *even more for the Church than for the women* their choice of other spheres of work than hers? "The ablest women of the day are not—with some notable exceptions—giving their lives in the direct service of the Church and, however valuable their service is to the nation, the loss of it to the Church is serious to contemplate."[7] Is that not true? And is it not disastrous? The churches are still filled (if filled at all) largely with women. But the leaders have gone or are going, and the young do not come. "The Church for her own sake, for her members' sake, and for the sake of those who through them might believe in God, should give every woman an opportunity of exercising all her gifts" (even if they be gifts of leadership—even if they be gifts of tongues). "No woman with her heart on fire to serve her generation according to the will of God should find her sphere more readily outside the Church than inside."[8] But women do find it so, and they go, not because they have ceased to love Christ, but because they do not find His Spirit in His Church, nor believe that in these petty restrictions, this grudging of opportunity, this insulting warning-off from holy places, there is anything in common with the spacious freedom of His teaching.

If we are wrong, let our error be shown to us with reason and not with abuse; but let those who oppose our claims realize that we do sincerely base them on the conviction that it is we and not they who in this matter have the mind of Our Lord. We have not made our claims lightly or unadvisedly, and claims sincerely made in the name of Christ should be treated with respect, even if they be mistaken.

If, on the other hand, we are right, let the Church take action.

Source

A. Maude Royden, *Women and the Church of England* (London: Allen & Unwin, 1916), entire pamphlet.

---

7. "Women in the Administration of Missions," 6. (MR)
8. "Women in the Administration of Missions," 6. (MR)

The Anti-Feminist's Last Ditch

In this selection from her 1924 book The Church and Women, *Royden argues that even though the Church of England officially declares that women are the spiritual equals of men, it treats them otherwise by refusing them Holy Orders. This is confusion at best, hypocrisy at worst. The only question when it comes to ordination should be whether or not God has called the candidate to ministry. The church's proper role is to recognize the call, not to make it. Royden concludes that there's no reason to doubt that women, just like men, are called to the ministries of prophet and priest, regardless of what church tradition says. "In a sense indeed," she writes, "if the vocation is a real one, no ecclesiastical order can prevent its fulfillment." Given Royden's own sense of priestly vocation, this is an especially poignant observation.*

What, then, is the real obstacle in the minds of Christians on this matter? In nearly all other fields women have won at least something like the right to use such talents as they possess. [. . .]

The medical profession and the legal profession have opened their doors to women, and although they have yet a long way to go, little remains for them to combat in the way of formal obstacles: and undoubtedly prejudice and custom will melt away.

Only in the Church the obstacle remains not one merely of prejudice and custom, and here we shall find the last ditch of the anti-feminist.

Even here a very curious change is to be observed. There are very few indeed now who have the robust courage to affirm that they desire to exclude women from spiritual office because they are honestly convinced that women are spiritually on a lower plane than men. This is rather curious, because St. Paul (on whom our opponents lean heavily) does at least once commit himself quite clearly to the belief that women are spiritually inferior to men (1 Tim 2:11–14). The extraordinary advance that has been made by women during the present century is shown in nothing more clearly than in the extreme reluctance of those who desire to see us go no further to commit themselves to the statement—so glibly made but a little while ago—that women are definitely the inferiors of men.

Today, at whatever point the opponents of the advance of women take their stand, it is nearly always with the careful assurance that they do not assert or believe in their spiritual inferiority. The position taken up by St. Paul has been, in fact, already abandoned. "Difference of function between man and woman in the Church, as in the world, and the relative subordination of the woman, in no way implies an inferiority of women in regard to man."[1] This argument has been urged again and again, and is embodied in the above phrase in the Report of the Lambeth Conference of 1920. The Report goes on to say that under the regulations laid down by St. Paul for certain local churches there lies "an abiding principle," and this principle is that it is for the Christian Church "to exercise unsleeping vigilance that in its regulations for worship in the congregation there lurk no occasion for evil or even for suspicion of evil; no occasion for confusion or strife; nothing which falls below the purest and strictest ideal of peace and seemliness and order."[2]

Certainly there must be within every social organization—even that which is divinely constituted—rank, offices, functions, and order. This is an "abiding principle." But it is surely a very strange mistake to suppose that these ranks and offices may be arranged in a purely arbitrary way. They must have some correspondence to the fundamental realities of things, or the "order" which they propose to create will be nothing but disorder. So long as men (and women) honestly believed that women were at all points the inferiors of men, it was at least logical for them to build their social organization on this understanding. But logic disappears, and the order based upon it is imperiled, when it is once grasped that men and women are in fact spiritually equals. To demand of one person subordination to another, in the name of the real superiority of that other, is to demand what is natural and right, and will in the case of any reasonable person appeal to the sense of justice of both. But to demand of one person who is the equal of the other a permanent subordination is to demand what is in fact unjust and must in the long run be resented. It is true that this error is frequently made. One often finds the inferior in

---

1. Lambeth Conference, 1920. Report of Committee on the Position of Women in the Church. (MR)

2. Report of Committee on the Position of Women in the Church, 98. (MR)

authority over the superior. The position may be accepted by the natural superior for various reasons, including, of course, the obligations of loyalty and of order. But to contend that this is in itself a right and proper thing, and that society does not suffer by it, is surely a very different matter, and permanently to subordinate equals to one another is to create trouble. It is to build both our social order and our ecclesiastical order not upon a reality but upon a denial of reality: and of course a denial of reality must in the end become a principle not of order, but of disorder. It is to create that very "occasion for confusion and strife" which the bishops of the Lambeth Conference so urgently deprecate. The constitution of the Church—beyond that surely of any merely social organization—must be concerned with the truths and not with the traditions of life. If men no longer believe women to be their inferiors they must embody that belief at last in the constitution of their Church, and cease to place in a position of permanent subordination those whose equality with themselves they are now willing to affirm.

Nothing is more surprising than the assumption that men may affirm this equality in principle and deny it in practice, and—to heap absurdity upon absurdity—that the result of this will be law and order, peace and quiet. It shows an almost childlike faith in the autocratic power of man. It assumes that, when a law is passed or a custom made, these laws and customs must of necessity be based upon eternal truth, or if not, that the truth itself is of less importance or validity than the law. As a matter of fact every law is wise, stable, and just, in proportion as it is an expression in human terms of some principle of greater than human creation. It is unjust, and therefore in the long run provocative of disorder, in proportion as it ignores such principles. In view of the continual appeal of the traditionalist to law and order in the enforcement of the subordination of women, it must be most clearly stated that such subordination is not, and cannot be, conducive to order unless it is in fact based upon reality. It is not an inherent perversity on the part of women that makes them rebel against it: it is their instinctive recognition of the fact that it is not based upon the eternal order, and therefore, whether they argue it out or not, women will, and in the long run must, resent it. They will and they must demand that the Church shall base her laws and frame her constitution upon divinely ordained principles and not either in contradiction to or in ignorance of them. To appeal to women to tolerate or even to approve a constitution which is based upon ideals frankly abandoned by the majority of Church people is to appeal in vain. In other words, if men were determined to enforce the subordination of women to men within the Church, they should never have been so foolish as to abandon their conviction that women are fundamentally their inferiors. Upon this conviction alone, is it logical or just to build up a Church in which the subordination of women is a permanent feature? When men ceased to believe in that inferiority, they had committed themselves, whether they realized it or not, to the necessity of conforming the constitution of the Church to the principles in which its members now believe.

Some perception of this truth has evidently been created in the minds of those who think clearly. They are now a little shifting their ground and contend, not so much that women are bound to be spiritually subordinate to men, although they are spiritually equal to them, as that there is a very real difference of function between men and women which expresses itself in the different scope given to them within the Church. If women are to be excluded from any spiritual office, it is not in the name of subordination or order, except so far as order is truly based upon a recognition of their differences of function. As men and women have different functions in life, so must they have in the Church.

Undoubtedly there is truth in the contention that between men and women, in the Church as in the world, there is a difference of function. There needs no assemblage of bishops from all over the world to tell us that women are women and men are men. So long as this is true—so long, that is to say, as humanity exists—there will be certain differences between the sexes, going so deep as the fact that one gives to the race fathers and the other mothers. It has even been urged that the vocation to the priesthood is to men what the vocation to motherhood is to women—a very curious confusion of ideas, since it could clearly be argued that what spiritual fatherhood is to a man spiritual motherhood may be to a woman. Indeed the whole argument is vitiated by this confusion of thought. No one will deny—at least I have never heard anyone deny it—that there are certain differences between men and women; differences as enduring as sex itself. Yet as we advance, it is certain that the common humanity of men and women has been increasingly emphasized, and is not even now sufficiently understood. What men and women have in common is very much greater than what they hold apart, and when it is stated that men and women are "different" the whole has not been said. No one would argue that they are entirely different: no one would suggest that the differences are so complete as to cover their whole being. Men and women work and rejoice, and eat and drink, are born and die, as human beings. When, therefore, any exclusion is proposed on the ground of the differences between them, it is necessary to ask whether this is a matter which concerns those differences.

If, for example, it is proposed to exclude women from certain spiritual offices or vocations on the ground of their sex, it is not enough merely to say that their sex makes them "different from men," and they have, therefore, different functions; we must ask, Is the difference of sex one that applies to spiritual things? No one, so far as I have read, has attempted to answer this question in the affirmative, except those who definitely believe and say that women are fundamentally inferior to men. Those who stop short of this, and admit that the spiritual nature of the two is equal, and that the differences are differences of function, must make it clear wherein they feel that this difference of function applies to spiritual work.

In order to decide this point it is necessary to consider the nature of the spiritual work which the Church regards as vocational, and to examine the nature of the vocation in each case. Broadly speaking, we are now discussing the vocations to the priesthood and to the prophetic office. We must ask ourselves what is vocation to the ministry? As it does not belong to all men, it must mean something more than the quality of masculinity. In what, then, does it consist? And may it not be found to exist in women as well as men, since it is not merely the quality of maleness that gives it to the latter?

It is a little difficult to define the vocation to spiritual work, because in the different branches of the Church it has been interpreted variously. Broadly speaking, however, I suppose that what women are claiming today is the vocation of the prophet and the vocation of the priest. And although these have sometimes been found in the same person, and are now commonly assumed always to be found there, at least by the Church of England, and in a minor degree by other branches of the Church, most people will agree that in fact the vocations are not exactly the same, and that one may be found in one man and not the other. It will be convenient, therefore, to consider them separately.

The vocation of the prophet may briefly be described as the possession of a message from God. A great prophet has a message from God to humanity: a lesser prophet a message to his own generation or to his own country. This is a question of degree. But it is the possession of the message that makes the prophet.

The vocation to the priesthood is more difficult to define, but perhaps it may be said that, as the vocation of the prophet is to the great mass of mankind, the vocation of the priest is to the individual: a passionate love of souls must be the prevailing note of the priest, and Christ was supremely Prophet and Priest in that he had both a supreme message to all mankind, and also a divine tenderness, compassion, hunger and thirst for every individual soul. These two vocations, perfectly united in our Lord, are not, as I have said, always combined in the same individual. One might suggest that they are found united in a St. Francis of Assisi, a Catherine of Siena. Perhaps it might not be rash to add that the prophetic quality was greater in St. Paul and the priest-like character in St. John. And among lesser men the prophetic quality is found in such as Savonarola, Luther, John Wesley; the priest-like character in a St. Francis de Sales or a Fénelon.

The commissions, both to prophesy and to exercise the office of the priest, were given by our Lord to companies representative of the Church, and including women as well as men. "Go ye therefore, and make disciples of all the nations, baptizing them into the name of the Father, and of the Son, and of the Holy Ghost: teaching them to observe all things whatsoever I commanded you" (Matt 28:19–20). "Receive ye the Holy Ghost: Whose soever sins ye forgive, they are forgiven unto them; whose soever sins ye retain, they are retained" (John 20:22–23). These charges were given not to men or women separately—not to individuals at all—but to the Church itself. It remained for the Church to authorize and send forth to the exercise of their vocation those to whom God had given it. [. . .]

The case against the ministry of women therefore falls to the ground so far as it is based on any exclusion made by Christ. He gave his "great commission" to the Church as a whole, and if individuals have the call from God to the ministry, it is for the Church to recognize and send them forth.

People, however, very generally argue as though the Church herself actually gave or created the vocation of the prophet and the priest. Clearly this is not the case. It is God who gives the vocation: it is the Church's duty to discover those who have it and to authorize them to exercise it. The service for the ordering of priests and of deacons in the Anglican Prayer Book clearly shows this. The candidate for ordination is asked: "Do you think that you are truly called, according to the will of our Lord Jesus Christ, and the due order of this realm, to the ministry of the Church?" The calling therefore or vocation is from above: the Church recognizes it and bestows the grace of Holy Orders. Ideally, of course, the vocation should always be recognized, and no man who has it not should be ordained. In fact, however, it must be admitted that men who have no real vocation have sometimes been ordained both to the diaconate and the priesthood: while others who had the vocation have for various reasons failed to receive ordination. But obviously the ideal is that the vocation, being present, should be recognized by the Church, and the man who is truly and in spirit prophet or priest should be authorized by the Church to discharge this function.

In a sense indeed, if the vocation is a real one, no ecclesiastical order can prevent its fulfillment. The prophet will prophesy whether he is authorized to do so or not. The priest will in some way find scope for his love of souls. He will have his unofficial, if he may not have his official calling. But it is well for him and for the Church also if the vocation is discharged with all the grace the Church can bestow, and within the limits of its order.

If, however, these things are so, it must not be contended that women are irreverent to the Church if they suggest that there may have been cases of vocation among women as among men which the Church has not recognized, and that the question really is whether women have such vocations, and not whether the Church may choose to deny their exercise. The most devout believer in the infallibility of the Church will hardly suggest that it extends so far as to protect the Church from having ever made a mistake in ordaining some man who had no real vocation, or in omitting to ordain some man who had. The question of inerrancy or infallibility therefore does not arise.

Neither does that of personal prepossession. It is quite usual to hear the question of the ordination of women discussed from the point of view of such prepossession. A speaker or writer will argue that he or she does not really like the idea of a woman priest or prophet: that he believes that the general public dislike the idea also: or perhaps that, whether they like it or not, such women priests are not really necessary. On the other hand, I have heard it reluctantly conceded—or even triumphantly claimed—that the difficulty of getting male ordinands in the Church of England (for example) will compel the Church to ordain women. Some have even suggested that the difficulty of raising sufficient maintenance for the men will make it advisable or necessary to ordain women, who have, since the world began, been cheaper! Such arguments—and although they will seem trifling to many, they are too common to be altogether ignored—show an extraordinary disregard for the sacred character of vocation. It would surely be a most deplorable thing if any Church proceeded to the ordination of women because it could not get men, or because the men were too expensive. One can hardly imagine a course of action more lowering both to the sacred ministry and to the women themselves. If the Holy Spirit is not calling people to the exercise of the priesthood, or to the prophetic office, it must be assumed that it is because they are not needed. If, on the contrary, the Holy Spirit is calling them, it is for the Church to recognize the vocation and to raise money enough to train and maintain the ordinands. No one who takes vocation seriously at all can possibly hold any other view than this.

On the other hand, the same plea to regard the question of vocation seriously must give pause to those whose opposition to women is based simply on the fact that the Church "does not want" or the general public "like" the idea of women in such offices. The question is not what the Church wants, or what the public likes—it is a question of what the Holy Spirit is doing for us, and the Church as a whole can have no other part in the matter than to find those whom the Holy Spirit has called, and ordain them to their work with the grace of Holy Orders. If this truth were more generally recognized, we should be saved from some of the extraordinary arguments that are brought to bear against the entrance of women into the ministry. Women who believe they have the vocation would not be met with the ridiculous assurance that they would have quite as much power, influence, or prestige if they were to become writers instead of speakers—poets instead of priests—Sunday School teachers rather than bishops.[3] The question is surely not whether a woman prefers a private life to a public one, or the pen to the pulpit: it is a question of the work to which God has called her. And it is curious to find some very "High Church" opponents of the ministry of women adopting such preposterous

---

3. In case those who are unacquainted with the niceties of ecclesiastical controversy find this quite incredible, let me quote an instance from *The Place of Women in the Church* [H. L. Goudge et al. (London: Robert Scott Roxburghe House, 1917)], where, on p. 138, we find the author assuring us that John Oliver Hobbes and other writers "have rendered more service to religion with their pens than they could have done in the eminently expensive business of platform speaking." She goes on to say that a poet can do greater service for God than a preacher. Would this extraordinarily irrelevant remark satisfy a man who believed he had a vocation to preach and none to be a poet? (MR) [Royden's quote is from Geraldine E. Hodgson's essay "The Ordination of Women," a repudiation of female ministry. John Oliver Hobbes is the nom de plume of Pearl Mary Teresa Richards (1867–1906), a popular novelist and dramatist.]

arguments as these. Surely if anyone takes the question of vocation seriously, it should be the High Churchman. Yet it is from this quarter that I have most frequently received assurances that, if only women would choose some other walk of life, they would find themselves abundantly blessed. It is not a question of what we choose, but of what God chooses.

I urge therefore that the whole question must be examined in this light alone—of whether women are capable of the vocations which some of them are now claiming, or not: whether there is something inherent in their nature which makes it possible for us to say with certainty that the vocation of the prophet and the priest can never in any case be given by the Holy Spirit to a woman.

Let us think of the two separately for a moment. Can anyone seriously doubt that God has sometimes given to a woman a great message for her age or for the world? In a Church which has given to the world some of the greatest saints in the form of women—a Church which has given to us a St. Catherine of Siena, a St. Theresa of Spain—is it possible for anyone to deny the prophetic office to women on the grounds that they are by their sex incapable of it? In modern times have we not known such prophetic women? Surely Mrs. Josephine Butler and Miss Ellice Hopkins, within the Church of England, have had the prophetic vision, and Mrs. Coltman has quoted innumerable instances from the other Churches.[4] In fact, the whole case against the prophetic office for women was abandoned when the Church decided that women might go forth as missionaries. These women go forth to carry the greatest of all messages to the world itself: who shall deny that they are prophets? Who that knows anything of their work can possibly contend that the Holy Spirit gives no message to women?

If the vocation to the priesthood be that universal and Christ-like love of souls which forever sends the lover forth to seek and to save that which was lost, to guide, strengthen, and save those who are already in the fold—can it be seriously contended that no woman is capable of such a love and such a calling? Was not the mother of the Salvation Army, Mrs. Booth,[5] such a priest-like soul? And though her ministry lacked the

---

4. Josephine Baker (1828–1906), Victorian suffragist and social reformer; Ellice Hopkins (1836–1904), Victorian philanthropist and reformer; Mrs. Coltman is likely Constance Coltman (1889–1969), pacifist, suffragist, and in 1917 the first woman to be ordained (Congregational Union of England and Wales) in England. (KW)

5. Catherine Booth (1829–90), co-founder with husband William of the Salvation Army. (KW)

sacramental element as understood in the Catholic Church, will anyone deny that she had the essential spirit? Indeed, if there be any difference between one sex and the other spiritually, I have sometimes thought it might be that women were more commonly priests and men more commonly prophets. Certain it is that the almost universal experience of woman teaches her a love of individuals, a knowledge of their needs, and a devotion to their interests, which may perhaps be complementary to the experience of men which has more commonly led them into a wider world.

Finally, let me urge that the question of vocation cannot be considered from any other point of view than this—is there anything in the essential nature of women which makes it impossible for them to exercise the ministry of the prophet or the priest? Does the admitted difference between the sexes apply to spiritual things? And if not, on what ground can they possibly be excluded?

Source

A. Maude Royden, *The Church and Woman* (New York: Doran, 1924), 149, 150–59, 160–66.

Part 3.

The Church Is "Christ's Society"

Selections from Royden's writings on church polity

The Church

IN THIS CHAPTER FROM her book I Believe in God, *Royden argues against those who would allow for no change in the church on the grounds that the risen Christ established it once and for all during the forty days between the Resurrection and the Ascension, as well as those who would argue that the institutional church is unnecessary and even undesirable. Humans are social creatures and Christianity is not a solitary kind of spirituality. Therefore, some kind of institutional structure—the church—is necessary. But it should be open to the promptings of the Holy Spirit and willing to change. Otherwise, it risks becoming burdensome and rigid. Royden contends here that all Christian sects necessarily have some kind of organizational structure despite their differences in belief and worship styles, and that this is both necessary and good.*

The most articulate theorists about the Church are of two opinions: one school believes that our Lord came to found a Church, and that the work of redemption must be done through that Church alone; the other that he never founded or thought of founding any Church, and that organized Christianity has been a mere perversion or caricature of Christianity as Christ meant it to be. Theorists of the first school believe that through the Church alone can any good thing be done; the second that its existence has been an unmitigated misfortune. Articulate as these two bodies of theorists are, I believe that the great majority of us believe neither of them.

The belief that Christ created an organized Church, in the sense that we now understand the word, is difficult to maintain without resort to the desperate expedient of guessing how he spent the forty days between the Resurrection and the Ascension. When we are asked to believe that the Church, with bishops, priests, apostolical succession and sacraments, was exactly and completely organized by Jesus in that time, and that what the Church now teaches on these and many other subjects was imparted to it then, we cannot help marveling at the extraordinary difference which would appear to exist between our Lord before and after the Resurrection. The differences which I have noticed already—differences which appear to have made it difficult for his followers to realize at first with whom they were speaking—were differences which did not affect his spirit. Indeed it was by his spirit that he was recognized in the end. Some characteristic word or act revealed him, and they knew that it was the Lord. But this ecclesiastical theory of the organizing of the Church changes him out of all recognition. The spiritual genius becomes the organizer—the proclaimer of principles, the framer of rules. A fellowship of friends becomes in a few days or weeks a highly elaborate organization such as, in ordinary circumstances, one would expect successive generations to create. And for all this we have hardly any evidence except the existence of such a society at a very much later date. The use of such words as apostle, bishop, priest and deacon, widow and virgin, is assumed to imply all that, centuries later, they were found to mean, and the extreme improbability of such an elaborate organization having come into existence except in response to the growing needs of Christian people is passed over by mysterious references to the still more mysterious events of "the forty days."

The result of this curious reasoning in a vacuum is that many developments which might reasonably have been expected from historical reasons to take place are regarded as having been divinely ordained by the express command of Christ himself, and any attempt to change or to develop further is met with the surprising objection that Christ himself laid down these rules and they can, therefore, never be changed. If it is urged that, in fact, they have changed, some change is admitted, and defended as permissible under the inspiration of the Holy Spirit; but none of these changes could alter what Christ himself laid down during "the forty days" and, in the case of the Church of England, none can now be made at all, as the Holy Spirit can only operate through a whole and undivided Church—which does not now exist. Ecumenical Councils alone could issue new orders, and no such Council can now be held for Christendom is divided into East and West.

It appears that nothing further can be done. As, in the case of the Bible, the loss of all the original manuscripts without a single exception makes it impossible for us ever to know which of the existing texts (if any) is the verbally inspired one, and so it seems we are deprived of the benefit of verbal inspiration altogether; so, with the Church, the division into East and West has obstructed the work of the Holy Spirit, and we have now no more to hope, at least until the Catholic Church is visibly and organically one again.

It is only human in such circumstances for ecclesiastics to decide rather arbitrarily what is and what is not divinely ordained and therefore insusceptible of change. I observe, for example, that if Christ consecrated bishops or ordained priests at all, he did so not only from one sex only, but from one class and one nation. His chosen apostles were all working class people; all Jews; all men. It has been decided that bishops and priests need not be Jews and had positively better not be working class people;[1] but they are still all men, and any proposal to admit women is met with a shocked reference to the fact that Christ ordained no women. As for the character of the episcopate and the priesthood, apostolical succession and the like, these were all decided during the forty days, and as there is no evidence of this, no one can call the evidence into question. The Sacrament of Baptism may be in case of necessity administered by any one; the Sacrament of the Holy Communion only by a priest ordained by a bishop consecrated by apostolical succession. There are other sacraments which stand in some dispute as to whether they are necessary or not. But all this we must decide on evidence which does not exist, unless we are to hold that the existence of these orders and sacraments in themselves proves their divine origin, since they belong to the Church and the Church was divinely instituted. If, however, facts in themselves are to be considered as evidence, we have the astonishing but undeniable fact that there are men and women outside any Church and unsustained by any Sacrament, whose lives are lives of convincing sanctity.

This leads us to consider the opposing point of view. It is quite usual nowadays to hear men discussing the decay of Christianity and attributing it chiefly or wholly to the existence of organized Churches. These, it is urged, have always distorted the teaching of Christ and exploited his personality for their own purposes. They have created vested interests, bound themselves up with discredited beliefs, and done all this because they are organizations, and organizations are bound to behave in this way. Christ, accordingly, must be believed to have created no organization or Church and is known to have been at war with the Church of his own day. We ourselves would be better Christians if we followed his example in this and, indeed, most of the people inside the Church are

---

1. This at least has been the attitude of the Church of England for many generations. (MR)

worse—more narrowminded, hypocritical, and uncharitable—than the people outside.

If I find myself as unable to agree with this presentation of the case as with the other, I hope it is not out of perversity. Indeed I believe that I am only one of a great number who also reject both extreme views, but are not, or not often, articulate about their own.

We believe that Christ founded a fellowship. Personally, it seems to me quite inevitable that he should have done so. How could he help it? With a personality like his, and a work like his to do, it was inevitable that people should come about him, drawn by the magnetism of his appeal: inevitable that some should not only be drawn to but wish to stay with him. This, in fact, is exactly what did happen. The scattered and not always consistent accounts of the coming of the disciples to Christ makes this at least clear. Some he called individually; some sought him out; some he rejected.

We are not to suppose that the maniac whom Christ healed and sent home was not sincere in his desire to remain with his Healer; nor that Lazarus whom Christ so greatly loved would not have been true to him had he been called to that fellowship. Neither of them was called; neither had a vocation, we must suppose. Others were called and hesitated or refused. The rich young man could not make the necessary sacrifice. Another was reluctant to leave his aged father.

Gradually, however, the little band of active helpers was formed. There is doubt as to who they were; lists of names do not agree. Twelve were probably more closely associated with Christ's work than the rest, yet seventy were sent out to preach the Gospel. Even among the twelve, three were called upon for special services—Peter, James, and John. Anyone can see how it happened. Anyone can see that it must have happened. But is this a Church? Is this an organization?

Certainly it is, and it is exactly the organization that was then and there imperatively needed. This is how organizations are formed. They are created—in the first stages it should rather be said they grow—out of the needs of persons and the work done by persons. Jesus needed friends and his friends needed him. He began to need workers also: some of his friends were suited for the work and others not. The ones who were so suited formed a band of ministers, and here is the Church. In the future lay its vast development, its increasing elaboration, its orders and sacraments. These things also arose out of its needs.

I feel bound to point out to the critics of organized Christianity that if our Lord did not foresee all this, he showed a singular ignorance of human nature—an ignorance quite unbelievable in one so supremely and profoundly wise. I do, indeed, meet people who believe that no organization is necessary and that, since it is unnecessary, it is wrong. These are people with whom it is impossible to work, for they refuse to recognize the limitations of our common human nature. We live in time and space and are subject to these, and it is really impossible to live at all without recognizing this fact. Few people of creative genius really like organizations, for they are always seeking to transcend recognized limitations and to lift all our powers on to a higher and more spacious plane. They recognize the danger of accepting the limitations of the present as permanent and by this means stifling the adventurous spirit by which humanity goes forward. They know, too, the strength of vested interests and shun the dead weight of a rigid past.

Vested interests are not only material; they can be, and often are, spiritual also. The man who has taught some opinion for years has a vested interest in its continuing to be held orthodox: the prophet who prophesies disaster an interest in the fulfillment of his prophecy. Jonah was not the only prophet to resent the merciful attitude of Jehovah to those whose penitence made his warnings void!

There are, in fact, a thousand objections to the organizing of a Church. But there is one consideration which overrules them all—it is that organization is necessary.

Christ chose the most suitable persons from those who came to him; gave them positions and work of varying importance; called the twelve to remain with him; "appointed" or "commissioned" seventy to go out to preach. The process continued after the Resurrection and Ascension and was bound to continue. At intervals the organization grows too elaborate and rigid, and prophetic spirits in rebellion seek to destroy or escape it. In vain. Organization of some kind cannot be avoided.

The Society of Friends is a typical example of this kind of rebellion. Desiring to be led always and only by the Holy Spirit, they tried to avoid all the elaborate government, organization, and ritual of the Catholic Church. They called themselves a "Society," rejecting the name of Church altogether. They permitted no priesthood or professional ministry. They substituted silence for sacrament and ritual. They called Sunday "First Day."

What difference does it make? The Society is a Church with a different name. First Day is no less Sunday. For priest and ministers elders are provided, and for their meetings of worship a building must be erected and a time appointed. I do not know if all Quaker meetings practice the same ritual, but, among those I have attended, it is the custom, rigidly adhered to, that when one prays aloud he rises to his feet and the rest fall upon their knees. The meeting ends with the hour, and the elders shake each other's hands before breaking up. The order or ritual is as rigidly observed as the order of the mass in a Roman Catholic cathedral. I can truly say that I should feel—and be—much more conspicuous if I failed to observe it in a Quaker meetinghouse than if I wandered at my own pleasure about a Roman Catholic church while mass was being celebrated.

The sacerdotal "priest" is ordained because he is believed by the competent authority to be called to the ministry. The "elder" of the Society of Friends is called to his post because he is recognized as a man of exceptional spiritual power. The method is different: the principle is the same. If I speak of Quakers and Roman Catholics it is only because in them we recognize the extremes. What is true of them is true of us all. Reduce organization to a minimum—dispense with a professional ministry—refuse to call yourselves a Church—all is vain. The Church, the ministry, the organization, all are needed and all reappear. What they gain in simplicity they lose in elasticity. To many of us the Society of Friends seems far more rigid than the Catholic Church.

It is impossible to believe that our Lord did not know what would happen. His emphasis on the importance of the Spirit in all things, not least but rather most in ecclesiastical matters, was insistent, but he never suggested that it was possible to do without organization at all. Some body (society or organization) the Spirit must have: we call it a Church or The Church. Whatever it be called it will still be a necessity.

Christianity is a social religion. It is not, as so many people have said it was and wished it might be, a "purely personal affair." Buddhism, the most spiritual of all religions outside Christianity, turns the gaze of the disciple inward. It is a religion of escape. Not so with Christianity. The religion of Christ holds the balance equally and the very consecration of the believer is to be for the sake of others.[2] Nothing can be done without that personal consecration: everything comes from within: the Kingdom of Heaven is within us, and it is the immanent Spirit of God which

---

2. "For their sakes I sanctify myself" John 17:19. (MR)

directs and upholds all our efforts. But still the Gospel of Christ is of the Kingdom. It is for others that we serve. It is the world itself that must be redeemed and we are not allowed to give it up as hopeless. God made it, and still it is very good.

The Church is a recognition of this social teaching. It affirms at once our inability and our refusal to live alone. It declares that we cannot be saved or damned to ourselves. The saying which fills many with horror—and has indeed been made a horror by the way in which it has been used—"outside the Church is no salvation"—is only horrible, when literally interpreted. It is used as though we perfectly knew who is and who is not of the Church—a thing we cannot know and must leave to God. Some, as Christ himself reminded us, are of the flock though they are not of the fold—they belong to him though they are not within one building or organization. In essence, however, this dread saying is true: no man lives or dies to himself alone. No man can love God without loving his neighbor. No man is religious whose religion is a purely personal matter. Salvation in the last resort depends not on our spiritual discipline or our orthodox belief, but on our service to our fellow men (Matt 25:31–46).

This is so surprising to the orthodox that they have never really believed it. We still argue about justification by faith and justification by works, as though Christ had never pronounced the parable of the sheep and the goats. The goats are still surprised to find themselves goats; the sheep astounded to be sheep.

The Church herself—irony of ironies!—forgets the purpose and meaning of her own existence and holds the acceptance of a creed more necessary to orthodoxy than the feeding of the hungry or the visiting of the sick.

Yet it must have been the sense of fellowship and the need of it that first drew close the bonds of union among Christians and created a Church. The spirit of fellowship does not come by looking for it, or by passing resolutions that in future we really must have it. It comes, without observation, because some men and women find themselves in agreement about an ideal which sets the world against them.

The soldiers had fellowship in the trenches during the war. Conscientious objectors had fellowship in prison. When there is a great adventure and great odds there is fellowship—there is a Church.

The followers of Christ had it in that upper room where, bereft of their Lord, they met with closed doors for fear of the Jews. No wonder the Holy Spirit descended upon them!

They "had all things in common." When we are in a common danger for a common cause, how can we call anything our own? I dare swear that if any one shall set out today to be a Christian he will find himself holding things in common with those who try to do the like.

When the fervor of the spirit cools, the organization becomes rigid and a burden. What is then needed is not an attempt to be rid of organization altogether, but a renewal of the Spirit which shall dominate the organization, and make it living again, and so able to change. Living, it will be adaptable to the needs of the Spirit and obedient to its commands. We waste our strength in pretending to ourselves that it is organization itself that is wrong. Those who have, in passionate rebellion, broken away from the Church have ended either in dissipating their strength altogether or in founding a new Church. Even the Quakers have not escaped this fate.

It is true that, at certain stages, men seem to be called upon to choose between holding to a Church they can no longer believe in or going out into the wilderness. This is a terrible alternative. It is true that if the only choice that remains to us is between isolation and dishonesty, isolation must be our choice. Let us never forget that the loss is irreparable.

An ancient Church unites us not only with our fellow men of today, but with those who have gone before. It is more truly democratic, however hierarchical its organization, than the modern sect, for it assumes the presence of the Holy Spirit in us all and not only in us of the twentieth century. It is in itself a recognition of the presence of God with us throughout the ages. That Presence demands indeed that we should still progress; it was to *lead* us into the truth that the Holy Spirit was promised; but the experience of the past is of profound value to us today, and when its exponents rise to prophetic heights it can no more be out of date than Isaiah or the Psalms.

To break away from the Church is to lose something of that deep-rooted unity which lies in historic growth. Some of the finest spirits have become ineffective in the world because they wanted to shatter the past with all its mistakes, and to begin anew. It is impossible to begin so, and to try is to be frustrated. We lose more than we gain. A Church is like a ritual—it cannot be invented or put together.

It seems so simple to some people, impatient of the defects in all organizations, in all forms of worship, in all expressions of thought, to make something superior to them all by choosing out what is good and rejecting what is bad from each. The result is the manufactured as against the living thing. Eclectic religions have to me a painful sense of artificiality.

They are "made up" when they should have grown. A historic religion has its difficulties, but it is a religion: the manufactured article is not. It refuses to come alive. It is like the carefully selected ritual which, instead of growing up in response to the needs and beliefs of worshippers, has been put together out of many rituals in the hope of getting the best and avoiding all defects. It seems such a good plan: the result is desolating. We are driven back to the actual facts and to ancient history.

Out of the necessity for organization arose the different orders and liturgies of the Christian Church. Its work increased. For what one could do at first several were needed. The work they had to do must therefore be divided. It was divided according to the capability of the worker. The apostles felt that it was a waste of their time to serve tables. Deacons were appointed. No doubt if a server of tables were found to possess great spiritual gifts he would by common consent and in course of time be released for service of a more definitely spiritual kind.

It will be said that this happens in every organization and that it is useless to labor the point. The work is sorted to the men and the men to the work. But this is precisely what we are not allowed by a certain school of thought to believe about the Church. We are expected to accept the whole organization, or nearly the whole of it, as divinely instituted, and therefore unchangeable. Nothing could be more improbable. Not in forty days but by degrees, different classifications or orders appeared in the Church according to the Church's needs. Why this perfectly natural and inevitable process in the organization of the Church should be made into a fetish and assumed to be of supernatural origin it is difficult to understand. Personally, I accept it because I see it is bound to happen and always does happen. Calling bishops elders or priests presbyters makes no difference to the fact that in a great organization there are varieties of work, some more, some less exalted, and that the good sense of the organizers and of the whole community will aim at calling the finest spirits to the finest work.

These finer spirits, just because they are finer, represent the Church more truly than the rest: but they are not the Church. They represent it when representative action or words are called for, but Christ gave the Great Commission to the whole Church, apostles and laity, men and women. It seems impossible to doubt this. And at Pentecost they were *all* filled with the Holy Ghost.

When special work had to be allotted to special workers and the different "orders" arose, it was and still is held that the Church recognizes the vocation of these special ones to their work and authorizes the doing of that work, but does not confer the vocation. In the ordination services of the Anglican Prayer-Book, the candidate is not called to the ministry: he is asked whether he believes himself to be so called by the Holy Spirit. The bishop does not, in ordaining a priest or deacon, bestow on him a vocation, but recognizes it and authorizes the ordinand to exercise his function. It seems hardly possible for any great organization to proceed otherwise. Forms differ, but the fact that men have different gifts and are not always able to judge their own capacity remains. In any Church orders, whatever called, will appear. It is better that those who have certain spiritual gifts should be set apart for their exercise by authority.

If these things arise out of the conditions of our human nature, it seems to me unnecessary to suppose that they have any other origin. Indeed to ascribe the development and organization of the Church to our common human needs, powers, and aspirations, is to ascribe it to a source noble and sacred enough. Whoever accepts with humble loyalty the nature of things as they are, will be willing to accept the necessity of order and organization even while he rejects the idea that any order or organization is perfect and in no need of development or change.

That orders arise out of the Church itself and are delegated in a representative fashion to those most fit to exercise them is shown in, for example, the recognition of the validity of baptism administered by lay persons. A priest is preferred—it is part of his priestly function—but if no priest is present anyone may admit the person to be baptized into the congregation of Christ's Church.

This is a tremendous admission. It involves the priesthood of the laity—a phrase which an extreme sacerdotalism in some parts of the Church has emptied of meaning. The primitive custom of confession in the presence of the congregation was a recognition of the same principle. Such confessions sometimes causing grave scandal, priests were made confessors, as representing the congregation and, in the name of the Church, pronounced absolution. I cannot think that the practice of confession to this day is based on any other principle than all the rest—the needs of Christian people and the ordering of the Church as to how they may best be met.

Confession of sin on repentance is a universal impulse. It is so natural and right that no religious body can ignore it. The penitent form of the Salvation Army and the sacramental confession of the Catholic alike bear witness to its necessity. Whether it is called confession or not, it is needed and it takes place.

The reason is that we are *solidaire*—social beings—whose lives are so knit together that every sin, however secret and however personal, is committed against the whole community. No man can sin to himself alone. The unuttered thought of evil lowers the spiritual temperature for all and is a sin against all. Whether people recognize this or not, they do unconsciously know it, and when they repent they are impelled to confess the fault and to ask for pardon, not only from God and not only from the person directly injured, but from the community itself, or at least from some person who is, by external authority or spiritual power or both, a representative person. This is why all religious leaders receive confessions, formal or informal. This is why the Church of England has appointed priests, who represent the offended and injured Christian community, to hear confessions and to give absolution.

To me, though I realize the great benefit derived from a wise director, it seems very human and right that any priest ordained by the Church should be able to hear confessions and give absolution. If he is not wise or holy, he is still the representative of the injured community. It is because the sinner has injured that fellowship—not because the fellowship is holy—that he wishes to confess and to be forgiven. The assurance of God's forgiveness through the lips of a human being is a most perfect means of keeping this in mind. We have injured not only the saints but the sinners. If we were to address our confessions to the congregation as at a "testimony meeting" we should still be addressing it to both.

If no priest could be found for those services to which the Church has ordained priests, the authority would still be found in the Church itself. If every bishop in the world were to be swept off by a pestilence, priests must still be ordained. If a band of Christians were left on a desert island with no priest among them, they would have authority to be married and absolved as well as to be baptized, for they would be in that place the Church. I am convinced that they could celebrate a Holy Communion and still find in it the communion of the body and blood of Christ. The sacramental idea is too human and too true to disappear with the organized method of expressing it.

The priest is still a priest even though the Church may fail to ordain him. Human beings will find him out and he will exercise his compassionate vocation and care for the souls of men even without its august authority. The loss is double: the Church loses his ministry; he loses her blessing, her guidance, and her prayers. There are, however, no means by which we can ensure that no one will ever be mistakenly ordained or mistakenly refused ordination. This is one of the limitations inherent in human life. It is a misfortune, but it only becomes a calamity when the infallibility of the Church is erected into an article of faith and nothing can be changed which has ever been decided. This assumes that perfection is possible on earth and has actually been realized.

Perfection, whether of churches, liturgy, or ritual, is not to be found on earth and, as we are ourselves so very imperfect, doubtless we should neither like nor recognize perfection did we see it.

I am often asked how I can remain a member of the Church of England. I have to admit that I do not know how I could enter it if I were not already within it, and this seems—not only to unsympathetic but also to sympathetic critics, and to myself—to suggest that I ought now to leave it.

But I believe in the necessity of organization. I perceive that however earnestly men try to escape it they cannot. It is in the nature of things, so long as we live in time and space. The loosest bond of fellowship demands a place of meeting and a time, someone to call the believers together, and so forth. If, therefore, I leave one organized body of Christians it must be to join or—hateful thought!—to found another. This other, unless it consists of myself alone, can never perfectly meet my ideas of a perfect Church. But least of all can it be a Church if it consists of myself alone! No people however—not even two—think exactly alike, and the ancient and honorable institution of matrimony itself had, so long as men insisted on complete unity of opinion, to be based on the suppression of one set of opinions altogether. Two people express their opinions and these opinions are found sooner or later to diverge at some point. This is inevitable. Everyone who joins a society must therefore sacrifice something.

The difficulty, of course, is to decide how much one has a right to sacrifice. It is not whether one can sacrifice anything, for this one must do; but how much? To me this further depends on the hope or possibility of changing some of the things disliked. A man must give up something to belong to an organization at all, but some things not fundamental he may feel it right to give up; others more important he is willing to wait for, if there is hope of attaining them later.

I suppose that those of my fellow churchmen who dislike certain things in the Church of England—more than dislike them, think them wrong—stay in it because they hope these things may be changed. They do not dream of getting a Church which shall be remolded to their heart's desire in all things. Even were it possible, modesty forbids them to believe that such a Church would be a perfect Church! But on some points, on which they feel a deep and intense conviction, they may hope for change and believe that change is possible.

This is fundamental. If a Church is dying or dead, the hope of change dies too: as long as it lives it can change. I believe the Church of England to be alive. Long contact with officialism may make this belief difficult for some, but it revives when one meets the unofficial Anglican. There are too many who care passionately for our Church, and care also for the things they want and hope to find in her, for us to believe that she is really dead or dying. Movements for reform, born of ardent spirits in love at once with what the Church is and what it may be, are captured by a prudent officialism; bishops are substituted for prophets, and the movement dies a respectable death; but still the rebels remain and their spirit does not die. If the Church of England should ever again be a living expression of the religious genius of the people of England, it will be because these rebels refused to be cast out. For the sake, therefore, of those who would like to be of us, but for whom at present the barriers are insurmountable—for the very sake, that is, of those who may perhaps wonder at us for staying where we are—I pray that all Anglicans who can stay will do so.

I have passed—not unintentionally—from the Church to the Church of England. It is because among other human needs I recognize the need of diversity. I see nothing desirable in an organization which imposes itself as the only possible organization by and through which men may approach God. Such an organization is as remote from human needs as is the refusal to organize at all. It is surely significant that different races and nations evolve different types of worship and therefore different "Churches." It cannot be because one nation or race is more truly good than another that these things happen; or (as I think) that one has a clearer perception of truth. Roman Catholicism is as natural to the Latin races as Greek Catholicism to the Slav. Anglicanism is the natural expression of the religious genius of the English people—as natural to them as Presbyterianism to the Scotch. I do not feel at home in a Presbyterian Church, nor does Presbyterian worship appeal to me, but I am not so stupid as to fail to see how profoundly it appeals to the Scotch! Anglicanism has its defects, and any Anglican may smile at them, but English people feel at home in the Church of England, and I for one pray that she may never cast me out.

I hope to be forgiven by my many Free Church friends if I say that I think the future of religion in this country lies with the national Church; that I believe there would have been little, if any, dissent if it had not been for the extraordinary folly of Church of England leaders in the past; that most forms of dissent seem to me as alien to the genius of the English people as Anglicanism or Presbyterianism to the Latin races.

I do not understand why Christians should seek to proselytize each other or send Protestant or Roman Catholic missions to Roman Catholic or Protestant nations. It is incomprehensible to me that anyone should really hope or seriously wish to make the South of Ireland Protestant or the North Roman Catholic. Does anyone believe that he has a monopoly of the truth?

I desire unity but not uniformity: a Catholic Church in spirit, of which no part or branch unchurches another; but not one set of doctrines, one liturgy, or one form of worship for all. One of the qualities that most appeals to me in my own Church is its exceeding toleration.

Once, in discussing some scandal in the Church of England with a Quaker friend, he said to me, "I do not know how you tolerate such people inside the Church. The Society of Friends would have found means of freezing them out long ago." With joy I realized that no one is ever frozen out of the Church of England: no one—or hardly any one—excommunicated from her altars. At her most sacred service, the Holy Communion, saint and sinner kneel together; the sweating employer and the slum landlord with their victims; the profligate with the virtuous. This scandalizes the virtuous sometimes. I do not know why, for nothing seems more certain than that we are quite incapable of judging who are the virtuous and who not. For my part, the social snobbery of the Church of England is less odious than the spiritual snobbery which is the besetting sin of more exclusive societies.

We shall never all worship in the same way, but I think we shall someday recognize that all who love Christ are of one communion, and we shall unchurch nobody. In the meantime, I cannot wish that differences of temperament and genius that exist among us should be ironed out into a flat monotony when we approach God in public worship, or even wish that we were all alike. I feel at home in a Church of England service: I do not desire all men to feel as I do, and I respect and even like the differences which I must believe not offensive to God who made us all so individual and different.

Source

A. Maude Royden, *I Believe in God* (New York: Harper & Brothers, 1927), 252–74.

What Hinders the Reunion of the Churches?

Writing in 1918, Royden argues that the horror of four years of war makes apparent the pettiness of inter-denominational squabbling. Uniformity among the various Christian churches isn't the goal. Differences are important and ought not to be washed away. Indeed, the particulars characteristic of each denomination, when shared with others, can only enrich the broader Christian experience. But these particulars should never serve as obstacles to interdenominational cooperation, much less as justifications for denominational chauvinism. Otherwise, churches fall into the "sin of setting small matters above great and rules above principles"—exactly the kind of absence of humility and charity that resulted in the Great War. What ultimately matters—what's non-negotiable—is the meaning of prayer and the character of Jesus. Everything else, although not unimportant to practitioners, is unessential.

We Christian people were once a single Church. We want to be so again. We have worked together and prayed together, and together we are faced with the problem of a world gone wrong. It seems to us senseless to go on insisting that we are all opposed to one another—some "right," some altogether "wrong"—when we all want the same thing and worship the same God.

Before the breaking out of war we were feeling this need for reunion. After all, the war is only a result of all our quarrels and our other kinds of war. No one who cared about his fellow men could really call the pre-war period peace. There was industrial and civil strife. There was an armed truce between the nations. That is not peace. We were at war all the time, and so we had already begun to long for peace, at least with our fellow Christians. And now the war has come and made us wish more passionately for peace, and realize more than we did before what a fight Christianity has before it, if it is to conquer the world for God. The greatness of the battle presses us closer together. "It is simply inconceivable to a plain soldier like myself," said an officer to his men far away on the Macedonian front, "that men who have stood shoulder to shoulder now for three years facing the most awful hardships which war is bound to bring, sharing these in common, and not only that, but sharing too in these supreme moments of our life a common religious service—those Holy Communion services in tent or dugout, in France, Egypt, Mesopotamia, all over the world—are we really going back to an eternal petty warfare of inter-denominational strife? It seems too ridiculous to be even thought of, and yet it is bound to happen unless we find an alternative." Too ridiculous to happen . . . and yet it is bound to happen.

It must not happen. We too, at home, have got our battle. To us also it begins to seem ridiculous that we should attach such supreme importance to our inter-denominational differences when we have got to fight the world, the flesh, and the devil. Our differences have their importance. If some people are afraid of reunion, it must surely be because they think that importance is not realized. Let such people be reassured. It is not uniformity for which we are longing—a dry and arid regulated sameness, rigidly imposed upon us all. There will always be differences of temperament and character. One man can best worship God in silence, another in free and spontaneous speech, another in the great forms of beautiful language and ritual. And these differences go deeper than mere temperament and forms of ritual. They reach our minds and hearts, and form our way of apprehending God.

Well, what then? Is this enough finally to divide us? I think not: unless we are prepared to say, "In our doctrine, our worship, our way of drawing near to God, the whole truth is to be found. We are right; the others are wrong. If they want reunion, let them admit this and join us." We twentieth-century Christians are not prepared to say this. We think we have some part of the truth; we think those who belong to other Churches than our selves have some part of the truth also. We believe that we hold a great deal in common, and what we do not yet hold in common, we should like to share. Each Church has a different history, a different spiritual experience, a different spiritual gift. Nothing can rob us of the wealth that experience has won, nothing lessen in our eyes the value of the truth we know. But we would share it now with our brothers, so far as it lies in them to receive it; and receive from them, so far as lies in us, what they—we are sure—have to give.

What hinders? Fundamental differences? What differences can be fundamental between those who love and follow Christ? How artificial these barriers between us seem in the light of our tremendous war! We take note, we who care about such things, of the teaching of men of spiritual power on subjects of fundamental importance. Does it matter to us or to anyone to what communion they belong when they speak to us of first and last things? A year or two ago we were all reading *The Meaning of Prayer*;[1] another year, *The Jesus of History*.[2] These books were commended to Anglicans by bishops. The one of them was published with a foreword by the Archbishop of Canterbury. By whom were they written? By two Baptist ministers.

Here are the things that matter; the meaning of prayer (we find it so difficult to pray!), the character of Jesus. Are there any subjects more important to the followers of Jesus? And if our Archbishops send us to a Baptist minister to learn about them, do they expect us afterward to get into a fever because we are not all perfectly at one as to the age at which we ought to be baptized, or unchurch one another because we do not agree about the importance of bishops or the meaning of apostolical succession? These things are important? Certainly they are important. We admit that. But we refuse to give them the first place, or say we "do not know" whence John Wesley had his commission to preach because he had it not from an Anglican bishop. We know whence he had it—he had it from God.

Let us get on a little faster: we have already started on the road. We no longer contend that Mr. Glover and Mr. Fosdick will be damned for their mistaken views on baptism or bishops. We have even got so far along the road to Christian unity that we do not really *want* them to be damned. Many of us would positively dislike the idea. Not a few Anglicans are convinced that they will themselves be very generously dealt with if they get into the same heaven as these two—at a considerable distance. We admit—nearly all of us—that these men are Christians, as good or better than ourselves. With shame we Anglicans find ourselves confessing that all the sacramental teaching and practice of our Church

---

1. *The Meaning of Prayer* (1915), by Harry Emerson Fosdick (1878–1969), prominent liberal Protestant. (KW)

2. *The Jesus of History* (1920), by T. R. Glover (1869–1943), Cambridge lecturer in classics. (KW)

in all its beauty has not been able to make of some of us Christians so good as these and many another. Who will contend today that the average Anglican is morally superior to the average Wesleyan? Or the faithful and frequent communicant to one who shares the fellowship of a Congregational Church? Or the man who was baptized in infancy to him that waited till he was of an age to experience conversion?

Let us make an act of devotion to the God of things as they are, and thereupon say boldly that these things have a certain importance, but not a fundamental one. It is right that we should take pains to think them out. It is right that we should give our allegiance where we deem ourselves nearest the truth. Of vague and sentimental thinking we have had enough and too much. But to assert that such matters are sufficiently important, and the truth about them sufficiently clear, to justify us in unchurching and casting out all those who come to a different conclusion about them from ourselves, is to fall into that sin which our Master never wearied warning us against—the sin of setting small matters above great and rules above principles.

The conviction that our differences are not fundamental strengthens every day among us, and strengthens the more for reading the words of those who still give great weight to them. "Catholic theology," says a certain type of Anglican, "is a complete and perfect whole." It is true: it is entire; it coheres. Once go outside it, and you get an unworkable theology, schisms, heresies, sectarianism, and the rest. "This," says he, "is my conviction. But when I emerge from the study in which I arrived at it, I behold—shall I say it?—Dr. Selbie. I cannot explain him. I cannot explain him away."[3]

The discovery of Dr. Selbie does not, however, destroy the conviction of this type of Anglican that "Catholic theology" is complete and perfect. The fact that Dr. Selbie is recognized as an inconvenient fact is in itself acclaimed as an instance of remarkable honesty in the theologian. Honesty! It may be so perhaps of a kind. It is at least an advance in honesty on the older assumption that Dr. Selbie or any other Free Churchman is really, in spite of appearances, a bad man, fit only to be broken on the wheel or burned at the stake. But there are degrees of honesty, as of cleanliness. One's hands may be "clean," yet not "surgically clean." One's attitude of mind, it seems, may be theologically but not scientifically honest. "How many a beautiful theory have I seen," said Lord Kelvin, "wrecked upon

---

3. William Boothby Selbie (1862–1944), principal of Mansfield College, Oxford, author, and minister in the non-conformist English Congregational Church. (KW)

the rock of a single impertinent fact."[4] Such is the scientist's honesty. His theory may be the result of a lifetime's observation and labor. It fails to account for "a single impertinent fact"? So much the worse for the theory!

But Catholic theology, majestic, complete, is unable to account for the fact of sanctity outside the Church. So much the worse for the fact!

Yet such sanctity exists, such holy and humble men of heart. We Anglicans are not content to cut ourselves off from them. God is with them as with us—*as* with us. Not by some mere whim of His benevolence, not by "God's uncovenanted mercies,"[5] are these our brothers what they are: but by that unbounded love and grace by which we know that those who ask shall be answered, those who knock shall have the door opened to them, those who seek, find. Not only to sacramentalists was this great promise given.

Shall not we, who are sacramentalists, and find in the sacraments of our Church a grace and strength on which we continually feed, admit at last all the facts, and admit their consequences? Certainly, if we fix the standard of theological honesty as high as that of scientific honesty, we shall admit that no theory, however great and whole, which leaves out of account one "impertinent fact" can be regarded as final. We have gone too far (God be thanked!) along the path of Christian charity to stop where we are now. We have opened our eyes to the existence of holy men and women in other Churches than our own, unnourished by our sacraments, unguided and unblessed by our priests. They are not of the Church of England; yet, too clearly for denial, they are of Christ. They cannot be consigned to hell. It is certain that we shall be glad if we find ourselves near them in heaven. What follows? That the sacramentalist is wrong, and must forsake the sacraments which have been to him meat and drink and life, forever? Certainly not; but that the way of approach to God that has been so infinitely much to him is not the only way, since these his brothers have come by another way. The Wesleyan, the Congregationalist, the Baptist, the Friend, have all found God, and have not found Him by His "uncovenanted mercies," except as all God's mercy and all His love are "uncovenanted."

---

4. William Thomson Kelvin (1824–1907), British physicist and mathematician. The line Royden quotes, or at least a modification of it, is also attributed to Thomas Henry Huxley. (KW)

5. The assumption that God can show mercy for even unbelieving "outsiders"—or, in the context of Royden's argument here, members of Christian denominations other than one's own. (KW)

I sometimes think that of all the intolerable things that Anglicans have ever said of Nonconformists, this talk of "uncovenanted mercies" is the worst. As though God were gracious to Anglicans because He was under contract to be so, and to Free Churchmen only because and when He felt inclined! As if His gift of grace to all of us were not the unchanging and unfailing expression of His nature! As if all they who truly seek Him shall not surely find Him because He is Love and cannot be other than Love!

I protest that the greatness and the glory of Catholic tradition have been caricatured into a lie by theologians. There is a great truth in the belief that "without the Church there is no salvation." Who can be saved alone? Who can be a Christian alone? In what deadly spiritual peril stands that man who holds that religion is the affair only of his own soul and God! How mean and poor are the ideals of him who is a law to himself, to whom humanity is nothing, and the experience of all the saints a trifle! How cheap and pert the heretic who forgets his common heritage and ignores his communion with his kind! *Extra ecclesiam nulla salus.*[6]

But when this great far-reaching truth is reduced to a rule and imprisoned in an organization, how quickly it becomes a lie. Outside the Church no safety? And what Church? Roman? Anglican? Orthodox? Outside one or all of these organizations none can be saved? It is not true. It is silly. We cannot go on pretending that it is true any longer. But if we cannot, let us let alone our niggling little explanations of the great sweep of God's freedom and love—explanations which only obscure the great Catholic truth about the Church, that all men are brothers and God is our Father, and no man can be saved or damned alone.

Source

A. Maude Royden, *The Hour and the Church: An Appeal to the Church of England* (London: Allen & Unwin, 1918), 15–25.

---

6. "Outside the Church there is no salvation." Attributed to Cyprian of Carthage, third century. (KW)

Churchmanship and Discipleship

*R*OYDEN ARGUES HERE THAT *the risk-aversive Church of England suffers from a "spirit of invalidism." Rather than venturing beyond ecclesial structures to transform the world into Christ's "kingdom of love and joy," the church plays it safe by focusing on a multitude of in-house religious practices that bore if not repel ordinary people and appeal only to those who possess a "religious temperament." The church's depressing, joyless, and business-like atmosphere will be lifted only when she embraces Christ's charge to proclaim the kingdom and succor the needy. True, in doing so she will be attacked by those who believe that such ministry meddles in the political and secular arenas. But just as Christ defied public censure to preach salvation and practice love, so should all those who call themselves his disciples.*

For the most part the Church has abandoned the attempt to turn the world upside down, and is content to preach resignation instead. Not that the sick should be healed, but that their sickness is the will of God, is her message; not that the humble should be exalted, but that they should enjoy their humility. The Church is to be a leaven, as Christ foretold, but with this curious property—that it never attempts to leaven the whole lump. Its work consists not in turning the world upside down, but in organizing the devotions of its people.

To this work its ministers devote an incredible amount of time and energy. The more earnest they are, the more services are multiplied. Celebrations in every church and at every hour; matins and evensong, litanies and intercessions, the importance of being baptized, the urgency of being confirmed, the absolutely desperate necessity of communicating—nay, even the heroism of being churched, of saying grace, of having family prayers—these themes are continually on the lips of the clergy, and loud is their condemnation of those who remain deaf to their entreaties and injunctions.

Nevertheless, it is increasingly obvious that those who do all those things are often not a whit better, and quite frequently very much worse, than those who abstain. If people went to Christ because they liked Him, it is equally true that they do not come to church because they do not like us. They think us stupid and conceited, snobbish and dull. They find us interested in the most preposterous trifles and largely indifferent to the things that matter. Above all, they find our society depressing. A priest once told me that the most gloomy spectacle he ever saw was presented by the faces of the communicants approaching the altar in his church. When, on one occasion, a boy who had just been confirmed, and who had gained the idea that to be in communion with God and his fellowmen was the most joyful thing possible, came beaming up the aisle, smiling at his acquaintances as he came, several members of the congregation complained of him, saying that his conduct showed him totally unfit to approach God's altar.

This strange attitude of mind repels the ordinary person. The churches are empty of congregations and the religious newspapers full of suggested remedies. It is hopefully supposed that a change in the hours of service, an alteration of the language, a larger number of hymns or a smaller number of sermons, will effect the change. None of them is of the slightest use—at present.[1] People stay away because they do not want to come. It is difficult, no doubt, to believe this, but it really must be believed before we get any further. I am quite sure that no large number of Anglican clergy attend—shall I say?—prize-fights. The reason is not that the prize-fights take place at inconvenient hours, or under rules which the clergy do not understand. They do not attend because they do not want to attend. If those who organize them, distressed at the persistent absence of the clergy, were to put their heads together to consider what time of day would suit the clergy best, and how far the expressive but perhaps hardly classical argot of the ring might be revised to meet their comprehension, or its rules altered to engage their interest, the spectacle would not be more ridiculous than that of the clergy anxiously seeking the hour of service most convenient to those who simply do not want to come to a service.

Let us realize that a Church whose chief emphasis lies on the importance of religious observances will appeal to those who have what is called

---

1. Of course, services should be at times convenient to the more hard-working members of the congregation, but, as things are, the alteration of the hour is the least important matter. (MR)

"the religious temperament," exactly as a concert appeals to those who are musical. And it will appeal to no one else. But there is no virtue—none whatever—in possessing the religious temperament. I myself have it and know what it is worth. I like to attend the services of my Church, her observances and her ritual appeal to me, I prefer to pray within her walls where I can find an open church. But this is merely temperament, not religion. I cannot believe that the Church gets at the root of the matter when she directs so much energy to getting people to "come to church," or organizes an impassioned appeal to them to have family prayers, or to say grace. These things should surely be the effect of a great spiritual movement: they can never be the cause of it. Yet, when a mission is to be begun, a special effort to arouse the conscience made, it almost invariably takes the form of an invitation to some form of religious exercise. Will it be believed that, during the National Mission of Repentance and Hope,[2] organized in face of the great and tragic catastrophe of war, a leaflet was issued in which—after a moving reference to the courage and devotion of the soldiers in the trenches—the writer reaches this climax in these terms: "Let us therefore lay aside all scruples begotten of timidity, and with great boldness make a personal resolution to live as Catholic Christians in the best sense of that word, and from this day forward let us say our night and morning prayers, and say grace before and after our meals wherever eaten."

No one who had much sense either of religion or of humor could possibly have begun by referring to the soldiers in the trenches and gone on to implore us with "great boldness" to "say grace before and after meals wherever eaten." It is this sort of appeal that makes one realize why religion seems a very trifling business to many deeply though unconsciously religious people. One wonders what sort of a spiritual movement our Lord would have created had He begun by urging His disciples to be more careful about the ceremonial washing of their hands before meals and attendance at the Temple services. No doubt, He would have achieved just what the National Mission did.

No one who reads the New Testament with an unbiased mind could possibly conclude from it that to have the religious temperament is to be religious, or that to organize the religious devotions of its people was to be the main business of the Church of Christ. But the moment it is proposed

---

2. Launched in the autumn of 1916 by the Church of England, the NMRH's purpose was to renew Christian faith in a nation traumatized by the devastating loss of life in World War I. (KW)

to go beyond this, our leaders assure us that we are now dealing with politics or economics or something else that is "secular" and therefore not the business of the Church. But if this is so, then almost everything that is interesting is secular, and the Church has abdicated her leadership in almost everything that counts. No wonder, then, that she occupies herself with ridiculous trifles such as saying grace in a restaurant: she has deliberately ruled herself out of the things that matter. No wonder men think of religion as a little thing: the "religious" have made it little.

It is true that, when thus challenged, Churchmen are apt to reply that though indeed all life belongs to religion, the business of the Church is not to advocate reforms or to lay down a program, but to create an atmosphere in which reforms can and must grow.

The answer to this is the atmosphere which has, in fact, been created. The Church of England has been called "The Conservative Party at prayer." An atmosphere more inimical to reform could hardly be imagined. Indeed, the mere thought of it appears to those within the Church shocking; to those without, comic.

You can no more create an atmosphere than you can create fellowship by wishing you could. [. . .]

To proclaim the kingdom of God upon earth, to heal the sick, to raise the dead, to make the blind see and the lame walk, to rejoice the heart of the poor with joyful tidings—these are the "aims and object" of Christ's Society as laid down by Himself. To achieve them would be indeed a mighty revolution! To attempt them, a glorious adventure! Do we require any bond of union but this? Is it not enough to make us all brothers, that we believe Christ's teaching truly carried out, His principles honestly applied, would indeed create a kingdom of heaven? Other great teachers have given other solutions—solutions often easier to attempt and more seemingly practical to the ordinary man. But Christ gave us His solution, and we are going to try it. Perhaps He was wrong. Perhaps we shall fail. But let us try! We believe in it enough to try it out until we die. Let us try! Is not this to "believe on Him"? (John 6:29). Is not this the test that He proposed? What do we want with another? The goal proposed is the true test of spirits. It is the ideal that attracts those who are like-minded into a living fellowship and society—not a rite or a creed. And such a society has the power of life to attract and to repel. It draws to itself those who in heart and mind are of it; but it also, and by the same power, repels those who are not. "They went out from among us because they were not of us"—that was true of the early Church: it is true of every living movement throughout the ages. Life attracts and repels by its own strength, and the Church which is alive will "try all the spirits" by the force of its own idealism and life.

A Church which seriously set itself to make of the world the kingdom of love and joy which Christ described would be its own test, as well as its own bond of union. Let all come in and help who desire to try. If the Church were an active and living force, an executive Society seeking at all points to apply the principles of Christ to every problem, there would be in her a force more than sufficient to bring to her all who "believe on Christ" in truth, and to drive out—if they ever came in—all whose solution or whose ideal was a different one.

Would it be safe? No, of course it would not be safe. There is no safe test possible. Has insistence on baptism or on the recitation of creeds been a very reliable test? Has it drawn to us those whom we desire, or repelled those who are not Christ's? But a living spirit has a force possessed by no mechanical test, and attracts and repels by its own vitality. "They went out from us, but they were not of us; for if they had been of us, they would have continued with us" (1 John 2:19a), is a statement of the same truth, from a different side, as that other—"I, if I be lifted up from the earth, will draw all men unto Me" (John 12:32). And to this truth Christ committed His Church. As here in the flesh, His life, His personality were the force which drew men unto Him; as love for what He was and thought and did was all the requirement He made of His disciples; so the life and spirit of His Church should be her sole persuasive force upon her children. Will it in after-ages be believed that for a desire to share in this abundant life men substituted, as a test of churchmanship, belief in an Empty Tomb?

Let it be admitted again that no test is infallible—that nothing can make us "safe." Christ's method brought into that first society St. John, St. Peter, St. Mary Magdalene: it also brought Judas Iscariot. Christ took the risk. Shall not we? Is there indeed any conceivable plan by which it can be avoided? Would Judas hesitate to recite the creeds *ex animo*—yea, even the more startling clauses of the Athanasian Creed? History does not lead us to suppose it: there is no comfort there. But Christ's method, though it admitted a Judas, at the same time rendered him harmless. To love so perfect, courage so sublime, Judas himself became subservient, and enthroned the Master he sought to betray.

But we are afraid of such risks, afraid of such a terrible victory. We treat the Church as one long accustomed to ill-health. "Do not open the window! Do not bang the door! You cannot take risks with an invalid.

Step lightly, speak softly. At any moment the poor thing might die!" At last the very idea of what health and vitality would allow seems to have disappeared. None but those who have worked with the dignitaries of the Church of England can imagine the lengths to which this spirit of invalidism has gone. They seem forever to count her pulse, to watch her breath, to calculate in a whisper how long she has to live, if rude and inconsiderate persons insist on speaking in ordinary tones or expect her to endure reform.

But if she were to cast aside her fears, and trust for her life and health to the living Spirit of God, would such faith not meet its reward? Then we should find the body of the Church so vital, so alive, that it would not need to be held together by bandages and ties. It would attract as life attracts—like coming to like, because they are one in spirit, and so desire to be one in fellowship also. All who love Christ would be with us if we really "showed Him forth." All who worship Truth would seek us out because we were inflamed with a thirst for Truth even greater than theirs. All who love their fellow men would desire to be in communion with us because we offered the most perfect service of all.

Source

A. Maude Royden, *The Hour and the Church: An Appeal to the Church of England* (London: Allen & Unwin, 1918), 69–75, 78–82.

The Heart of Worship

IN THIS SELECTION, ROYDEN compares the practice of magic with genuine worship. Magicians and, perhaps, early religionists who had no distinct concept of deity, seek to harness and exploit what they take to be forces of nature. But once an awareness of the existence of a personal God arrives on the scene, a God who is responsible for natural forces and who remains faithful to humans no matter how far from Him they stray, the urge to exploit is necessarily replaced with gratitude, awe, and love, all of which are defining characteristics of worship. The magician seeks to augment his power by tapping into nature, but the worshipper gladly sacrifices some of his in worship by acknowledging the majesty of God. Implicit in this essay is a criticism of Christians for whom formal worship is primarily a way of placating or exploiting God rather than an opportunity for expressing love and gratitude.

It is fashionable nowadays to say that you can have religion without God and that the earliest forms of religion did not have any God. I suppose that is true if one thinks of God always as a person. I think Miss Jane Harrison, in her latest publication, is obviously right when she says that it is possible to be religious, and that people have done religious acts and had a religion when they had no God.[1]

If she means—and I think it is clear that she does mean—"when they have no personal God," I agree with her. She says the first beginnings of religion were generally some form of magic, and that magic does not imply a god at all in the sense of a person. Magic is an effort on the part of the magician to use some kind of power to bring about the things that men mostly desire—a good harvest, success, sun or rain, or fertility in

---

1. Jane Ellen Harrison (1850–1928), British classical scholar at Newnam College, Cambridge, and suffragist. The book Royden is referring to is most likely Harrison's 1921 encyclopedic (despite the title) *Prolegomena to the Study of Greek Religion*. (KW)

the tribe, or victory in battle, or any of those first things that all human beings desire, and which they have a sort of feeling some people can get for them. By some kind of magic, by hearing some sort of a conjurer, by going through certain rites, by drawing lots, by imitating the thing that you want to happen, you can perhaps make it happen. And she says, and I repeat it seems to me quite rightly, that these acts are religious acts, but they do not imply a god, at least not a person.

Of course, it all depends on our idea of what God is, and most of us have got so strongly hold of the idea of a personal God that when Jane Harrison says these things can be done without any God we think, Yes, that is quite right, they can be done without a Person. But they cannot be done without a belief on the part of those who do them that they are invoking some power that is invisible, that is really spiritual, and that is stronger than they are themselves. All magic, I think, implies that. Some people have a certain gift, perhaps, which enables them to heal, or some kind of wisdom in using herbs; or they want a good harvest and they think some medicine man or conjurer can get it for them. Sometimes, I think, these magicians are aware that they are using a power which is not exactly themselves. It is something beyond themselves, a spiritual power, therefore the act they do is a religious act. Only I would say that that perception of a spiritual power which they do not understand, which works rather capriciously, but which they always hope they can conciliate or bribe or deceive—because a great many magical feats are based upon an attempt to deceive—that power does really exist; and I would say that that power of God is, to the magician—though he would never call it by such a name—an operative cause. If you do certain things certain results will follow; but then, in my philosophy, the cause of this is God, because God is the operative cause behind all creation. Personality is, in my creed, one of the attributes of God, but I would never say a person had not a god because he had not a personal God. But I think it is perfectly true to say this is not realized by the magician. I think very often he does not realize what it is that he does.

Some of you will have read Browning's great poem about Mr. Sludge, the medium,[2] in which a fraudulent spiritualistic medium admits his fraud, and yet he says, "All the same there was some truth in it. Of course, I couldn't help deceiving people; they were asking to be deceived,

---

2. Robert Browning's poem "Mr. Sludge, 'The Medium,'" is an ambivalent indictment of spiritualism inspired by the poet's fascination with the nineteenth-century medium Daniel Dunglass Home. (KW)

but all the same there was something there"; an impression I suppose most of us get when we hear of fraudulent mediums. There have been many fraudulent mediums, but all the same isn't there something there? And so with these magicians, although many of them may have been frauds—because it is very difficult to be a magician without deceiving somebody—yet they knew there was something there, and that was their first primitive idea of God. It is not worship, but religion, and worship comes later. Worship comes when the nature of these powers becomes partly known to us. Behind the power that makes the harvest, that sends the rain or sun, or makes the tribe have many children or gives it success in war: behind this power of evading God, of getting round him, or bribing or frightening him, it may be (because all these things are resorted to by primitive religions), there is something which is constant, which is trustworthy, and I feel that no one knows better perhaps than the magician himself that underneath all the chances he takes, and underneath all his uncertainty as to whether his magic is going to work or not, there is something faithful, something that he cannot get round, some laws that cannot be broken.

You get the first joy of that discovery, as far as our religious literature goes, right at the beginning of the Book of Genesis, after the flood. Suddenly we hear that as long as the earth endures seed-time and harvest, summer and winter, day and night, shall not cease. Now the idea of God in the Old Testament is often most capricious, most uncertain. Again and again we get the impression that the Jews simply did not know what it was their God wanted them to do.

But nevertheless again and again in the history of man, with all his efforts to evade or frighten his God, to coerce, to persuade, or push Him into doing what He does not want to do, there is continually this discovery that underneath it all there is something or someone who is faithful. As long as the earth endures the natural processes will not fail. With all your magic you cannot stop them. Seed-time and harvest, cold and heat, summer and winter will not cease. And after all the horrible, cruel, fantastic ceremonies of magic, the human sacrifice, the fetish, the ju-ju man, all the bloodstained imbecilities and cruelties of human religion, we draw near to God. By what strange and miry paths have we come home, and from what immeasurable distance has God seen us coming and made haste to meet us!

Through all this tangle of superstition and folly and cruelty and fear, and a desire to exploit the spiritual things and to work the oracle, there dawns on the human mind the realization that there are some things that cannot be worked, some gods who cannot be bribed, and some laws which cannot be violated; just a few things in the universe that can be trusted. The growing consciousness of that trustworthiness of God is one of the glorious things in the history of religion. It grows and fades, comes and goes. Some religions have had more than others. Some seem hardly to have had any at all. But all have a little, and gradually as the mists begin to clear away we see that God is in fact power and order and love and strength, and when we see that, when we see any part of it, then suddenly comes the possibility of worship. "Thou hast said, Seek ye my face. Thy face, Lord, will I seek" (Ps 27:8). Religion you can have, but the impulse of worship comes only when God is seen to be worshipful.

We may worship false gods; we do; incomplete gods, shall I say. We may worship God as power, or as beauty, or as wisdom, or as might, but I believe that the history of human progress lies in those moments when humanity suddenly perceives some glory in the nature of God, and worships it with so disinterested and perfect a love that the desire to exploit or make use of Him disappears, and at least for an hour man desires nothing but to see the glory of God. Just as magic is an attempt to exploit God, so worship comes at the moment when the desire to exploit Him vanishes, when the sudden realization of His beauty, majesty, or power becomes so lovely, so adorable, that the beholder ceases to want to make anything out of it and has nothing more to ask, but his heart goes out to God just because He is so beautiful. "We praise Thee, we bless Thee, we glorify Thee, *we give thanks to Thee for Thy great glory.*" Not for anything Thou hast done or we want Thee to do. We give thanks because Thou art so glorious. And whenever that happens in the world it involves sacrifice. Suppose you are somebody who can secure a good harvest or ensure the fertility of the tribe. If you suddenly come to the realization that God is law, and you cannot alter His laws, you have got to give up something of your own power, something perhaps even dearer and lovelier than that, the thought that you can help other people. If you were a magician and thought you could produce a good harvest, and you suddenly learned what this great phrase meant, "Seed-time and harvest shall not cease," and you had to stop the "magic" of making a harvest, you would not only give up that bit of power which is dear to you, but you would give up that dear thought that you could serve other people.

Worship must be very disinterested, because whenever that impulse for worship is invoked in humanity by some revelation of the nature of

God, it always means that something dear, lovely, or noble as far as it goes, has to be sacrificed. It is not only in your individual life, but it is in the whole history of humanity. Men must claim Him in such disinterested love that they forget what they have to lose.

The great prophets who have moved the world along its path are those who have revealed to us the worshipfulness of God, and if they reveal it to a generation which can forget its own loss, which can cease to desire to exploit God even for its own consolation, can forget it all in the glory of the discovery that God is greater than they knew, such a generation is worthy of a prophet.

Source

A. Maude Royden, *Prayer as a Force* (New York: Putnam's Sons, 1923), 3–9, 10–11.

Must the Church Always Be Last?

The church, argues Royden, is called to "lead, inspire, and inform" by preaching the "revolutionary Gospel of Christ." But from a combination of theological conservatism and moral timidity, she too often accommodates herself to secular public opinion rather than obeying the dictates of the Holy Spirit, thereby "leading" from behind. Why, then, does the church exist? To rubber stamp the latest fashionable intellectual current or political program, or to serve as spiritual leaven to the culture as a whole? For Royden, the answer is clear.

Must the Church of Christ be so exactly like the world? Must she trot always in the rear of public opinion, deride where it derides, and give her blessing with its applause? Must she wait until *everyone* has decided and then decide as they do, to avoid "a humiliating defeat"—a defeat which might seem as terribly decisive as the defeat of her Master on the Cross?

For what, then, does the Church exist? To tell us what we already know? To ratify what is already done? It seems an expensive and cumbersome way of doing superfluous things. Is God dead, or has His promise failed, that we, instead of confidently expecting to be led by His Holy Spirit, must be led by the public opinion of the world instead? Shall Christ bring, no longer against a renegade race but against a renegade Church, the accusation, "Ye build the sepulchers of the prophets, and garnish the tombs of the righteous" (Matt 23:29)? Is it our duty to be more anxious to be safe than eager to be right?

I urge that this conception of the Church is a mistake. It is her work to lead, inspire, inform. She is to be the leaven leavening the whole lump, the light set on a hill, the salt giving savor to all. It is not an old but a new delusion that organized Christianity must always labor in the rear of secular public opinion. Throughout the Middle Ages the Church of England again and again led or shared the fight for liberty. She was the champion of public right. She stood stoutly against the encroachments of regal power. She gave the people education—true ferment of revolution!—she established that great tradition which made it possible for Newman, hundreds of years later, to assert, "There is not a man who writes against the Church but owes it to the Church that he can write at all."[1]

Democracy was invented by the Church. The Stoics had said "All men are equal." The Church believed and practiced it herself. Any man might become a priest if he had learning; and the Church gave learning to all. Any man might come to be Pope; and the Pope was God on earth. Truly the Christian Church turned the world upside down. Here, in our England, the Archbishop of Canterbury was the champion of the people. Anselm, Lanfranc, Thomas à Becket, Stephen Langton[2]—these are names to point to when men say the Church is bound to be reactionary. It has become so, God knows. That it must remain so is not true. If it does remain so, it has not long to live.

It is useless to shut our eyes and repeat that the Church is a Divine institution which can neither fail nor die. The Jews held fast by the same kind of belief. "We have Abraham to our father," they repeated. "We are God's peculiar, chosen people. The Divine promise cannot fail." Neither did it fail. The Messiah came indeed, and the promise was fulfilled; but while they reminded each other of Abraham, they inadvertently crucified Christ.

And we? If we refuse to preach the revolutionary Gospel of Christ, if we lag always in the rear, if we leave to others the difficult and dangerous work of the pioneer, if we must depend on the State to preserve a little decency, a little respect for freedom, a little toleration in our border: may we expect a more merciful judgment than the chosen people? We have the promise; true. We have also the warning "God is able of these stones to raise up children unto Abraham" (Matt 3:9).

Source

A. Maude Royden, *The Hour and the Church: An Appeal to the Church of England* (London: Allen & Unwin, 1918), 41–44.

---

1. St. John Henry Newman (1801–90), British cardinal and theologian. (KW)

2. Royden names Roman Catholic archbishops of Canterbury: Anselm (ca. 1033–1109), Lanfranc (1005–89), Thomas à Becket (1118–70), Stephen Langton (ca. 1150–1228). (KW)

Church and Politics

IF THE CHURCH MUST forswear a spirit of accommodationism, as Royden concluded in the previous selection, what's its proper relationship to politics? In this sermon preached at the Guildhouse, she argues against a church that bends over backward to avoid offending or alienating "good and Christian people" on either side of a political issue by speaking for or against it. The church's custom is to preach general and abstract Christian principles while avoiding discussion of their concrete applications. But the Hebrew prophets never backed away from making political statements that offended the people of their time, and neither did British campaigners against palpably evil social institutions such as slavery, child labor, or sexual exploitation. They recognized that sometimes "good people" can defend immoral political policies. For the church to take a neutral stance when confronted with such policies is to forswear its responsibility.

Last Sunday when I was describing what the work of our Fellowship would be, I said among other things that we should sometimes discuss and I should sometimes preach on political subjects, and though some of you agreed, I think—in fact, showed that you did—others doubted, and some quite frankly dissented. I want to make it clear why I sometimes feel bound to preach on political subjects, and I want first of all to say that I do understand, I think, because I used to share, the feeling of those who do not like to hear politics discussed at a religious service. [. . .]

There is a feeling that when we come here in the presence of God, we want to leave outside these perplexing and difficult questions and to seek for those deeper truths which underlie all political problems, and which are not discussed—or rarely discussed—on political platforms, which if not given to us in a church or at a religious service may perhaps never reach us at all. There is a feeling that after all in the application of Christian principles people may very well differ; that on certain political questions now before this country it is certain that there are good and sincere Christians on both sides. Not only good and sincerely religious people, but people who are definitely Christian, may be on either side—will certainly be found on either side of the question. Therefore a preacher should rather seek the underlying principle than proceed to the application of a principle about which his congregation may very well differ with him and with themselves, and may differ without any moral blame. In church we are to discuss great moral principles and not politics, since good people are found on either side.

I remember very well hearing violent anti-suffrage sermons preached when I was working in the suffrage cause, and my indignation was a just indignation, because I felt what I often have said—that I should equally deplore it if I heard a suffrage sermon preached. I said, "There are good and Christian people on both sides, and when they come to church they ought not to have their feelings outraged by hearing a person they cannot answer back." (It increased my sense of impatience that I could not "answer back" to a political question!) Yet I changed my mind about that, and I want, if I can, to explain tonight why. It is true that if you apply your principles, you will almost certainly hurt somebody's feelings. You may talk for ever in the terms of the Sermon on the Mount, but as long as you do not apply them to the world in which you live, nobody will resent it. When you begin to apply them, you are absolutely certain to hurt somebody's feelings, and that somebody is quite likely to be a more religious person than the preacher, and a person whose Christianity is both real and deep. [. . .]

The point I want to bring home to you is that our own great religious writings—the Bible from which we read every Sunday and in some churches twice on Sunday—are full of denunciations which to the people who heard them seemed political: the indignant denunciation of the foreign policy of one king, of the policy of having a king at all over the Jews, the denunciation of moral wrongs, of economic injustice, of international politics, all those things which you and I call political—though perhaps the Jews did not have an equivalent word for it—all things that were very sore in the people's conscience. These great prophets from whom we read Sunday after Sunday and draw from them religious ideals, seemed to the people to whom they were addressed to be profoundly and most tactlessly political. So tactless were some of these prophets that the people took them out and killed them! They enraged public opinion to such an extent that it became, as you know, a proverb about the Jews that their fathers had slain the prophets and that they had built sepulchers over them.

And in our own country also, again and again, a great political question has arisen on which there was a moral issue. For instance, take the question of slavery. Take the question of child labor, or the Contagious Diseases Acts.[1] All these were political, for about all of them there was legislation. People standing for Parliament were accepted or defeated on platforms connected with these subjects. They were political in the sense that they were discussed and debated on every political platform and that, as I say, men made or lost their political career according to their position with regard to slavery, or child labor, or even the Contagious Diseases Acts. Now, in regard to the question of slavery, there were good and religious and Christian people on both sides. There were people who pointed to the Old Testament to show that slavery was a divine institution. There were Christians who quoted St. Paul's Epistle to Philemon to prove that slavery had the approval of the early Church.[2] And in the same way with regard to child labor, there were perfectly sincere and honest Christians who felt it was inevitable that children should spend their waking hours in a mine or a factory. It seems to us incredible, but it is literally true. These people were persuaded that economic necessity demanded that these children should be sacrificed. They pointed out that the industry—the factory or the mine—would collapse but for the work of these children; that they could not afford to do without it; that it would cause the narrow margin of profit to disappear; and they suggested that after all the industry exists for the sake of the people.

In the children's own interests, they argued, the mines should be run and factories should be kept going, and they could not be kept going without child labor. Therefore, it is a painful necessity that these children should be there, and to strive against it is to strive not against the wicked employer, but against God. Really, honestly religious people thought that

---

1. Thanks largely to the efforts of William Wilberforce, Parliament finally passed a bill in 1833 to gradually abolish slavery. In the Industrial Revolution, it wasn't uncommon for children under the age of ten to work in factories and mines. England's first child labor law, the 1819 Cotton Factories Regulation Act, set the minimum age at ten with a maximum of a twelve-hour shift. Subsequent child labor acts were passed in 1833 and 1847, despite the protests of factory owners. The Contagious Diseases Acts, passed between 1864 and 1869, legalized and regulated prostitution, especially for soldiers and sailors, in an effort to control the spread of venereal disease. (KW)

2. In the epistle, Paul mentions that he's returning a runaway slave, Onesimus, to Philemon, his owner. (KW)

and said it. And I do not doubt that many ministers and preachers up and down the country were silent on the question of slavery, were silent on the question of child labor, not out of fear, though no doubt there were many subject to fear, but I am certain that there were many who were silent because they realized, as I do every time I speak on political subjects, that there are good and Christian people on both sides; and held that the preacher ought not to attempt to lay down the law as to the application of Christian principles. But all that is so long ago and so far away that we see now how splendid it would be if the Church of Christ had been the defender of these helpless children!

If a Wilberforce, or a Lord Shaftesbury[3] had not been left to fight his battle almost alone; if a Mrs. Josephine Butler[4] had not been cast out by nearly all the people who called themselves respectable; and if the Churches of Christ had always spoken out for the oppressed and the abused and the exploited! How proud those of us who belong to any Christian Church would be, if we could have claimed that they had always spoken for those who could not speak for themselves, for those who were exploited and destroyed by civilization! The Churches did not do it for the most part, and everyone says how unreal the Churches have become. They do not seem to touch life at any point. You go into a church and there seems no contact with the world outside. [...] [But] the Church of Christ should be concerned with men's bodies as well as their souls and should care when people suffer, not only to bind up their wounds, but to get rid of the cause of trouble. And, my people, the moment I try to do that, I am bound to preach what you would call a political sermon. [...]

There is in my home a little Austrian boy. When he landed in this country a year ago he was four years old, and he had never walked. He was so rickety that he could not walk. I never looked at him without being haunted by those lines of Mrs. Browning:

> They look up with their pale and sunken faces,
> And their looks are sad to see,
> For the old man's hoary anguish draws and presses
> Down the cheeks of infancy.[5]

---

3. William Wilberforce (1759–1833), abolitionist crusader; Anthony Ashley Cooper, Lord Shaftesbury (1801–85), author of the 1833 Tenth Hour Act, which limited child labor to a ten-hour shift. (KW)

4. Josephine Butler (1828–1906), social reformer, suffragist, and campaigner against sex trafficking. (KW)

5. Elizabeth Barrett Browning, "The Cry of the Children" (1842). (KW)

That little boy's face was like a little old man's. He had that terrible, anxious, harassed look that is pitiful on any human face, but is heartrending on a child's. He was only two years old when the war ended. He was not born when the war began. His fathers, you will say, made the war. Yes, perhaps. But we made the peace, and it was the war and the peace together that made Freddie look like that. He says at night the Lord's Prayer. He is rather young for such difficult words, but he is a Roman Catholic, and the priest asked us to teach it him, and he says: "Forgive us our trespasses as we forgive them that trespass against us." I suppose he cannot understand such long words. I wonder when he does understand them, whether he will still be able to say them. All the world has trespassed against that child. His own country and our country and all the world has taken from him the healthy little human body that he should have had. The mark is on his very soul. You cannot be starved for the first four years of your life and be just the same in your soul at the end of it. Well, he is lucky, isn't he? He has come here; at least he can have enough to eat and he can be loved. But he has a little brother in Vienna who is seven years old, who is almost an idiot through lack of food and care. And that is a political question. Am I to be silent when the world treats children like that? Am I to stand here before Christ, who said it was better to be drowned in the depths of the sea than to offend against a little child, and not tell you why these children are starved (Matt 18:6)? [. . .]

It seems to me that a preacher has this responsibility. There is a right side and a wrong to all these great questions. That is what we shirk. All these questions have good and Christian people on both sides? Yes, that is true. But this is also true: that one side was wrong. You see that is what we are afraid of. The people who were on the side of slavery, God knows, might have been people infinitely more religious than I, but they were wrong. The people who held that it was necessary for this country to build her prosperity on the work of children in mines and factories might have been convinced of it from the bottom of their hearts; they might have held it with all the earnestness they were capable of. They might have been sure they were right, but they were wrong, and time has proved them wrong. The people who defended the Contagious Diseases Acts, who thought it right that the State should regulate the sale of the bodies of women—I know that many of them believed sincerely that they were right, but they were wrong. They were damnably wrong.

I think the Church, in fear of making a mistake, has ended in making nothing. "You may make a mistake!" Yes, indeed, I may, God knows.

I may, in believing that one side is right and one is wrong, take the wrong side. But is it not a fact that if you will not try to decide, if you will never face the issue for yourself, you will never do anything in the world at all? I ask you to forgive me beforehand, when I say something that is stupid, unjust, or wrong. I promise you that I will do my best to be honest and fair. I will not let myself off any hard thinking that I can do. [. . .] I do not mean to weary you with political sermons. The other side—the theological side—often interests me far more, and I know you care about it. But when there comes a great moral wrong, or what seems to me to be so, I owe to my own vocation the duty of applying what I believe to be the Christian principle—not only to declare the principle, but to apply it. [. . .]

I have heard it said by a very distinguished business man, who is also a politician, that while people sneer at commercial morality, he found it as heaven to hell compared with political morality. That is what we have reduced politics to, so far as it is true—it is not true of everyone, thank God. But it is to that standard that we reduce it when we do not try to bring our politics into the presence of God where, if anywhere, we can give our opponents credit for desiring to do what is right; where, if anywhere, we can abandon the silly habit of scoring off one another, of getting our own back, of trying to make each other look a fool; and together, approaching from whatever opposite ends of opinion you like, can bring our difficulties to the feet of God. I cannot believe that in such circumstances the solution would be impossible. We do not need to be afraid of politics, not even, I think, of party politics. What we should be afraid of is the party political spirit, and to get rid of that here might make it possible for us when we go out into the world to the election, to the work of municipal or national politics, not only to carry with us a new spirit, a spirit of desiring to find out what is right, but, as I said, a willingness to give our opponents credit for decent honesty, for well meaning, for a desire to arrive at a right judgment; and it is possible that if such a spirit were generated in the churches, our churches would not become more secular, but our Parliaments would become more religious.

Source

A. Maude Royden, *Political Christianity* (New York: Putnam's Sons, 1922), 3, 4–5, 6–9, 10–11, 11–13, 14–15, 16–17.

Sacramentalism

A SACRAMENT IS AN act or material object in which the glory of God is revealed. For Royden, the entire material universe, reflecting as it does the divine presence, is sacramental, a channel for the sacred. It's a mistake, consequently, to draw hard and fast distinctions between the material and the spiritual. That's why Jesus himself praised simple natural creatures like lilies and birds and simple artifacts like bread and wine. Royden believes that the sacramental quality of reality is especially obvious in artistic and liturgical beauty. The Eucharist, often called the sacrament of sacraments, is especially, for Royden, an opportunity to intuit communion with both God and one's fellows. It lies at the heart of the church's worship.

The sacramental idea has given us sacraments, but is more profound than any of the methods by which we express our belief in it. Even though some Christian communions have no sacraments, it is true of them also that Christ's religion is sacramental.

Sacramental religion is religion based on the belief that God made the world and that he found it good. The sacramentalist believes that God is revealed through the world he has made, and that it is still, in spite of its failures and defects, able to declare the glory of its Maker. It should be the perfect expression of the Holy Spirit, as the bodies of men and women of the spirits whose temples they are. This is not so: the material universe (again like the human body) does not perfectly express the mind of God; but yet it is good.

In this belief—that the material universe is the sacrament of the presence of God—Christianity differs from some other great Eastern faiths. All the great living religions of the world today were born in the East; Christianity not in the heart of Asia as Buddhism was, but on the very edge of it, between East and West, at the center of the known world of that time. The universality of Christ is perhaps symbolized in this. His conquest of the West has been due, I believe, to that quality of hope and joy which is characteristic of a religion of redemption. The note of renunciation is there also—"He that hateth not his own father, and mother, and wife, and children, and brethren, and sisters, yea, and his own life also, cannot be my disciple" (Luke 14:26)—but it is never one of resignation or despair, nor is Christianity a religion of escape. The world is good and its redemption possible. Even now it is a revelation of the nature of God. Nature itself bears witness to his glory and his love.

To the sacramentalist, then, matter is the sacrament of the spirit, the outward and visible sign of an inward and spiritual grace. This is clearly the teaching of Christ. Material things, therefore, are also spiritual things, and the belief that we can draw a sharp distinction between them is mistaken. What the scientist is proving today, the poets perceived long ago, and Christ (who was both) based his religion on this truth. In all discussion, whether of sacramentalism or of sacraments, we must follow him and avoid the mistake of supposing that we are making real distinctions when we use such words as "material" and "spiritual," "natural" and "supernatural," "objective" and "subjective." We cannot avoid using them, but we must bear in mind that they do not represent reality. A sacrament is "the depth beyond the depth and the height above the height," where "our hearing is not hearing and our seeing is not sight." It recognizes that "soul is form and doth the body make." It is the "power beyond" of which Tennyson wrote:—

> How far beyond that grove and brake
> Yon nightingale is heard.
> What power beyond the bird could make
> Such music in the bird?[1]

All art is sacramental for it sees in material things the presence of the spirit and, being creative, compels matter to express that spirit. The difference between a paint-box and a picture is that the genius of the artist has made of paint the expression of his spirit. The artist takes paint

---

1. Alfred Lord Tennyson, "The Ancient Sage" (1885). Royden either misremembers or consciously rewrites Tennyson's stanza:

> How far thro' all the bloom and brake
> That nightingale is heard!
> What power but the bird's could make
> This music in the bird?

Either way, she completely changes its meaning. I suspect it's a deliberate riff on Tennyson. (KW)

and canvas, marble or wood, brass or strings, and creates a work of art. We use our spirits to carve our own bodies into an expression of what we are, though often we do it unwittingly or unwillingly.

There is little or no great Christian art where Christianity has been taught without emphasis on sacramental thinking. Where the stress of theology has been on the wickedness of the world or the total depravity of man, the beauty of created things has not been noticed or valued, and art has been regarded rather as a temptation of the devil than a revelation of God. The Roman and Greek Catholic Churches, even at their gloomiest and most monastic, have been saved from this belief by their emphasis on sacramentalism. They have produced some appalling art, but they have also produced the great cathedrals, the noblest music, the most glorious painting and statues, where Protestantism has produced little or nothing. Even in poetry, of which for some reason Protestantism has not been so suspicious, Dante outsoars Milton. We cannot think ignobly of the world and its beauty and then make beauty out of it.

We should see this more clearly if we had not so atrophied by disuse our power of mingling spirit and matter in creation. Industrialism has almost robbed our Western civilization of arts and crafts, and many do not understand that matter must be wrought upon by spirit if it is to be beautiful. Our materialism has gone near to undo the progress of spirit in other matters. People actually believe that matter can be made beautiful by machinery and without spiritual labor. If we are ever to unlearn this, it will be by a recovery of the sacramentalism of Christ, and those who have most quarrel with Catholicism should remember how deeply we are indebted to it for keeping this always in mind. Even the accusation of magic, so justly brought against some of the cruder forms of sacramentalism, must not outweigh our sense of gratitude. The instinct that makes the High Churchmen of the Church of England spend money on beautifying a church in a slum is a Christlike instinct. If we cannot, in Whitechapel or Shoreditch,[2] consider the lilies, let us at least make something beautiful which we may consider instead.

Our Lord, believing that all material things are revelations of the divine, took the simplest and humblest of them as in a special sense sacramental. He calls his hearers to consider the lilies because they were so common and valueless;[3] the sparrows because they were sold at two

---

2. Parts of London that, in the Victorian and Edwardian periods, were slums. (KW)

3. They were not, of course, costly blooms like ours, but the wild flowers round Jerusalem. (MR)

for a farthing. He took water and washing for the sacrament of baptism, bread and wine for Holy Communion. We have lost something of the beauty of this, because wine is not the drink of the poor in this country as in the East, and there is unfortunately no drink that is in universal use as bread is for food. Nothing, therefore, can quite replace the wine. Water cannot, because it owes nothing to man, and in this Holy Communion Christ shows that we should be in communion not only with God but with one another. Both bread and wine convey this meaning. Wheat and grapes are the gift of God, but as bread and wine owe something also to men's hands, and no food or drink of which this is not true has the same sweet and touching significance for sacramental use. If God is our Father, all we are brothers. We learn this from Christ who first taught us to pray in this sense. Thus we are in communion, through him, at once with God and man.

The danger of thinking not sacramentally but magically is real in fact, though there is no trace of it in our Lord's teaching. In baptism nothing magical happens. We are not "made" the children of God—a dreadful doctrine still enshrined in our Anglican catechism and baptismal service—we *are* his children, all of us, good and bad, baptized and unbaptized. Our Lord did not say to those who brought their children to him, "take them away and baptize them and then suffer them to come unto me," but "of such is the kingdom of heaven" (Matt 19:14). I do not know how men have found it possible to refuse baptism to children after this, or to argue that we must have attained some higher spiritual level or deeper spiritual experience before we receive this sacrament. The baptism of babies—all babies, any baby—before we know whether they are going to be good or bad, spiritual or unspiritual, is a recognition of the tremendous fact that every baby is a child of God—it is not a magical process by which the child becomes one.

A friend of mine, who is the head of a large school, once assured me that she "could tell" which of her children had been baptized and which not. This is a staggering assertion. I rather think she could tell which of them had been brought up in Christian homes or not: and as this would generally, though not always, coincide with the baptizing or not baptizing, it would be easy to assume that any child who did not exactly fit the supposed classification was an example of those exceptions to our theological rules which, unfortunately, exist in so inconvenient a manner! The existence of these exceptions ought, however, to dispose at once of the magical view of sacrament. It is extraordinarily difficult to understand how it has survived the existence of the Society of Friends, among whose members have been some of the best Christians and truest saints. If only we had a little of the scientific spirit of our Lord, we should not be content merely to admit the fact of these exceptions, and continue to hold a theory of the Church which assumes that the facts do not exist. It is this form of dishonesty which makes people, to whom Church membership would be a source of joy and a real and needed spiritual discipline, give it up in despair. If the scientist has taught us by his example to give up the most cherished theory if it is "wrecked on one inconvenient fact," he has also taught us to demand a like uncompromising honesty from the theologian, and to turn with disgust from a religion which seems content with so much lower a standard of truth.

Sacraments are not magical in their effect, and an unbaptized Quaker may be as true a saint as a baptized Catholic. Yet sacramental grace is real. The prayers of the Church, the reception of the child into its fellowship, of the communicant to a deeper unity with God and man—these are realities. Because I believe this, I would have no one excluded except by his own choice. I have known many people who were unaware of their own loss till they received the Holy Communion, who then realized the meaning of the value of Christ's sacramentalism as they would never have done by merely hearing it spoken of or described.

The value of a sacrament is therefore not wholly subjective: it has an absolute reality like the reality of beauty in a picture. A picture is not merely material; paint and canvas are not the whole of it. To a blind man, or a color-blind man, or a man devoid of any sense of beauty, it may seem no more and it is no more; but that is his defect, and his defect does not destroy the beauty of the picture: it exists independently of him. So the defect of the communicant may make the Holy Communion meaningless to him, and he will contemptuously affirm that the experience of the sacramentalist is purely subjective: but it is not so. It is as "real" as beauty.

A Nonconformist friend of mine, discussing the more liberal attitude of modern Nonconformity to the arts in worship, assured me that when he realized how much some of us were helped by (the instance actually used) the music of Westminster Cathedral, he had no wish to deprive us of it. "One does not take a doll from a child," he said indulgently.

This ignorant tolerance of the greatest of all the arts is the opposite of what I understand by sacramentalism, and, while I admit that, like all great teaching, it is dangerous—dangerous because a sense of the supernatural may easily decline into magic, and often has done so—I still believe that to be indifferent to beauty in worship is a lamentable defect. The arrogance of those who speak of beauty and order, ritual, architecture, and music, used in the service of God, as though they were concessions to an undeveloped and childish state of spiritual development, are not more advanced than others but merely more defective. Certainly one should be able to do without these things: a saint can, though with a deep sense of loss, live in a slum and give up considering the lilies. God can give up heaven and enter the slums of the universe. Heaven and the lilies, the echoing music of the mass, the soaring voices of the choir, the storied windows, architecture itself, are not the less divinely inspired and inspiring for that, nor the less to be desired.

I am, without doubt, deaf, blind, and stupid to many things: I pray that I may not be so stupid as to be proud of being stupid or think it a proof of superior spiritual development.

I have learned to value the silence of the Quaker: I rejoice to realize that—though the Quaker may not take our mass from us—we, if we are not too proud to learn, may take his silent worship for our possession.

I have learned to value the free prayer of the Nonconformist: I hope I need not for that reason cease to love the majestic forms and words of our Anglican liturgy. It is to me a glorious experience to use the very phrases the saints have used throughout the ages. When I repeat the Psalms or the Lord's Prayer, the *Gloria in excelsis*, or the Confession, I am conscious that I draw near to God by the path the saints have trod, and realize with humble joy that what was true for them is true for me also. With an experience immeasurably less deep and full in content, I still share their spiritual life. Its phrases and prayers and thanksgiving are valid for me also. The Communion of the Saints becomes a reality to me, and I, trembling, take their words upon my lips.

My Church is sacramental. The Quaker will declare that his is also. I have heard him claim that silence is his sacrament, as the Free Churchman maintains that the sermon is his. In a sense no doubt they are so: it is a sense which allows the High Churchman and the Roman Catholic to place confession among the sacraments: but I think that this makes the idea of a sacrament too wide and vague. Sacramentalism is a recognition of material things as the channel of spiritual things, and where the material is lacking the full force of the sacrament is unexpressed. It is, I believe, a sound instinct which has made the Church of England set the sacraments of Baptism and Holy Communion by themselves. In them the material is actually the sacrament, and the commonness of the things chosen recalls us to the truth of the Quaker view that everything is sacramental, without allowing our sense of it to become so vague and nebulous as to be easily lost.

The commonness of washing and eating as religious rites has even shocked some people. Learning that such an initiatory rite was common to many of the mystery religions—some of them superstitious and degrading—they feel that the sacredness has departed from Christian baptism. When further informed that eating and drinking the flesh and blood of their god as a means of sharing his power is almost universal, and has been found in some of the most primitive religions of savage men, reverence for the Holy Communion becomes impossible to them. This is strange to me—as strange as though we should cease to believe in God because all men everywhere have believed in him. Instead of rejecting a rite which recalls our first human striving after some relation between man and his Maker—between physical and spiritual powers—I receive it with a greater reverence. It binds me to the past of my race where most we are one—in our aspiration toward God.

I realize that, so soon as men became human, they sought, no longer altogether blindly but consciously and of set purpose, to find that right relationship between themselves and God which they were dimly but surely aware that they had lost. It shows me those forefathers of ours realizing that there is a link between the material and the spiritual. It shows them on the right road, not despising or escaping from material things, but seeking a way to the Spirit through matter. If it was a crude and gross belief that a man could become one with the totem of his tribe or the god of his worship, by eating him, it was not much more crude than many of the thoughts we have today about God.

I try now to put into words what our Holy Communion service means to me, and I realize how crude I shall seem to minds more spiritually developed than my own: but I think that such minds will no more despise me than I my rude ancestors, nor will they contemptuously decide that my spiritual dullness makes their sacrament invalid.

To me, then, the sacrament of Holy Communion expresses a truth and conveys a grace which neither words nor silence alone can adequately convey. At this holy service body and soul alike are fed, because body and soul alike belong to God. The sacredness of material as well as spiritual things is recognized. This is why many of us prefer to receive the Holy Communion fasting. We go early because we wish our thoughts to be undistracted by other matters: almost instinctively, it seems to me, the desire that the spiritual reception of our Lord should be the first thought in our minds is accompanied by the desire that the food he gives us should be the first to pass our lips. I cannot see why this very natural and spontaneous impulse should seem superstitious or gross to so many critics. I was not brought up to go to Holy Communion fasting, but I was taught to go early in the morning and to exclude other thoughts from my mind as far as possible. To go fasting, and bring my body into the same worship as my mind and spirit, seemed and still seems a natural corollary. But to insist on doing so when the probability is that the fasting communicant will proceed to faint and disturb the whole congregation is to convert reverence into irreverence, and to refuse the Holy Communion altogether to people who, for example, can only come in the evening and therefore not fasting, is surely to make the word of God of none effect through our tradition.

I do not myself like evening communion, and I intensely dislike to receive the Blessed Sacrament except fasting; but to go without it altogether, or cause others to go without it, because they are prevented from doing as I do seems to me really horrifying. Our Lord said nothing about fasting communion and nothing about the time of our receiving it, but he did say "Do this in remembrance of me . . . drink ye all of this" (Luke 22:19-20; 1 Cor 11:24-25).

Everywhere the common meal is a rite of friendship. Christ takes this old and beautiful idea and lifts it on to a higher spiritual plane. He makes of this common act of eating and drinking a communion with God and man.

This is the deepest and highest communion of all. It arises, not out of the eating and drinking, but of a unity of spirit. Christ gave his life—his body and blood—for us. We, if we receive this sacrament, must offer ourselves to share in it. We "offer and present to God our souls and bodies to be a reasonable holy and living sacrifice" (Rom 12:1). He asks us, "Can ye drink of the cup that I drink of?" (Matt 20:22; Mark 10:38) and we answer, kneeling before him at the altar, "Lord, we can." Then we are entitled to receive the food necessary to us for this service—food for both bodies and souls which we here present. If we are not willing to share his sacrifice we have no claim to receive that food. We receive his body and blood because we are willing to give our own. This is a fearful thought. I cannot go further than a prayer that I may be willing; I trust this is accepted. James and John did not know what they were saying when they declared their ability to drink of the cup from which the Lord was to drink, yet he accepted them. "Ye shall indeed drink of the cup that I drink of" (Mark 10:39). They failed and fled in the hour of danger, but afterward they triumphed over themselves and followed their Lord to death. The Holy Communion is our offering of ourselves—all ignorant for the most part—to share the sacrifice of Christ, but, as we make the offering, we know we must fail unless he gives us himself. We ask him to do so because we desire to be and to do what he asks of us. This is our Holy Communion. I think we should not receive it unless we mean this.

The sacrament is a recognition of our common human need. We must all eat to live. But for what purpose do we live? That we may serve. Christ also had to eat and drink, and he lived only to serve. The institution of the Holy Communion is not recorded in the Fourth Gospel but the symbolic act of the washing of the disciples' feet by Christ is there. It is the other side of the Last Supper. We have only a right to our share of the world's food if we take our share in the world's service. "If any will not work neither shall he eat" (2 Thess 3:10). It is a sacramental thought. "Bless these gifts to our use and us to thy service." Our Christian prayers are penetrated with this idea. By it, all meals become sacramental, for sacramentalism is based on the knowledge of our common human needs; it accepts and consecrates them. The first Christians hardly distinguished between the Holy Communion and the Agape; but one has become more and more a mystical communion with God; the other has disappeared, or survived only in the habit of saying grace.

My experience of Free Church communion is that the sense of fellowship with one's fellow men is emphasized, and that the communion of God is attenuated: in the Anglican service the reverse is true. To most Anglicans, Holy Communion is an intensely individualistic act. We are inclined to go alone to it, or at the least in silence. We look neither to right nor left for fear we should see someone we know. A boy who approached the altar for the first time, smiling with pleasure at the friend whom he recognized in passing, was the subject of complaint on the part of his fellow communicants, who told the priest that he was "in no fit state to approach the altar of God."[4] At a Free Church communion, on the other hand, I have, I confess, felt a difficulty in recognizing the supernatural at all. It has all seemed to me very friendly, but in no sense awful.

I do not know if it is humanly possible to conceive a form of Holy Communion in which both elements are equally present—the sense of

---

4. Royden also tells this anecdote in the earlier selection entitled "Churchmanship and Discipleship." (KW)

communion with God and men equally real. Perhaps it is not. The very act of kneeling to receive the bread and wine seems to emphasize the one at the expense of the other—of sitting, to have a like defect. Perhaps in a perfect Church we shall recognize the limitations of human words and acts, keep the awful Communion of the body and blood of Christ, and revise the ancient friendly Agape to follow a friendly human meal and bring home to us the meaning of our eating and drinking together. Whatever is gained or lost, I believe that Christianity in the future will never lose its sacramental idea: I believe, on the contrary, that it is becoming more real and more necessary to most Christians. We can unite silence, freedom, and ritual in our worship; but the fundamentally Christian belief in the beauty and reality of material things, the conviction that in them we see God for they are the channels of his grace, the belief that sin is the failure to see this, and redemption the recovery of a right understanding of the relation between matter and spirit—this will deepen more and more.

Source

A. Maude Royden, *I Believe in God* (New York: Harper & Brothers, 1927), 275–89.

Part 4.

Theology "Can Never Rest Content"

Selections from Royden's writings on theological issues

Orthodoxy's Quest

IN THIS REFLECTION FROM 1918, Royden contends that orthodoxy isn't a repetition of frozen creeds but a dynamic, ongoing process of discovery. The human mind and heart are too limited to fathom the infinite mystery of God. Our understanding of things divine will always be incomplete; there will always be a "further" when it comes to knowledge of God. Consequently, orthodoxy or "right belief" must be humble enough to admit its inescapable limitations and receptive enough to embrace new insights.

Orthodoxy is right thinking: it is not complete and final knowledge. Knowledge of God is the supreme concern of orthodoxy, and the Gospel of Christ and of His Church is the revelation of God to us. But while it is of supreme importance to know God, and our search for truth is a continual search for Him, no one can know Him finally and wholly. This at least is certain. We are human, and our brains are not of a kind to apprehend completely the divine, nor so long as we are human shall we ever do so. It is not a want of orthodoxy that makes our thought fall short of God's divinity. It is the nature of our thought, which, finite, cannot grasp the infinite. If we cannot measure love with our yard-measure, it is not because the measure is not long enough. It is because love is not measured so. If we fail to apprehend God, it is not because we are unorthodox, but because we are human and can only understand the Godhead so far as it is revealed to us in terms of humanity.

We can therefore think rightly as long as we know that we are not thinking completely. We can trust our knowledge of God, and live by it, as long as we realize that it is incomplete. An understanding may be true as far as it goes, and valid as long as one remembers that there is a "further." It becomes untrue—it becomes a lie—the moment we believe it to be complete.

A man who says he knows that God is Love says the truth—so we Christians believe. A man who says that what he knows about God is all that there is to be known tells a lie. The first man is orthodox: the second is a liar.

This is where we have made our mistake. Catholic theology is great, beautiful, profound, and true. The moment the theologian says "This is all: the whole truth is here" his truth becomes a lie.

Orthodoxy, therefore, is only possible as long as our "right thinking" includes a right consciousness that we have only a part of the truth—not other than true, but yet only a part. And it must mean, to every lover of truth, a continual pressing on to more. The theologian, like the scientist, can never rest content. He must continually press on. He must always obey the guidance of the Holy Spirit leading Him on into the truth. He must bear in mind Lord's promise—"I have yet many things to say unto you, but ye cannot bear them now" (John 16:12). He must forever listen to those "many things," and strive to be more and more able to bear them. The hunger and thirst of the man of science after knowledge must be surpassed by that of the Christian thirsting after the living God. He must never say "It is enough." He must never abandon the quest. He must never tire of purifying his soul of self-interest, his mind of confusion, his life of error, that he may be of those pure in heart who see God. The humility of the man of science must be pride compared with the humility of the man of religion; the courage of the explorer in the face of physical danger be exceeded by the courage of the theologian in danger whether of body or of soul.

Such an adventurer will never say, "Let us not search here, for we may lose our faith," or "Shut now your eyes and ears lest you see a devil." Neither the advances of science nor the researches of biblical criticism will alarm him. He knows that it is the truth that makes us all free. He knows truth is another name for God, and he will go down into hell to find it.

But then it is clear that orthodoxy is dynamic and not static. It is a tremendous adventure, a continual effort of the mind. Those who realize this, and know that the mind as well as the heart belongs to God and must forever seek Him, stand amazed at the discovery that people calling themselves orthodox think or act as though they thought that orthodoxy consists in the repetition of a number of statements called a "creed." How easy a means of attaining so amazing a result! Alas! Orthodoxy is not so easily won. Not when Christ called him from his fishing-nets, but after long and closest intimacy, did his Master ask St. Peter, "What think ye of Christ?" (Matt 16:15). The answer was received with too much joy for anyone who loves Christ ever to dare to think that it was unimportant, that it does not matter what we think of Christ. It matters tremendously. Perhaps nothing else matters at all. But to think rightly about Christ—about God—was the result of long companying with Jesus. To the last, how "unorthodox" were some of those who had been with Him in such close companionship! "Have I been so long time with you, and yet hast thou not known Me, Philip?" (John 14:9) was Christ's sorrowful question to one who should have come nearer the truth because he had been "so long time" with Jesus. It matters profoundly that we be orthodox—that we "think rightly" of God. But such right thinking is not a test imposed upon the sinner; it is the supreme achievement of the saint.

Source

A. Maude Royden, "Orthodoxy," in *The Hour and the Church* (London: Allen & Unwin, 1918), 33–37.

Incarnation

If God is love, and God created everything that is, then love is supremely creative: this is Royden's foundational assumption in her reflections on the Incarnation. Jesus, she argues, is unique, "altogether possessed by God," the "one point of perfect communion with God." Two things follow from this: the Incarnation is a creative act in which God seeks to love humanity into wholeness, and the perfect human Jesus is the Incarnation of the pre-existent Source of love and creativity, or what Christians call the Second Person of the Trinity. Proportionate to our embrace of the spirit of love manifested in Jesus, we too become incarnations, although imperfect ones, of divine love. As such, there is "no final gulf" between humans and God. Jesus Christ, and the creative love he embodies, is the bridge.

Divine love, pressing in on us on every side, is immanent everywhere. Nowhere and in nothing has the Spirit been altogether driven out or altogether defeated.

And only once has God been perfectly received. Only once has he been able altogether to enter in and take possession. This is the Incarnation.

Why was this little earth chosen as the scene for the great drama of the Incarnation? It was not chosen: it needed God, as all the universe needs him; and God sought it as he seeks all.

The nature of God could not be perfectly revealed in lifeless or non-spiritual creatures. Neither in the stars nor in the lower animals, beautiful and revealing as they are, could he be altogether shown. Nor yet could he be revealed in human beings before human beings had reached a certain stage of evolution. Had Christ appeared among the bushmen of Australia he could have achieved nothing: but then he could not have appeared among them. It would have been impossible. Humanity at that point of development could not so have responded to God as to produce such a person as Christ.

Why were the Jews chosen? Again, they were not chosen: they had sought God with a persistence and understanding greater than that of other men. And "if with all our hearts we truly seek him we shall ever surely find him" (Jer 29:13). They found him who was seeking them and all humanity, because they sought more earnestly than the rest. They learned that he was Righteous and Lawful and One and a Father. They had no more evidence before them than others, and certain aspects of the Divine they did not see. But they saw the significance of the facts on the whole more completely than others did. Some of them saw so much that Christ himself, questioned on certain points, could do no better than quote from their great prophets. When one asked him: "Which is the first commandment of all?" Jesus answered him: "The first of all the commandments is, 'Hear, O Israel, the Lord our God is one Lord, and thou shalt love the Lord thy God with all thy heart and with all thy soul and with all thy mind and with all thy strength': this is the first commandment. And the second is like, namely this, 'thou shalt love thy neighbor as thyself'" (Mark 12:28–31 and Luke 10:27).

Even where he had to go further than they, Christ took the moral standard of the Jewish race as his starting point. In paragraph after paragraph of the Sermon on the Mount we read—not, as Christians often suppose, that the Jews were wrong and he was going to set them right, but that the fact that they had got so far already in the understanding of God's laws enabled him to show them more. They had realized that justice was allowable but not revenge: Christ said they must now realize that not justice but love is the will of God (Matt 5:38–44). They had learned that it was wrong to commit adultery: he told them that it was wrong even to have an adulterous thought (Matt 5:27–28). They had learned that it was wrong to break an oath: he told them that they should be so upright that no one would trouble them for an oath (Matt 5:33–37).

At each point Christ accepts the evolutionist's position: it is because the Jews have pressed on so far that they are now able to go further. And the Jews, thus knowing God, gave us Jesus Christ. This was neither a piece of favoritism on the part of the Almighty nor a mere accident. It was after the nature of things and according to law. Evolution is proceeding to its goal.

This Christ, going far beyond his people—who had gone far beyond the rest of us—saw God and revealed him to us perfectly. We now know what God is like. We have reached a point at which the human race was fine enough and spiritual enough for God to be able—at last—wholly to enter in at one point and in one person. This is why, in looking at Jesus Christ, we see God.

Is Jesus God, then? Can we believe in the divinity of Christ?

Yes; for God—his love neither destroyed nor decreased by his world turning from him and casting him out—had never rested "in his home in heaven" (Heb 13:14) but sought us out. This is the truth of Immanence and Incarnation, and it was inevitable that love should act so. No one who loves can keep away from those he loves when they suffer. No one who is a lover can be content to send help from a distance. Neither does he hurry to the side of the loved one from a sense of duty, or because no other help is obtainable. He is drawn there by the irresistible compulsion of love. Even if he can do nothing at all to help, he wants to be there—he cannot keep away. Let him, he would urge, at least share, even if he cannot avert, the suffering. If it be asked why he does not keep away, the answer is because he cannot—he loves. God who is Love itself could not see the suffering race of men and keep away from them. He came to seek them—all of them everywhere.

> He sent no angel to our race
> Of higher or of lower place,
> But wore the robe of human frame
> Himself, and to this lost world came.[1]

In parable after parable, of the lost sheep, the lost coin, the prodigal son, this truth is set before us. The shepherd seeks his lost sheep, not for a long time, but *"until he finds him"* (Luke 15:4). He finds us—the human race—but none of us receives him wholly, except Jesus Christ.

God, therefore, was able in Christ to reveal himself perfectly, and in such a way as we, also human and also the children of God, could best understand or least misunderstand.

This seems to me most beautiful and wonderful, but not difficult to understand. I do not see how God could have acted otherwise. I have to confess that many of the difficulties about the divinity of Christ seem to me now a matter of words. I believe we have really gone past them, and they are no longer difficulties and no longer real: but, unfortunately, while we now think scientifically, we still use the language of the Middle Ages

---

1. From the hymn "O Love, How Broad, How Deep, How High," Benjamin Webb (1871). (KW)

for our theology, and this language does not fit our thoughts. I believe that, if we realized this change in our way of thinking, we should change some of our words and our phrases, and no longer have the feeling of dislocation from which we moderns are so apt to suffer when we turn from reading a book on science to a book on theology. I perfectly realize that the next stage of our evolution may bring us beyond the scientific method of thought to something deeper, higher, and more true. But I humbly submit that *now* we are going through a scientific stage of our development, and that we are right in believing that the astounding truth and beauty revealed to us by science is a real revelation of God; a revelation which, until we get further on still, governs our thoughts.

This is specially true in the case of what is called the divinity of Christ.

To the medieval world, God and man were entirely separate beings; "divine" and "human" totally different ideas. Christ, who was both God and man, was therefore a really incomprehensible being who, in a sense, bridged the gulf between God who was "up" in heaven and man who was "down" on the earth. It was terribly difficult to keep the mind fixed on a being who was at once God and man, because God and man were in medieval thought so utterly different and apart. Consequently, endless discussions took place and countless heresies arose, some sacrificing the divinity and some the humanity of Christ. Men were really trying very hard to believe something that was so contrary to reason that they hardly could "believe" it.

Today we do not think of God as "up" in heaven and ourselves as "down" on earth, but of God as everywhere. We believe he is in all things, and therefore we must believe he is in us. There is no final impassable gulf between God and his creation; neither, therefore, between God and man. We really are his children, and therefore it is only recognizing a necessary truth to say that we have something of the divine nature in us, poorly as we reveal it.

Christ revealed it perfectly. No part of his being was in darkness. All was possessed by God. In him God was perfectly manifest. His spirit was wholly one with God's. In him, therefore, God became Incarnate.

What is the difficulty? That this makes no "final" gulf between Christ and ourselves? But then there is no final gulf between God and ourselves.

Is Christ then no longer to be regarded as unique? Certainly he is unique. No other has been altogether possessed by God. He is God's only-begotten son—the son in whom God is well pleased. In a large family of children it may happen that one only is like his father. One alone bears the stamp of his father's spirit in looks and thoughts and ways. It will be said of him: "that is his father's child!" Or even: "that is the only one who is his father's child!" All of them are the children of their father by physical generation, but this one by a deeper tie—by an identity of spirit.

So are we all the children of God of whom Christ said that he is "my Father and your Father, my God and your God" (John 20:17). He even quoted with approval that startling saying from the Psalms: "I have said ye are gods and all of you are the children of the Most High" (Ps 82:6). Christ was in no doubt of his own unique position, but he showed us that it consisted in his perfect spiritual unity with God. When we are in such unity of spirit with any one, we say we are "at one" with them. Add one thing to another thing and you make two things; but spirits so added to one another make "one spirit." Twins may be so much alike that they cannot be known apart, yet no one says they are "of one body." If two people are as much alike spiritually, we do say they are "of one spirit." So Christ and the Father are one; and so our Lord tells us to think and do as he does "that ye may be the children of your Father which is in heaven" (Matt 5:45). At the close of his life his great prayer for us was that we might all be one—"as thou, Father, art in me and I in thee, that they also may be one in us" (John 17:21).

Expressing thus my belief in the divinity of Christ, I am confronted in the latest form of theological controversy by the word "deity." I believe in the divinity of Christ: good: but do I believe in his deity?

The deity of Christ: what then is meant by the deity of Christ? That Jesus of Nazareth is transcendent God, absolute, unconditioned, infinite, eternal? People really seem to mean this, and to demand that I should mean it, and yet it is to deprive words of all meaning to say so. If Christ be God transcendent, what difference is there in our thought of God the Father and God the Son? Is not one God transcendent and the other God incarnate? But if the divine becomes incarnate, it ceases to be absolute and unconditioned: it is conditioned by the mere fact of incarnation; it is conditioned by the flesh.

So Jesus Christ was conditioned. It is meaningless to speak of transcendent deity as "increasing in wisdom" (Luke 2:52), or of being unable in certain conditions to do certain mighty works. Yet St. Mark tells us: "He could there do no mighty works because of their unbelief" (Mark 6:5). Transcendent Godhead could not say: "My Father is greater than I" (John 14:28). Nor could Omniscience marvel at anything ("he marveled at their unbelief" [Mark 6:6]) or be ignorant of anything ("of that day and that hour knoweth no man, no not the angels that are in heaven, neither the Son, but the Father" [Matt 24:36]). Such a deity would not say: "Of myself I can do nothing" (John 5:30), or "All things that my Father hath given me I have made known unto thee" (John 15:15). It is not on any one of these sayings that I lean but on them all together, and on our Lord's attitude of continual and complete dependence upon God the Father. This is perfectly compatible with the belief that he was divine—one in spirit with God Almighty—a revelation of him to us: but all this also is compatible with the humanity of Christ—which the other belief is not. If Jesus knew all things, and could do all things, his humanity becomes a mockery and his hopes and beliefs, surprises of joy and grief, a mere pretense.

It is in the Gospel of St. John that we find the divinity of Christ most clearly stated. It is indeed his theme throughout. Christ was the expression of the mind of God—the eternal Word made flesh—the pre-existent only-begotten Son of the Father—it is with him that the Gospel is concerned. But all this is described as a profound unity of spirit, and it is this same Gospel which most strongly insists on the divinity of the ordinary man!

In proportion as we share the spirit of Christ we, too, are the sons of God. As he is one with God in spirit, so should we—so must we—become. Again and again this glorious note rings out: "Even as thou, Father, art in me and I in thee, that they all may be one in us" (John 17:21). "I have said, ye are gods and all of you are the children of the most High" (John 10:34; Ps 82:6). "At that day ye shall know that I am in my Father and ye in me, and I in you" (John 14:20). "And to as many as received him, to them gave he power to become the sons of God . . . which were born not of blood nor of the will of the flesh nor of the will of man but of God" (John 1:12). "That was the true light which lighteth every man which cometh into the world" (John 1:9).

Or, as Dr. Moffatt has it, "The real light, which enlightens every man, was coming then into the world" (John 1:9).[2]

Mr. Middleton Murry writes:

> What was Jesus to his own inward eye? Above all things else, the son of God, who had sought in vain for earthly brothers. By

---

2. James Moffatt (1870–1944), translator of the New Testament (1913) into popular English. (KW)

bitter experience he had proved himself God's only son.... Of his communion with God he could not doubt. But other men had communed with God. None knew so well as he the authentic voice of God as it came from the lips of the prophets of old. But his communion was different, strangely different: he had known God, not as a servant knows a master, but as a long lost son his hidden Father.... For him God had to be one in whom all his love could find satisfaction and rest. To him no other God was possible; and to all other men such a God was impossible. So he had become, inevitably, God's only son.... Perhaps the splendor of that loneliness is unthinkable. Yet somehow we must imagine it, even though it be, as it can be, only for a single moment. We must know that it was not some mysterious and unimaginable delusion. He had become what he had become by an inexorable necessity. Once grasp the fact of this man's communion with God as he came up from John's baptism—and who, that has eyes to see, can deny it?—then he was inevitably bound to become verily and indeed the only son of God.[3]

I believe that Christ claimed for himself just this. He knew that no other had ever been in such communion with God as he: no other was so "one" with him. He was therefore the only-begotten Son of God. He warns us against any other interpretation. He says that if anyone "shall speak a word against the Son of Man, it shall be forgiven him: but unto him that blasphemeth against the Spirit it shall not be forgiven" (Luke 12:10; see also Matt 13:31–32 and Mark 3:29).

It is a text seldom preached upon. I understand it to mean the converse of what Christ meant when he said: "Not everyone that saith unto me Lord, Lord, shall enter into the Kingdom of Heaven, but he that doeth the will of my Father which is in heaven" (Matt 7:21). We are to believe in love and to act as though we believed in it: this is to believe in the Holy Spirit. To blaspheme against the Holy Spirit is to put evil for good and lies for truth. As long as we are in this state of mind we are, simply, in an unforgivable state. We cannot be forgiven, not because God refuses to forgive us, but because we cannot receive forgiveness.

On the other hand, to recognize truth, to give our worship to love, this is to be forgiven and accepted, even though our doing so does not include our acceptance of Jesus Christ. We may actually reject him—we may "blaspheme against the Son of Man." Even so, we may be forgiven.

---

3. *The Life of Jesus* [London: Butler & Tanner, 1926], ch. 18, 159. (MR)

I think that Christ must have had in mind those people to whom his religion should be presented in such a guise and by such teachers as made acceptance the more impossible the nobler were those to whom it was presented. There are people to whom Christianity has been presented as a religion of fear, of injustice, of stupidity, of narrowness, of dishonesty. Look at Shelley's rendering of it in "Queen Mab" and see what a monstrous thing Christianity can be made.[4] Those who reject Christianity and Christ when it is presented to them in this way are assuredly not far from the kingdom of God. They reject it because it is indeed a horrible thing. Not knowing what Christ really stood for, they reject him with indignation: they blaspheme against the Son of Man. They are not, therefore, without forgiveness.

In nothing has the divine love of Christ shone forth to me more radiantly than in this amazing teaching. Not everyone that calls him Lord or God is a follower of Christ; not all such will be received by him. Again and again they may find themselves rejected as "workers of iniquity" (Matt 7:23). It is the Spirit that they must recognize. Those who do the will of God—whether they use the name of Christ or not—are the children of God, for they, too, have his Spirit.

Has any other founder of a religion spoken words so Godlike as these? So selfless? So perfect in love?

"He that dwelleth in love dwelleth in God and God in him" (1 John 4:16). So writes the beloved disciple, and makes us all divine, since all of us love someone or something. But he goes on: "for God is Love" (1 John 4:8), and so makes of Christ God himself, for Christ's whole message, life, and being were Love.

Here we begin to understand how it is in and by Christ that "all things were made and without him was not anything made that was made" (John 1:3).

Love is the principle of creation. No other power exists by which it is possible to create, except love. Indifference can create nothing: hatred actually destroys.

But love creates and must create. It can no more not create than light can refuse to shine. It is light because it shines, and it shines because it is light. So love creates. It is really as meaningless to ask why God created

---

4. Book 7 of Shelley's "Queen Mab" is a particularly harsh critique of religion:

"The name of God
Has fenced about all crime with holiness . . ." (KW)

the universe as it is to ask why light shines. Love must create because to create is the nature of love. To me it seems in the end as foolish to ask whether—in spite of all—the Creator of the universe is Love since no one ever did or could create anything except by love.

There is a wonderful unity of truth in the Bible. It begins with the words: "In the beginning God created the heaven and the earth" (Gen 1:1). In one of the books of the Apocrypha it is written: "Never wouldst thou have created anything if thou hadst hated it" (Wisdom 11:24). Finally, almost the last word of the Bible: "God is Love" (1 John 4:16).

God then creates because God is Love. Christ is the Incarnation of the Spirit of love. In this sense I humbly believe that he was indeed pre-existent, "begotten before all worlds," and that "by him was everything made that was made" (John 1:3). Of no one else could this be said, for of no one else could it be said that he was the Incarnation of Love. Of Christ it is said and is literally true. Nothing of hate or indifference was mingled with his love. No resentment, no revenge, no selfishness, no love of power, no greed—nothing shadowed that love or diverted it from its purpose.

The heart of the religion that Christ taught and the nature of the God he revealed are the same—they are love. Other great revelations of God have been made before Christ came, and have been made since. Egypt had thought of God as Truth, Persia as Light, India as universal Spirit, Islam as Unity and Power. To the Greeks God was Beauty, to the Jews he was Righteousness and Law. Christ showed that Beauty is the expression of Love, and Righteousness and Law are Love itself.

The value of any religion to humanity is simply the value of its God. All these great revelations were and are true, and they all form part of the spiritual education of humanity. The revelation of God as Love sums up all the rest, and beyond it I cannot see how it is possible to go. If, for the sake of argument, we consider the possibility of another and a higher revelation by another and a greater Messiah, I ask how, in actual fact, there could be any revelation of God more glorious or more complete than this—that God is Love?

Christians have made the grievous mistake of setting Christ against Confucius, Zoroaster, and Buddha, and the teaching that God is Love against the teaching that he is Light or Power or Law. Determined to be right, they have imagined that their rightness demanded that everyone else should be wrong. They denounced the world's great educators and prophets of the past, as though God had indeed left all men without a witness until the first year of our Lord. The only exception they made was in favor of the Old Testament, for the first Christians were all Jews. Christendom, indeed, made up for this afterward by treating the Jews with more concentrated hatred and cruelty than any other race on earth. Everywhere, however, they have consistently held that if Christ and Christianity were right all other teachers and religions were wrong.

This is to rob Christianity of its true supremacy. For Christianity is the consummation of all other revelations. Christ's method was quite other than ours. As I have shown, he addressed himself to the Jews as to people who had gone a long way and were certainly in many respects ahead of the human race in their conception of God and of goodness. He led them forward from that point. It was because they had "heard that it was said by them of old time" (Matt 5:21, 27, 31, etc.) that he was now able to speak to them of yet nobler things. And these nobler things that he told them were simply that God is Love.

Love includes righteousness, beauty, power, light, and law. Therefore it is the final revelation. To denounce other revelations as false is to exclude from our own idea of God and of Love the qualities or aspects they proclaim: it is to impoverish our worship and to narrow out God.

The disastrous consequences of this narrowness are seen in the fact that Christians have often been afraid of Beauty and have built hideous churches where they sing bad verses to false music. They have been afraid of Truth and struggled helplessly against the advance of science, giving the impression that to be religious is to be silly. They have ruled out Power and their religion has been reduced to a vapid sentimentality, well expressed by the drooping and effeminate Christ of modern religious art. Love itself shorn of Wisdom, Power, and Beauty has seemed merely a weakness.

Christ's God of Love was not so. In him was gathered up all the revelations of God the world had ever yet accepted. It is a final revelation because no higher can exist.

To this revelation the whole of Christ's life and being were given. He then is both unique and final. Thousands, perhaps millions, of years may be needed before we understand or practice all that this revelation means to the human race and to the universe, nor shall we reach the goal of our evolution till this is done. But the revelation has been made, and by Christ. All else—all progress—all redemption—all evolution—now turns upon this belief in love. On Christ, therefore, creation itself depends.

Unbelievers sometimes say that if we Christians would stop saying "God is Love" and begin saying "Love is God" they would be willing to join with us. Would they? Do even Christians—does any one—really believe this?

Love is God. I am ready to say it. I want—I desperately want—to believe it. I admit that Christianity will never be Christlike until we Christians do believe it. But it is a hard, even a terrible saying. What does it mean? On the lips of our critics it seems to mean that love is the thing they give their homage to, the thing they find most beautiful, most divine, most worthy to be called godlike. This is good; but to say that Love is God is to say much more than this. It is to believe that the creative power in the universe and throughout the universe and beyond the universe is love.

It is to believe that love creates, sustains, and keeps us. It is to deny the power of hate. It is to refuse to rely on hate or force or cruelty. It is to believe that love—since love is God—must at last prevail. It is to believe this when everything seems to deny it: to look at innocent suffering and wrong, the defeat of high purpose, the wreck of great ideals, the sacrifice of the good and pure—and still to say love is God. It is to believe in love as the supreme power in the universe, not only on Easter Sunday, but on Good Friday.

Christ did so because he was love and love dwelt in him. He lived out his belief and saw his life close in failure. Around him on the cross he saw the hating faces of the crowd he had lived and died to serve. So far from creating in them the response of love, it seemed that he had evoked nothing but hatred. Seeing it, he felt that even God had deserted him. Yet he believed in love when God himself had gone. Forgiveness and pity inspire his latest words. No anger or resentment was found in him. If the weapons of love broke in his hands—if God himself abandoned him—he would use no other weapon, worship no other God. Even in his dying agony he knew there were no weapons and no Gods that were any use if these failed. He staked all on love and, seeing beyond the anguish and failure, at the last, when darkness covered him, "he knew that he had won."[5]

This is to believe that Love is God. No one has ever believed it but Christ.

---

5. G. A. Studdert Kennedy, *The Wicket Gate, or Plain Bread* (London: Doubleday, Doran & Co., 1923), 230. (KW)

Yet, in my heart, I too know that it is true. I know that Love is God and God is Love. I know that there is no other power in the universe to create or to sustain in being. I know that if I rely on any other power I must fail. I know it, because Christ has demonstrated it to me in his failure and his victory, and I acclaim him the Incarnation of that divine Power which was with the Father before the worlds were made, by whom the worlds were made, and without whom nothing has been or could be made.

I cannot read the Gospels or any part of the New Testament without realizing the awful loneliness of Christ's perfect love. This is the miracle of the Incarnation to me. How could a perfect life be lived in an imperfect world—nay, an imperfect universe? Must we not be all of a piece and all infected by the general imperfection? And if we find Christ—as I do find him—thus perfect, he becomes of more than earthly meaning: he becomes of cosmic significance. Here, perhaps, in all the universe, has been found the one point of perfect communion with God. Here God has penetrated the barrier of materialism set up at the fall and comes in to take possession. The human race on this little planet may be the only race in the materialized universe—whatever may be true of beings on another and more spiritual plane—which has struggled upward to the point at which it was possible for a Christ to be born, and this the one point of perfect communion of God to the universe.

If this be so, I understand a little better the meaning of St. Paul's strange saying: "The whole creation groaneth and travaileth in pain together until now. And not only they, but ourselves also, which have the first fruits of the Spirit . . . waiting for the adoption, to wit, the redemption of our body" (Rom 8:22, 23). In the redemption of the material world by the Spirit we have these first fruits. We ourselves are able to give the command again to the Spirit as regards one material thing at least—our own bodies. Through this, will the universe itself at last be wholly repossessed by God?

Does this terrific responsibility lie with us? No one can go forward without incurring the responsibility of leadership. If God has been able to give through the human race a Christ, humanity itself has now the leadership—is now the point at which God can take possession of the world and make, not only this world, but all the universe completely his own again.

This is the cosmic significance of Christ. In this sense he was "pre-existent" before the world first began. How shall we understand such a saying as this? Theologians and philosophers may do so, and may discuss and dispute it to eternity, but we also—we lay people—have to come to some sort of an idea about it all. My belief is that this Christ was (in untheological language) the embodiment of love—the incarnation of God, who is Love. In all his thoughts and words and acts—in his whole life—he was inspired and guided by this Spirit. And "he that dwelleth in love dwelleth in God and God in him; for God is love" (1 John 4:16).

Source

A. Maude Royden, *I Believe in God* (New York: Harper & Brothers, 1927), 101–19.

Atonement

"LET US SAY BOLDLY that God is not angry with us, nor has he ever demanded satisfaction for our sins." In affirming this, Royden rejects the penal substitution theory of atonement, the claim that Jesus, an innocent man, died as vicarious punishment for human sinfulness. Such an interpretation of the atonement, thinks Royden, ignores the parable of the prodigal son, Jesus' own life and ministry of love, and the love revealed in human interactions. All these ought to persuade us that the atonement was an act of love, not of punishment, much less vengeance. God's willingness to die at our hands is the supreme act of love—vicarious suffering, not vicarious punishment—and in recognizing it we repent, worship, and are healed. This is the heart of atonement or reconciliation with God.

One of the greatest difficulties in the minds of Christians today is created by the doctrine of the Atonement. Great and illuminating books have been written about it but, for those who have no time to be learned, it remains obscure and even horrifying. I wish that it might be purged once and for all of those elements which make it horrible, for I believe the doctrine in itself to be one of the loftiest and most moving of all Christian truths.

To many people the Atonement still means simply this: that God is angry with the whole human race; that his anger demands a victim, a sacrifice, a "propitiation"; and that he could only be satisfied when Jesus Christ offered himself as that victim and, by an agonizing death, atoned for all the sins that he had never committed.

This frightful doctrine is still preached, and even preachers who are willing to soften it down a little cling to the idea that the wrath of God (or "divine justice") demanded some victim, and that we are only forgiven because Christ offered himself as that victim. We are "saved by the blood of the Lamb." The idea of substitution (i.e., of the punishment of an innocent person for the guilty) is not abandoned.

It is, nevertheless, an idea so abhorrent to our sense of justice that it must be abandoned.

Let us say boldly that God is not angry with us, nor has he ever demanded satisfaction for our sins. The idea of an angry God is childishly human: the idea of a vindictive one is horrible. God is the Father of Lights, in whom is no variableness neither shadow cast by turning. It is we who have been angry with God and it is we who needed a mediator.

There is no mediator, no advocate, no victim in the story of the prodigal son (Luke 15:11–32). This story contains the heart of the Christian faith. It has been said of it that if all the rest of the Bible was lost and this alone remained, we should still have in it the heart of the Christian faith. This is a picturesque way of putting it, but in a sense it is true, at least in so far as any teaching without the life behind it could convey the heart of Christ to us. Yet this sublime and perfect parable contains no Christ at all! There is the Father; there are his erring sons, the prig and the prodigal; there is the wandering away from the Father, the fall and the recovery, the return, the welcome home, the full and free forgiveness. No sacrificial blood is shed, no altar and no victim are required. Yet the son who was lost is found and he who was dead is alive again.

In all the sermons preached on the prodigal son I have never once heard one which emphasized this point; and yet how moving it is—how adorable the God it proclaims—how easy, how inevitable to worship him!

God is not angry with us; we have been and still often are angry with him. "God was in Christ reconciling the world to himself" (2 Cor 5:19)—not himself to the world.

We have wandered away from God and now no longer clearly see either him or his purpose for us. We suffer because we are away from him who is the source of life and beauty; and our suffering bewilders us further. Stupidity is the inevitable consequence of sin, for sin darkens the understanding. The very thing that makes us suffer—our alienation from God—makes us resent our suffering, for we cannot understand what makes us suffer. We arraign God. How can he, we ask, endure to see us suffer? Does he not realize that the innocent are suffering too? Is he unable to save us or does he not care to do so? Is he loveless or merely weak? Does he suppose that by making us suffer he will make us love him?

These and a thousand other taunts, reproaches, or entreaties are hurled at God and have been hurled throughout the ages. From the savage who offers his human sacrifice to appease his terrible deity to the infuriated rebel of the nineteenth and twentieth centuries—a Shelley or a Swinburne—and the Christian church-goer who under his breath confesses to me that he "hates God," there has been incessant witness to the fact that it is not God who must be persuaded to forgive us; it is humanity which can neither understand nor forgive God.

If we have ever understood him, even a little, it has been through the love revealed to us by human beings. The fundamental need of the whole human race has been the love of parents for their offspring. Without this, humanity must have perished, or rather would never have succeeded in becoming human at all. The evolution and survival of our race is knit up with the long infancy of human children and the need of self-sacrifice on the part of human parents.

To this basic fact Christ appealed. "When ye pray, say Father" (Luke 11:2), he said, and said it to Jews whose finest quality is their devotion to their children. "Will any man of you being a father," he says, "when his son asks for an egg give him a serpent?" (Luke 11:11). From this try to understand God! Attribute to him no more such infamies as undying resentment of savage punishment. He is our Father. Our brothers may desire to see us suitably punished for our sins[1]—may grudge us our forgiveness. Our Father does not do so. He is more glad when we repent and return than determined to exact the penalty our human justice would demand.

A child who has never known love finds it difficult to believe in the love of God. Many men and women have told me they first realized what love meant because of some sublime act of self-sacrifice or of forgiveness on the part of a father or a mother. They saw love there, and God is love, so they saw God. Many have said to some injured friend: "If you can forgive me, I will believe that God can."

But still this was not enough. We needed a love more perfect still. Christ came, and so loved the world as to convince the world. In him we have seen a love which would never coerce, either by violence or by signs and wonders; which would never defend itself or use any weapon except love; whose forgiveness of injuries demanded no reparation; who pleaded for those who tortured and killed him. Shall we think that this is the love of God? Or are we to suppose that in this the creature surpassed the Creator, the fountain rose higher than its source?

"Greater love hath no man than this, that a man lay down his life for his friend" (John 15:13). In spite of all that we can say—and truly

---

1. As the elder son in the parable of the prodigal son did. (MR)

say—about the merit of living for one's friends being more needed and more serviceable than dying for them, it remains true that greater love hath no man than this that a man lay down his life for his friend. It is not a thing one can argue about: it is a deep imperious conviction that one must feel. Death is final. In death we give all: there is an end. Living, we keep the power to change our mind, to waver, to take back the gift; dying gives everything at once. Greater love hath no man than this.

So, by his willingness to die, Jesus has conquered. Could he have conquered in any other way or won us at any smaller cost? I do not think so. The gracious, reverend, and beautiful old age of Gautama Buddha has not moved the world as has the agonizing and shameful execution of Jesus Christ. Literally, we love him because he died for us.

Christians have divided the life of Christ from his death in a way which robs death itself of meaning. The mere fact of death—even death by crucifixion—is nothing. All men die and many thieves have been crucified. The whole meaning of Christ's death for us was his life; and to emphasize his death as a thing apart, by which alone we are saved, is to make nonsense of the Gospel. But this is true—that it was such an end to such a life that breaks every barrier down and gives to Christ upon the Cross a power to win us to love and worship greater than, without it, he could ever have possessed. If, then, it is love which is God, and to love is the first and great commandment, that which evokes our love is truly that by which we are saved. We are "saved by the blood of the Lamb" (Rev 12:11): I believe it with all the conviction of those who use the phrase most familiarly, though they may reject my interpretation of it.

To me this is the Atonement. Christ has revealed to us what love really is, to what heights it can rise and what it can and must achieve. I believe that love is God, and in Christ I see what God is. He does not, I now see, abandon us to our grief. He is not content to let us suffer. He does not argue that we have deserved all that has come upon us. He is not concerned to judge but to save (1 John 3:17). How childish and how small seems all our concern for his offended Majesty! How meanly human our idea that he is weighing our sins in a balance and demanding a victim!

God in his home in heaven could not rest, being love: he must seek for the lost and try to re-enter and repossess the universe. We do not know how that loss was possible, but, seeing ourselves lost in perplexity and pain, we do see, dimly in one another, perfectly in Christ, how he has sought to win us again. This is the meaning of that ancient majestic phrase: "The Lamb slain from the foundation of the world" (Rev 13:8).

When God gave us freedom of choice he took the risk which ended on Calvary. This is what the gift of free will has cost him. This is the cost at which we grow noble. The drama of the incarnation is repeated everywhere, for everywhere God seeks to become incarnate and make us all his own again: the tragedy of the Crucifixion took place not nineteen hundred years ago at Jerusalem, but wherever any one has seen God and received him, and tried to show him to mankind, and been stoned or stabbed or crucified for his pains.

Today, as always, men cry out in derision: "If thou be the Lord of the Universe, come down from the Cross! Save thyself and us!" (Matt 27:40). And the reply today is always the same: "He saved others; himself he cannot save" (Matt 27:42).

This is the Atonement. Vicarious punishment is a horrible imagination: it is a lie. Vicarious suffering is a fact. God could save us by no other way than this, and at no less cost. He could, indeed, put an end to our suffering by putting an end to us. This would be simple, but it would not be love. I marvel that those who cry out against God for not stopping the war, or preventing the infliction of suffering by the guilty upon the innocent, do not see it. If I were God, surely I should weary of the human race and put it out of its misery! No one with a heart of love can look on at our suffering and not pity us. Even if we have brought it all upon ourselves even if it is all our fault, we must be pitied. How simple to put an end to it all—to destroy the freedom which we have used so ill! Why does not God save himself and us from all this pain?

I believe he could. I do not share the modern idea that God himself is helpless or at least not omnipotent. I find what Christ said of Pilate true of us all: "thou could'st have no power at all against me except it were given thee from on high" (John 19:11). It has actually been given to us by God, this dread freedom to do right or wrong, this power to crucify him; and it will not be taken away. In this is the last proof of God's love.

Omnipotence is not the power to do contradictory things but to do all things that are possible to be done. To make us at once free and not free is not possible, and to demand it in the name of the omnipotence of God is not to invoke omnipotence but chaos. God can leave us free or he can destroy us—for to destroy our free will is to destroy us—but he cannot make us free and unfree at once.

I believe, moreover, that God cannot destroy even one of us without in some mysterious sense maiming us all. The worst cannot be sacrificed without loss to the best. If one member suffers all the body suffers with it.

We find it hard to bear this in mind—hard to accept—but it is true. If we forget the basic facts of life, God does not. We are *solidaire* whether we choose to remember it or not. This is God's answer to those who plead for the destruction at least of the most wicked among us.

He will not destroy us. We, when we see some small tormented animal for which we do not care, will put it out of its misery. An impulse of compassion will make us hastily kill the fly whose wings some heedless child has torn away. It is nothing to us, but we pause a moment to put it out of its pain and very likely suffer in imagination more than the fly can. We hesitate to kill an animal we love. An injured dog or horse we take to the surgeon, and, though we may say, "if you cannot cure it, put an end to it," we give it a chance. We let it suffer, even a good deal, in the hope of recovery. We think its recovery worth that suffering because we love it.

We never say of a child, "put it out of its pain." The child is too precious for that. We may suffer in watching it suffer; because of our superior knowledge we may suffer much more than it suffers. I think grown-up people often do. But we dare not say "let it die." We must let it suffer even when our hearts cry out against the suffering. Even when love hardly plays a conscious part, some instinct rises up against the destruction of a human life. We dare not, even to spare the cost of agony, put an end to it.

Shall not the patience of God with all our evil and our pain be interpreted in terms of love? Is it not because we are too precious in his sight to be destroyed, that he allows us to suffer—and is willing to suffer with us?

That he does suffer I cannot doubt. It may be heresy, but, if God is love, how can he stand apart from our pain without sharing it? It is inconceivable. It is of the essence of love that it shares, and though I cannot conceive the suffering of God—because it is altogether beyond my human mind—I can see that Christ suffered and was bound to suffer—could not escape suffering. The anger I should feel against a God who could, omniscient, know all our pain and be unmoved by it, dies when I see Christ on the Cross. I know God cannot be less—less loving, less pitiful—than Christ. Once more I realize that God is in Christ reconciling me and all the world to himself.

I do not know how all this pain and sin has come about, but I know that the cost of it to God is so much more than to me that I cannot measure it. Why does he endure it? Why did he accept crucifixion "from the foundation of the world" (Eph 1:4)? Because he loves us enough even for this. "Herein is love; not that we loved him but that he first loved us. . . . We love him because he first loved us" (1 John 4:10).

Seeking his lost world, and entering in wherever he could find a way of entering, it was inevitable that the Crucifixion should come. When Christ, his only-begotten Son, the one who perfectly received him and is perfectly his own, tried to show us how we also should live so as to be in truth the children of God, the beauty of the vision was too much for us. In this sense we may say that Judas was foreordained to betray Jesus. If he had not done it someone else must have done it!

Yes—someone would have done it. It did not take Judas alone to crucify Christ. The priests who accused and condemned him, the Roman ruler who delivered the judgment, the faithless friends who forsook him and fled, the fickle mob who demanded the Crucifixion, the soldiers who carried it out—it took all these to kill Jesus Christ, and among one or other of these we all have stood at times. Was it all foreordained? In a sense it was: it was foreseen: I think it was inevitable. Those who receive God are too glorious to be hidden. We see them and at first we love them; but then we envy them, or feel they ask too much of us, or shrink from the dread contrast between their lives and ours.

This is what happened with Christ. In him men saw the spirit of God himself revealed. In him they saw also what all men ought to be. He told them how they too should live and what manner of kingdom they would, if they so lived, bring about on earth. They flocked to him and listened with joy to his words. Who could refuse to love him? Who fail to be ravished by his great promises? The common people heard him gladly.

And as they listened and he spoke they began to understand him better. They began to count the cost of the things he promised. The Kingdom of Heaven is like unto a merchant seeking goodly pearls who, when he heard of one pearl of great price, sold all that he had and went and bought it (Matt 13:45–46). All that he had! But this is terrible! Who is ready to give so much? It is impossible to give so much!

A chill fell upon them. They walked with him no more. Then they began to wish they had never walked with him at all. It was not easy to forget, once they had heard; not easy to give up that heavenly vision and return to the dull round of a narrow, sordid life again. If he had only let them alone they would never have thought of anything better. If they had never seen him they would have had no haunting sense of loss. They began to hate him—to be sure that he was wrong—to hope he might be wrong—to wish at least that he should be silent—that they might be rid of him and his terrible love and beauty, and be free to go back to their comfortable materialism.

> For O, the Master is so fair,
> His smile so sweet to banished men,
> That those who meet him unaware
> Can never rest on earth again.[2]

This is why the slaying of the prophets is so certain. God comes into the world at his peril! We ask to see him, but we dare not when we can. His beauty is too great for us: we cannot cease to desire it and yet we cannot pay the price. We wish to be left in our complacent smug materialism: we dread the advent of the Spirit. We cry out in pain against it. We turn in fury upon those who show us its power. We too join in that age-old shout: "Crucify him." Let him be dead and buried. Put a stone upon his sepulcher. Make it as sure as you can.

We cannot look upon ourselves in the light of God's love—we cannot see humanity as he would have it to be—without an agony of shame and grief. As Peter, when he saw it, cried, "Depart from me for I am a sinful man, O Lord" (Luke 5:8), so do we; and since he will not depart we seek to kill him.

This is the cost of our redemption to God. Vicarious suffering is not a doctrine; it is a fact. When we have done our worst and killed the one who alone was truly godlike and God, then only will we see and repent and worship. By his stripes we are healed.

Human beings in an agony of shame and resentment put Christ to death. If they had not, they could never have known how altogether perfect he was. Afterward, they did know, and saw that the man they had put to death was the man we would all be if we could. They knew that once at least a human being had been perfectly what God desired. When, therefore, they draw near to God they hide behind this Christ. They put him forward as the one who can show that humanity is worth saving. They make their prayers in his name. They feel that they are justified in him. This is why we pray to God "in Christ's name" and "for his sake."

This is why we think of him as the "propitiation" for our sins.

Since this word, like the "Atonement," has become a horror to many people, let us consider it not as a theological doctrine at all but, like the Atonement, as a fact in human experience.

Vicarious suffering does, as a matter of fact, redeem us: we have known it happen. The suffering of the innocent, brought about by our

---

2. Attributed in some sources to the "poet E. B." and in others to verses found in "an old missal." (KW)

sins, has again and again checked us in mid-career and brought us to our senses again.

Atonement was needed between God and man, for men were angry with God. It was achieved by Jesus Christ, for no man could be angry with him, and in him we can all see God.

So also, as a simple fact, we do find in Christ the propitiation for our sins. No words are more true to Christian experience than these—

> Look, Father, look on his anointed face,
> And only look on us as found in him.
> Look not on our misusings of thy grace,
> Our prayer so languid and our faith so dim;
> For lo, between our sins and their reward
> We set the Passion of thy Son our Lord.[3]

Let us rule out the theological doctrine. Let us forget the idea of God and the idea of sin and think of it in another way. Suppose there is not any God: suppose there is not any sin. These are theological terms, and we are looking for something purely human—something in our own experience. We have friends, and to these friends we sometimes have done wrong; and when we realize that we have done wrong we want to be forgiven. On what grounds do we ask for excuse? With what words shall we say "forgive me"? We ask to be believed when we say that we will not so offend again; or if, perhaps, we cannot even promise that, knowing how often we have failed already, at least we ask that it may be believed of us that we do not want to do it again. We would not do it again if we could help. We ask to be forgiven, not so much for what we are as for what we wish to be and may be.

In a sense, what we hope to be and intend to be is what we actually are. We have a sort of shadowy right to be forgiven when we are sorry, because when we are sorry we reject the fault—our will rejects it; our will is right; and that shows what we may someday become. Can the injured person care enough for the "me" that does love him and that does not want to injure him? Will he perceive that the good "me" is the essential "me," and, for the sake of that, however small it is, forgive?

Whenever we ask to be forgiven it is on such grounds that we find courage to ask it. We do not argue it all out in this way, perhaps, but it is what we really mean. "Believe in me enough to think that I shall someday become a good friend." The wish does imply the thing. The acorn is not

---

3. "And Now, O Father, Mindful of the Love" (1874), William Bright. (KW)

the oak, and yet it is the oak in a sense that the beech-nut is not. The beech-nut is not the beech, and yet it is the beech in a sense that the acorn is not.

> All the music of the moon
> Sleeps in the plain eggs of the nightingale.[4]

What does the poet mean by that? Can an egg sing? Or is there music in an egg? Is there even any sentient being in an egg? Yet it is true that all the music of the moon does sleep in the plain eggs of the nightingale as it does not sleep in the eggs of the thrush, the cuckoo, or the sparrow.

There is truth in our plea when we say, "Because there is something in me that is good, since I do love you and am sorry for what I did wrong, will you believe that that is really myself, and for the sake of that forgive me?"

Christ is to humanity what that spark of goodness is to us. Christ is in us individually in that spark of goodness. That is his Spirit and, in a little way, it is ours also: and in a great way it passes from the individual to the human race. We recognize Christ as the best that we have done. We believe that Christ is the divine Idea of Humanity, the Word of God to Man, made flesh. Or we think only: "this is the best that humanity has produced." In either case Christ is to the race itself what the spark of goodness in us is to us individually.

The goodness of Christ belongs to the human race just as my little spark of goodness belongs to me; and since humanity has produced this perfect human being, it has as much right to claim to speak in his name as it has a right to blush for all the sins it has committed against him. We have a right—a sort of right—to ask to be forgiven for the sake of the fact that we repent these things. There's goodness enough in us to be sorry with, and so we have a right to be forgiven. There is goodness enough in the human race to have made it possible for the Spirit of God to become incarnate in Jesus of Nazareth, and so, instinctively, we say: "for the sake of that, for that which after all humanity does share in—for that which we recognize as the best of all—be pitiful with all the human race!"

> Look, Father, look on his anointed face,
> And only look on us as found in him.

If we humans could only produce a Judas Iscariot, or an impenitent thief, or such weak friends of Christ as forsook him and fled, it is an

---

4. Alfred Lord Tennyson, "Alymer's Field" (1870). (KW)

open question whether it would really be merciful of God to let us go on existing. What do such creatures as we, crawling between earth and heaven—if that were all!

But it is not all. There is Christ also. "Look on his anointed face and only look on us as found in him." After all, it is worthwhile to save us. There is something of Christ in all of us—something, in spite of all that we have done that is wrong. It is worthwhile to bear with us and to forgive us, for such as Christ is we, who are also human beings, may one day become. We recognize in him our elder brother, but we also are the children of God—his very little brothers and sisters, but still of the same family and the same race. For his sake be not weary of us!

How weary we are of ourselves! How impatient of our own failures! Is it conceivable that God should be patient still? Yes; because he sees in us, even when we cannot see it in ourselves, that spark of goodness which makes us Christ. In the sense that the acorn is the oak and the nightingale's eggs are the music of the nightingale, in that sense humanity is Christ. It will someday grow up to the measure of the stature of the fullness of him. How then should God be weary of us? He sees Christ and knows that this also, this alone, is the final truth about the human race. Christ is the propitiation for our sins.

Whatever any human being does, in that we are entitled to claim a share: it belongs to us all. Somewhere in the back of our minds we feel when we read of some heroic act (of which in fact we are incapable) a kind of sympathetic and generous pride that we also are human beings. A young painter, seeing a supremely great picture, said to himself with proud humility, *ed io son pittore*—"I also am a painter!"[5] I, too, belong to the glorious band of which one of us has produced this perfect thing! We rejoice to read of great and glorious deeds, to recognize the doers of them as our brothers, and take a not wholly vicarious joy in what they did.

This we do when we are at our best. When we do not feel so, it is because we are moved with a mean spirit of jealousy: we are vexed to think that someone can do so much better than we. But at our best we take a pride in thinking that we too belong to the race of men, as did they who did these things.

So we say to God: "Will you not look at us as part of the same great family—as having the spirit of Christ?" Against our vindictiveness, our resentment, our rancor, we set the Christ who said when he was crucified,

---

5. The young painter was Antonio Allegri da Correggio (1494–1534). (KW)

"Forgive them: they know not what they do" (Luke 23:34). We ask God to look at that, and he does. Against our lack of love we set the love of Jesus. We ask God to look at that, as something which in a sense we share when we love any one at all. We, too, are of that great company of lovers whose head and chief is Jesus Christ, and God is just and sees that it is so. Christ is the propitiation for our sins. God recognizes and admits our plea.

> Look, Father, look on his anointed face,
> And only look on us as found in him.

(and we are found in him)

> Look not on our misusings of thy grace,
> Our prayer so languid and our faith so dim;
> For lo, between our sins and their reward
> We set the Passion of thy Son our Lord.

Source

A. Maude Royden, *I Believe in God* (New York: Harper & Brothers, 1927), 181–98.

Personal Survival

IN THIS 1933 REFLECTION on life after death, Royden draws a distinction between spirit, "God Imminent" within us, and soul, or individual personality. Influenced by evolutionary theory, she argues that spiritual progress leads to "a more and more perfect individuality," a cleansing and refining of the soul's faculties of mind, will, and emotions. When the spirit of a cleansed person returns to God, it's accompanied by the person's soul or personal identity. For the Christian, to be "lost in the All-ness of God" is undesirable. Royden is not a universalist. She argues that just as there are physical consequences to our health if we mistreat our body, so there are spiritual ones if we mistreat our soul. To presume that all souls, no matter how corrupt, eventually return to God is a bit of sentimentality that trivializes moral responsibility.

In that strange and cynical book, the Book of Ecclesiastes, there is a passage, one of the loveliest and the most haunting in the Bible:

> Or ever the silver cord be loosed, or the golden bowl be broken, or the pitcher be broken at the fountain, or the wheel broken at the cistern, and the dust return to the earth as it was, and the spirit return unto God who gave it. (Eccl 12:6)

There are three ways in which men think of the soul after death. There is the old-fashioned Christian way of thinking that the soul goes either to Heaven or to Hell, to a place of eternal bliss or a place of eternal torment, and there remains. There is the agnostic's way of thinking, that the soul is annihilated, dies with the body, being no more than a by-product of our physical life. There is the more modern Christian way which believes that the soul, though unfit for perfect bliss, is equally unfit for eternal torment, and therefore supposes it to go "from state to state," forward through eons of ages, but always at last returning to God.

There are many modifications of each of these beliefs, but they represent broadly what people think about the soul.

What is the soul? Christians are taught to think of man as being body, soul, and spirit, but in common speech we have so misused the word "soul" that we have lost its distinctive meaning, and frequently use it as though it were the same as "spirit." This is an error. The body is our physical life, the flesh and blood form in which we live; and the spirit is God Immanent in us, the Holy Spirit of God by whose indwelling presence we are the children of God; the soul is the emotions, the mind and the will. It is the soul which gives personality, not the body or the spirit. The spirit is impersonal, it comes from Deity, it is that which links us with God. It is the soul which is our individuality, the thing which makes us *you* and *me*.

It is clear that Christ attached a very sacred importance to personality. Mrs. Besant,[1] when giving a course of lectures in the Queen's Hall on the great religions of the world, dwelt in each case on the particular gift of teaching that each religion had given to mankind; and she chose as the most characteristic gift of Christianity the sense of value of the individual soul, that deep sense of its infinite possibilities and worth that made medieval theologians say that if only one man had fallen from grace, God Almighty would have thought it worthwhile to be crucified for that one.

This comment from one who is not of the Christian faith is very significant. Of course those of us who call ourselves Christians would say that the gift of Christianity to the world was the idea of a God of Love, but certainly the second thing we should say, was that Christianity had given an enhanced sense of the value of personality. Although, looking at the glaring defects of our civilization we may think it holds life very cheap, we have only to go to the East, where other great spiritual religions have held sway, to realize that human life is precious here compared with what it is in oriental countries.

This is the result of two lines of thought. First of all, it is the result of centuries of Christian teaching, which taught in parable after parable, saying after saying, act after act, the worth that Christ set on the individual soul, however lost, however degraded, however mean. He would seek, he told his followers, for one out of a hundred sheep, for one out of many silver coins; would not abandon one soul, one great was his love of each. [. . .]

Then, more recently, science has taught us the same thing. We see in the course of evolution the development of individuality. Coming up

---

1. Annie Besant (1847–1933), suffragist, socialist, and theosophist. (KW)

from the very slime of creation, through uncounted millions of years, the human race has at last been evolved. Through blood and sweat, through agony and toil, through aspirations and errors, the human being has come. And the higher his development the more distinctive he appears. He does not evolve into the mass, he evolves into the individual. The finest men and women are the most individual, unlike other people, distinct in themselves. So has science itself endorsed the teaching of Christ: so has science set its seal on the high value of personality.

To suppose that, at death, the soul goes back to God who gave it, in the sense that a drop of water falls into the ocean and ceases to be, is to suppose that the spiritual world reverses all that we know of the world in which we live. It makes chaos of knowledge and reverses all that experience has taught us.

If we can reason at all from what we here know, the line of advance is not to extinction but to a more and more perfect individuality. This, the teaching of science, that the higher we rise in the range of being the more distinctive, the more individual, the more significant we are, is the demonstration in the physical world of what Christ taught two thousand years ago—that the supremely important thing is personality. It is strange to realize that the "heaven" of Buddhism is the nearest approach to "hell" for the Christian. To be lost in the All-ness of God as the drop in the Ocean still seems to many devout minds heaven enough. To Christ it was not gain disguised but loss; for to him personality was supremely precious.

These two converging lines of thought, of the love of Christ for the individual person and of the knowledge of the long ages of struggle that have gone to the evolution of personality, have created in many people the conviction that we all survive and all ultimately find our way to heaven, to peace, to God. Not the spirit only, but the soul "returns to God who gave it."

Yet it seems to me impossible to claim that this was the belief of Christ. The view for which there is the least direct evidence is that held so widely by modern Christians; that everybody is ultimately "saved," that all souls born into life go forward by a process more or less painful, more or less laborious, but go forward until they reach the goal which is God himself.

I can only suppose this "universalism," as it is called, this belief in the universal salvation of all human souls, is due not to any one saying or parable—for of these there are very few to justify it—but to the general impression that Christ attached infinite value to the human soul, and that it is impossible to believe that a God of Love would allow even one to be destroyed.

It is an attractive belief; yet I do not believe it. Is our moral responsibility so unreal? Are the choices that we make of good and evil, of life and death, so unmeaning? In the sphere of the spirit is nothing eternally significant? If one treats his body amiss the consequences follow as the night the day. The means he takes to remedy the ill have also their certain consequences. Everything we do in the physical world follows a law which cannot be broken. There, there is cause and effect, effect and cause, in a succession so certain that if we only perfectly knew and understood it we should be masters of life, and in fact we are becoming so in exact proportion as we know and accept the law of cause and effect in everything that we do. Can this be so in the material world, and in the world of spirit our choices have so little reality, our actions no meaning at all? It is true that when we say "God gave us freedom," we mean a limited freedom, for all of us are limited by the very conditions of human life. Still, even so, most of us believe that we have some kind of freedom. It that freedom *wholly* a delusion? Can we really never make a final choice? Is God, who is the Truth itself, so careless of the truth that he can let us imagine we are free, while in fact we are free only as a child is free who moves about in one of those little wooden pens that they make for children just learning to walk? They pull themselves up by the railings and walk round and round, quite happy and contented at first, thinking they are doing a wonderful thing. Have you ever put a child in such a pen and, when the day came that the child has found out the object of the pen, did you have another moment's peace? Not one! That pen was no further use from the moment that the child found that its freedom—which seemed so great when first it pulled itself up on to its feet and wandered round the little wooden railing, thinking itself "lord of infinite space"—was a delusion. If God has really so conditioned us that in the end we *cannot* choose anything but God, what reality is there in our freedom more than in that child's?

I sometimes think there is an element of unreality, of sentimentality in this conception of a benevolent and amiable God in whom nothing is real, nothing is true; he has us on a string and will pluck us back to himself at last, our choice a delusion, our freedom a lie.

There is no sentimentality in the teaching of Christ. That God is Love was a truth for which he was prepared to live and to die—a truth of which he was so certain that death became to him a victory. Great love and utter truth go hand in hand. If there is no final moral responsibility in us for what we do or leave undone, for the laws we obey or disobey, for the life we accept or refuse, our religion is a sham. But it is not so. Again and again Christ warns us of the possibility of utter loss. Again and again he tells us that the *soul* may be destroyed—self-destroyed—and the spirit go back to God who gave it. This gives an urgency to his Gospel that many of us have lost in the vast amiability of our religion. It gives a sharp reality to our deeds and our decisions which can never be found in them if it is true that in the long run they do not matter, for God will put everything right whatever we do and "save" us all whatever we are. Life was not so meaningless to Christ.

> God created man to be immortal and gave him the image of his own eternity. *Nevertheless, through envy, of the devil, came death into the world, and they that do hold of his side do find it.* (Wisdom 2:23–24)

It may be that we have chance after chance, opportunity after opportunity; that the death of this body is but a small event in that long progress which, God helping us, ends only with him. It may be through eons of ages, it may be through choices as unnumbered as the stars, that God waits for us; but that, in the end, we have *no* choice, I find it impossible to believe. There is a relentless logic in all we do and choose and reject, and if, through age after age, and eon after eon, we continually choose death, is our freedom so unreal, our moral responsibility so utter a delusion, that in the end God will force eternal life upon us.

In the parable of the choice of plucking out the eye, of cutting off the hand or foot, Christ conveys his sense of the infinite value of the soul—not the spirit, but the *form* that the spirit takes within us—which makes us each different as the stars differ from one another in glory. There is also the stern reality of the thought that to attain good is not an easy path to which God will always lead us back, but something for which we are ourselves responsible. He who taught us that if we did not use our talents, we are condemned, said also, "If your eye offend you," that is to say, if your eye cause you to stumble, "cut it out and cast it from you. It is better to enter into eternal life having one eye than having two eyes *to go to destruction*" (Matt 5:29). "If your right hand offend you, cut it off and cast it from you. It is better to go into eternal life having one hand than having two hands *to be destroyed*" (Matt 5:30). What can that mean? It is not mere drama! If Christ spoke as a poet—only the poet can deal with things so deep and true—surely he meant that though it is of infinite importance to use that right hand and that eye that God has given you, yet, if that same gift should cause you to be cruel and brutal to other people, if it should make you offend against the law of love, it is better to cut it out and cast it from you and enter into everlasting life.

We have a right to choose, we must choose, and our life here is immeasurably more significant than we realize. The vague amiability which makes right and wrong almost the same thing—because in the end God will force us to choose right—robs it of reality. It is possible that in the end "the *spirit* returns to God who gave it" because the *soul* has been destroyed. Herein is reconciled the love and the truth of God. It could not be a God of Love who should condemn any child of his to everlasting and therefore senseless punishment; but it is quite consistent with the love of God that we may, if we choose, quench in ourselves the spirit. The soul, the individual personality, the *form* the spirit took in us, ceases to be, and "the spirit returns to God who gave it."

What is it that makes us immortal? What is it that we have to choose? We think, perhaps instinctively, of some spiritual interest, some kind of belief in spiritual things. We make a distinction in our minds between the "spiritual" person, and what we all the "materialist," and sometimes the religious person is much less attractive to us—much less lovable than the materialist. We swing over to the "universalist" side and say "these people cannot be lost, they cannot really be lost, because although they are so materially minded, they are often so kind, so charitable, so generous-hearted." But these are the people who in the eyes of Christ *are* immortal! It is not necessarily the people who believe in and care for spiritual things who are saved. It is the people who are kind. The immortal spirit in us is not what we, with our stupid standards, regard as religion. The immortality within us is love, for God is love, and they that dwell in love dwell in God, *and God in them.*

To reject love, to refuse love, to be turned in upon yourself even from the most religious motives, to be self-absorbed, self-regarding, self-centered, this, and only this, is death.

Source

A. Maude Royden, *Here—and Hereafter* (London: Putnam, 1933), 228–37.

A Soft Theological Revolution

IN AN EARLIER SELECTION, *"The Anti-Feminist's Last Ditch,"* Royden argued that the church was diminished by denying women Holy Orders. In this one, from a 1920 pamphlet, she contends that the discipline of theology is diminished because it neither trains nor takes seriously women theologians. Especially after the trauma of the Great War, she argues, theology is in need of a "lovelier message," one that sees justice as love rather than retaliation. Unfortunately, male theologians tend to think of the relationship between God and humans exclusively in legalistic terms of judge and offender. Women, on the other hand, see the relationship as more intimate than legal in nature. They think of it in terms of parent and child, and so are better attuned to reforming theology in what Royden calls a "soft revolution." In drawing the distinction she does between male and female styles of theologizing, Royden anticipates Carol Gilligan's later argument that women's moral reasoning is in "a different voice" than men's.

The entrance of women into the learned professions will have a much greater effect on the thought of those professions—and through them, on the thought of the world—than is realized by those who regard it merely as the fortunate opening of new careers for women, or the deplorable invasion of yet more of the sphere of men. The only one in which women have already entered in sufficiently large numbers to create a corporate as well as an individual impression is medicine. Those who have watched their progress will probably agree that their most valuable contribution to the great science of hygiene has been their repudiation of the ancient heresy that "woman is a natural invalid." I do not forget the brilliant work done by individual women physicians and surgeons, or the high level reached by medical women as a whole, when I say that this beneficent revolution (it is nothing less) outweighs in importance to the race of the future anything else that has been done.

That the coming of women into the legal profession will result in another peaceful revolution in thought, I have no doubt at all, and I believe that here it will be along the lines of a much greater emphasis on the sanctity of life as compared with property. But here, since women have not yet begun practice in either of the legal professions, one is in the dangerous region of prophecy.

Prophecy, too, is all that is possible in the case of women in the ministry, for the number who have entered it, in any Christian communion, is too small, and their entrance too recent, for them yet to have exercised this kind of influence. But I believe that theology has been and is the poorer for the almost complete lack in it of the influence and experience of the ordinary woman.

It is true that there have been distinguished women who have shared in the building up of our theology; but here, as in medicine, it is not the exceptional woman's individual work that I am thinking of, but rather the contribution of many women—women in numbers large enough to give something of the point of view of their sex as a great part of the community, as well as of their individual minds.

One is inclined at first to argue that since intellect and spirit have no sex, women as women neither have nor ought to have any such contribution to make. The same argument might be applied to medicine; but it has been shown to be untrue, and the whole race will benefit immeasurably from the fact that women doctors have, on some matters, a different point of view from men, and are able to give effect to it. I do not attempt to make generalizations about the "fundamental differences" between the sexes. No one yet knows what they are, and no one can know until artificial differences have ceased to be created by convention. But apart from "fundamental differences," there is no doubt that the actual lives and experience of women as a whole have been different from that of men as a whole, and that this difference has either been created by, or has created, differences of outlook. Men have been more active in public and women in private life: men in creating States, women in creating homes; men in making and administering laws, women in bringing up families.

It is possible that our depressingly legalistic theology may suffer something like a peaceful revolution when women begin to interest themselves in it. Let me take a single instance to show what I mean.

It is a commonplace that the great and adorable doctrine of the Atonement has suffered such incredible distortion and perversion at the hands of theologians that it has become, to many seeking minds, the worst stumbling block of all, in the way of their acceptance of Christianity. This doctrine is sublimely stated by St. Paul: "God was in Christ, reconciling the world to Himself" (2 Cor 5:19). But St. Paul's doctrine has hardened into a legalism so harsh, so un-divine, so remote from the spirit of Jesus Christ, that it has become unrecognizable.

Partly, no doubt, this has been due to the influence of Rome and the majesty of Roman Law; but has it not also been due to the fact that men naturally think of our relation to God in terms of king and subject, judge and offender, creditor and debtor, lord and servant, rather than in terms of parent and child? All these analogies were used by our Lord in His teaching, and all, obviously, convey something of the nature of our relation to God. But all will agree that the very heart of His revelation was the great assurance that God is our Father. Compared with this, the others are mere incidents of His teaching—figures of speech used to point to a particular moral, or throw light on some single perplexity. Transcending all is the sublime truth that we are the children of God, that He is our Father, and that His "Kingdom" is in fact our home.

If the doctrine of the Atonement had been seen and interpreted in this light, it could not have become the terror that it has been for so long and to so many. It would have been interpreted, surely, in the light of that master-parable of the Christian life—the parable of the prodigal son. It has been said that if all the rest of Christ's teaching were lost, this parable alone would give us the heart of His revelation. It is an exaggeration, but it is a striking testimony to the character of that revelation. Not God as king or judge or lord or creditor is the God of Jesus; but God as Father: not man as subject, offender, servant, debtor; but man as son, even if an erring son.

It is at least remarkable that this story, which has so seized the imagination of the world, was recorded by one evangelist only—St. Luke—and in that part of his Gospel which biblical criticism has now assigned to a woman![1] The "great interpolation" may have been given to St. Luke by our Lady, by Joanna, by the group of women who ministered to our Lord: but that it was from women or a woman is very widely believed. Is it a coincidence merely that while (male) theologians have darkened understanding with their strange and harsh interpretations of the doctrine of

---

1. Royden is referring to a theory that Luke's Gospel, which focuses much more than the others on women, was written in part or whole by a woman. Scholars generally identify two "interpolations," a "Lesser" (Luke 6:20—8:3) and a "Greater" one (Luke 9:51—18.14). (KW)

the Atonement, a woman saved for the world that perfect revelation of the real attitude of God to man—the story of a father, an erring son, and no mediator at all?

I take this single example to show what I mean when I prophesy that the coming of women into this last of the "learned professions" will have its effect in ways we do not dream of. It may be argued that theology has always been open to them; that they have never been forbidden to read; and that in St. Catherine of Siena and St. Theresa of Spain[2] alone, there is proof enough that women could, without entering the ministry of the Church, both study and influence the direction of theological thought. It is true; and many names hardly less great could be added to these. But it is also true (a) that women have generally been discouraged not only from study in general, but especially from the study of theology (vide, almost in our own day, the prohibition of Ruskin in *Sesame and Lilies!*[3]); and (b) that it has never been their business to study theology. This is more relevant than it may seem. People do not study subjects which can lead them nowhere for the obvious reason that life is too strenuous, except in the case of persons of exceptional leisure. And life seems always to have been fairly strenuous for women, even women of the richest classes, during the Middle Ages! Women are not beginning to turn their attention to theology, but this is precisely because it does now seem that there will be a possibility of their using such knowledge in the service of their fellow men.

And for the few outstanding women theologians of the past, whose bent was too strong to be denied by adverse circumstance, it must be repeated that it is not so much the individual work of exceptional genius that we are thinking of here. Such work will generally not represent the normally characteristic experience and point of view of women, because it comes from women whose experience has been as exceptional as is their genius. Neither St. Catherine nor St. Theresa lived the ordinary life

---

2. Catherine of Siena (1347–80) and Theresa of Avila (1515–82). (KW)

3. John Ruskin (1819–1900). Although Royden's longtime friend and eventual husband Hudson Shaw adored Ruskin, she couldn't abide him because of his views on women. In *Sesame and Lilies* (1871), he's particularly offensive. "There is one dangerous science for 30 women—one which they must indeed beware how they profanely touch—that of theology. Strange, and miserably strange, that while they are modest enough to doubt their powers, and pause at the threshold of sciences where every step is demonstrable and sure, they will plunge headlong, and without one thought of incompetency, into that science in which the greatest men have trembled, and the wisest erred" (Boston: Silver, Burdett & Co., 1900), 89–90. (KW)

of women, and their genius transcends sex. The pressure, the molding power, of women as a whole, will be felt and only felt when women in considerable numbers are studying, writing, teaching and preaching theology.

It is possible that this influence is not only an important one in itself, but actually the essential one for the world of today. Looking at the ruins of our civilization, seeking the new hope and the new vision which shall lead us to a better, the hearts of all Christian people turn again to their Lord. Here and here alone is the Light of the World. But this civilization that has ended in such tragic wreck, it also was called Christian, it also was built up by nations nominally Christian. And horrible as have been its crimes, awful as is its failure, we cannot help believing that there is an element of hope, a possibility of effort, in people born into a religion so full of promise, which cannot let us despair. We build again; but it is reasonable to ask where and how our building failed before. I believe it was in a too prosaic and legal interpretation of the gospel of Christ; a greater insistence on the sovereignty than the Fatherhood of God; a tendency to reduce the relation of Father and child to a legal contract, a harsh bargain, a dwelling on justice human rather than divine. To a new world, Christians must preach the lovelier message of a God, who, though Judge, King, Lawgiver, is more still, and more completely, Father. They must learn that there is a Divine Justice not less just than ours but more divine—a Justice which is not retaliation but Love.

I am reminded that in Mr. Homer Lane's "Little Commonwealth,"[4] that great pioneer found a tendency among the children to elect girls rather than boys as judges. After the first shock of seeing so monstrous a regiment of women, they found—or so they believed—that girls were more just than boys. The boy was inclined to regard chiefly the outraged majesty of Law! The girls were more apt to consider every circumstance that accounted for the human offender. After all, should not justice consider all these things? But it is not in the law courts—it is in the home—that one realizes that.

There must be some way of reconciling Justice with Mercy; some way of showing that they are the same thing. There must be a possibility of building the new civilization on Love, without weakness, since only Love can ever create at all. If it be true that in the past, we have gone astray through too lawyer-like a theology, then it is possible that the age

---

4. Homer Lane (1875–1925), American-born educator and founder in Dorset, England, of the experimental school Little Commonwealth. (KW)

now dawning will be "the woman's age" in a much deeper sense than has been realized.

We are all beginning to understand how much the East has to give the West; how much each nation has to give to our idea of God. Until all are Christian, can we be perfectly orthodox? And until both sexes share equally in the interpretation of our religion, will not one aspect always be over-weighted, over-stressed?

Source

A. Maude Royden, "Women and Theology." Pamphlet in the *Women and Church* series. (London: League of the Church Militant, Anglican, 1920).

Part 5.

"Called to the High Ascent"

Selections from Royden's writings on matters of faith and morality

Being Christian

IN THIS GUILDHOUSE SERMON, Royden argues that to be a Christian is to imitate Christ in love, faithfulness, joy, serenity, and hope. If that sounds platitudinous, she says, it's because we confuse being a Christian with "making a fuss about trifles which God doesn't care about" or alternatively focusing too obsessively on important but nonfundamental "rites and ceremonies." Don't confuse churchiness with being a Christian, she warns. One can imitate Christ without going to church or even without ever having heard of Christ, because to love and serve others is to be filled with Christ's spirit. Professed Christians are called to reveal to others the God that Christ reveals to them. How shameful, then, when they so betray that commission as to turn other people away from Christ.

What is a Christian? If you take one of the greatest chapters in the Bible, you will find the answer to that question:

> Beloved, let us love one another: for love is of God; and every one that loveth is born of God, and knoweth God. He that loveth not knoweth not God; for God is love . . . . Beloved, if God so loves us, we ought also to love one another. No man hath seen God at any time. If we love one another God dwelleth in us and His love is perfected in us. (1 John 4:7–8, 11–12)

Therefore if you come to the Guildhouse and do not see God—if neither in the music, nor the sermon, nor the prayers is there any message or vision of God for you, yet if you have felt friendly to other people, God dwelleth in you, for God is love. "No man hath seen God at any time. If we love one another, God dwelleth in us; for God is love."

Christ revealed God to us just as a human being could. At least I believe that he worked under the ordinary limitations that human beings have to work under. He did not know everything. He did not know what modern science has taught us. About the ordinary facts of the formation of the world and the nature of the stars, and theories of evolution, and so on, our Lord did not know more than any other man of his time and age knew. He was asked once when the end of the world should come, when he should return to glory. He said he did not know. He worked under human limitations of power and strength. He had to deal with individuals. He healed people who were able to be healed. He was sometimes tired. Not often. He evidently had magnificent health. But he was sometimes weary; he had to rest; he had to sleep. He needed to eat and drink. He could only be in one place at a time. He could not see all the people who wanted to see him. They often pressed upon him; he had not time to see them all. He worked just like any human being who should be filled with the divine spirit. Of course, he seems to transcend human limitations, but I do not believe that he did. I believe when he told us we ought to be able to do as he did he meant it. He meant that every human being had as much control over circumstances, over his body, over the world in which he lived, as he himself, and that he was showing us what God meant humanity to be like. But his spirit was the spirit of God. "In the beginning was the Word, and the Word was with God, and the Word was God" (John 1:1). Christ shows us what the spirit of God was like. And what was it like?

It was a spirit of power and love and joy; of serenity and hope and faith; a spirit of service, a spirit of love for every human being and for every created thing; a spirit of wisdom which understood what was important and what was not important; a spirit divine, joyful, wise, loving, merciful, strong. "That," says Christ, "is what God is like." And when I ask the question, "What is a Christian?" my answer is, "A Christian is a person who is like Christ."

Well, you say, what a platitude! We did not come here on a frightfully hot Sunday evening to listen to such a platitude as that! I wish to God it were a platitude, for every day I find people whose idea of what constitutes a Christian is quite different and absolutely heart-rending. It is heart rending because it often makes them feel that they themselves can never hope to be Christians: more heart-rending because it often makes them feel that they have no desire to be Christians. Someone told me the other day that a friend of hers was going into an office—where, I do not know or how it happened to be what she described—but she said with some alarm that that place was a "perfect den of Christians," by which I gathered that she meant it was a place of profound gloom, of people who make mountains out of molehills, who thought that God cares about such futile, ridiculous trifles as none but a very foolish and tiresome human being could make a fuss about. "A den of Christians!" Is it really a platitude to say that a Christian is a person who is like Christ?

A member of the congregation once described to me her mother. She said, "She is the kind of woman to whom everyone takes their difficulties." Not a rich woman, not perhaps, a highly educated woman, but a woman to whom you instinctively went, knowing that she would never leave you in a hole. And after having described to me this mother, she said sorrowfully, "But she isn't at all religious." Good God! What is religion if that is not religion? What do you mean by a Christian if that is not a Christian? I said to her, "What can you mean by saying that a woman whose whole life is full of service to God and man is not religious?" And after some thought, she said, "Well, she never goes to church." I do not think our Lord said very much about going to church. He went himself, I suppose, until they drove him out. And I am certain that every Christian desires to find fellowship with other Christians and sometimes to meet them and worship God together. But that is because we want to do it, because we like to do it. To do it because it is a duty seems to me to be a most extraordinary idea of God. As though one would go to see one's friend from a sense of duty! One goes because one wants to go, and in any case our Lord said very little about it. But he continually taught us in every parable, in every saying, and in the whole of his own life that religion consisted in serving our fellowmen. In that great parable of the sheep and the goats, you remember, the ones who were welcome in Heaven were the ones who had served their fellowmen, and the ones who were cast out were the ones who had not served. There is nothing whatever about going to church, or about believing any special doctrine, unless you call believing in love a doctrine. It is, of course, the greatest of all beliefs. But that is the only one on which our Lord laid very much stress.

On the other hand, some years ago I heard a man discussed who had just resigned his bishopric, and two clergy of his diocese were nearly frantic with joy because he was going. They kept interrupting themselves, because they were really very kind, good men, and saying, "It is a shame to talk like this, because he really is such a Christian." I said, "In what sense is he a Christian?" "Well," they said, "of course he is dreadfully narrow-minded and domineering." I said, "But surely Christ wasn't narrow-minded and domineering?" "Well," they said, "no, that is true. But, you know, he does say so many prayers." Afterward they added thoughtfully,

"It is generally when he has said the most prayers that he does something outrageous." I said, "I should like to know what he is praying, what his God is like, and in what way this person resembles Christ, who is narrow-minded and domineering." I sometimes think our Lord's hatred of making a fuss about trifles was one of the strongest things in his character. You remember that when the Pharisees objected because his disciples plucked ears of wheat on a sabbath day, they said it was against the ecclesiastical law, and I feel that almost anyone else would have said to his disciples, "Don't pluck ears of wheat on the sabbath. You are offending very sincere, religious people, and after all you cannot really mind whether you pluck ears of corn or not, so just don't." But he would not. He said to the Pharisees in so many words, "Do not make a fuss about trifles. That is not what God cares about. That is not religion. The sabbath was made for man, not man for the sabbath." Almost always people today, when they find great importance attached to some trifle, say, "Well, it is only a trifle after all. It is better to yield on these points." I wonder if it is. I sometimes think that the really important issue is that nobody should be allowed to think that God cares about such little things, about such trifles as whether a person plucks ears of wheat on a Saturday or a Sunday. It is the disfiguring of God in our minds that made Christ so angry, that made him refuse to yield to what we should say was such a little point. After all, he came to reveal God to us, and to be a Christian is to be able to reveal God also to other people. It does not really matter about the rites and ceremonies of religion. I do not say they have no importance. I think they have: they have a psychological importance: they have an importance also from a religious point of view. But they are not the first things.

I think of another friend of mine who became a Christian in very difficult circumstances. Her family practically cut her off, cast her out. She had not much health. She had not much education. But they turned her out and left her to earn her living in a poor state of health, without any training. She really did sacrifice about as much for Christ as most people do! Yet another woman told her she was not really a Christian at all, because she had only been baptized by having a little water poured upon her instead of by total immersion! Is that not un-Christlike? Some people would rule out the whole of the Society of Friends, which has in it some of the best Christians in the world, because they have never been baptized at all. They have only loved God and served their fellow men. They have only done those things which our Lord did all his life, and which he told us were religion.

People come to me who want to join some Christian Church, perhaps they want to join the Church of England, and they take up the Confirmation Service and find they have to believe in the Virgin Birth, and they do not. They do believe in Christ, and they are Christlike. And we have to wonder whether they can stretch their belief enough to fit the creed, instead of stretching their lives enough to fit Christ! Christ only asked of his disciples that they should love him, and to love him is to be like him, because you cannot love a person with whom you have nothing at all in common. If you love anyone, you have something of their spirit. It is true that our Lord loved clear thinking as well. When St. Peter answered that he knew who Jesus was, one can see from the joy with which our Lord hailed his words that he does care that we should care about the truth. But he did not turn to the other disciples and say, "You have not found this out, so you must go away. You have not got the right Christology. You have not given the right answer." He said, that St. Peter had had it revealed to him by the Holy Spirit of God and that gave him joy. But all the disciples loved him, and all of them had a little of his spirit, and that was what he asked of people who were going to follow him.

Do not these other things matter? Yes, of course, they matter. It matters tremendously what you think of Christ. But let us put first things first. To be a Christian is to be like Christ. You may never have heard of Christ. The great Catholic poet of the Middle Ages, Dante, looking for the best in mankind, could not refrain from taking four or five of the great noble pagans who had never heard the name of Jesus Christ and putting them into his purgatory or his paradise because they were souls naturally Christlike. And all over the world there are lovers of Christ who have the spirit of God in them, and have never heard of Jesus of Nazareth. Yes, and there are people here who reject him. I will tell you why they reject him in what is called Christian England. They reject Christ because Christians—so-called Christians—have so misrepresented him. It is as true of them that they have never seen Christ as it was of Plato, or Confucius, or Buddha. It is almost worse, because they have seen Christians—so-called Christians—who are such a caricature of Christ, whose whole idea of religion is bound up with little rules and ceremonies, and who are cruel, and hard, and intolerant to others. It seems to me that these two sets of Christians, the Christians who have never heard of Christ and the Christians who have seen Christ caricatured, and therefore reject him, come under these great sayings of our Lord: "Other sheep I have, which are not of this fold: them also I must bring..., and there shall be one fold, and one shepherd" (John 10:16).

Or again, "Whosoever shall speak a word against the Son of man, it shall be forgiven him: but unto him that blasphemeth against the Holy Spirit, it shall not be forgiven" (Luke 12:10).

Source

A. Maude Royden, *The Friendship of God* (New York: Putnam's Sons, 1924), 103–12.

What Is Prayer?

Prayer, argues Royden, is a request, and as such it points to a desire on the part of the person who prays. But in authentic prayer, the desire is sincere—something we genuinely want—and honest—something we're willing to pay the price of receiving. Many of us pray, for example, for courage or humility. But if we're not willing to embrace the lifestyle changes they would entail, our prayer is neither sincere nor honest. No wonder, then, that it goes unanswered by the God who sees into our hearts.

Prayer is a request: it is asking for something. There are many people who think it is a very childish idea to think of prayer as asking; but I think that that, if they will forgive me for saying so, is juggling with words. To pray is to ask. "I pray you" means, I ask you; and prayer is asking; and everybody who prays asks. A person may ask for a bicycle, or he may ask to pass an examination, or he may ask for the Spirit of God; but whatever it is that he may ask for, prayer means asking. It is "the soul's sincere *desire*." If you contend that prayer is rather that act of communion with God when you cease to ask, when you have come so near to the Divine that your will is one with God, and you ask for nothing, I would say that you are confusing the prayer with the answer. That sense of absolute communion with God, which leaves you nothing to ask for, nothing to desire—that is not prayer; that is the answer to prayer; that is the complete and final and infinite answer to your asking. It is joyfully true that most of us sometimes know that perfect union with God in which we cease to ask. It is true that great saints reach it so often and so easily that they may live in a state of contemplation; but that is because their prayer is answered. It remains true that to pray is to ask. [. . .]

That is my idea of prayer. Is it Christ's? Yes, I think it is. "Ask, and it shall be given unto you; seek, and ye shall find; knock, and it shall be opened unto you" (Matt 7:7). Even though your Father God knows what you want, yet ask! "Your Heavenly Father knoweth what ye have need of before ye ask Him" (Matt 6:8), says Christ; and yet in the same breath He says, "Ask, and ye shall receive" (Matt 7:7). "After this manner, therefore, pray ye: Give us this day our daily bread; forgive us our trespasses as we forgive them that trespass against us; lead us not into temptation, but deliver us from evil" (Matt 6:9–13). One petition after another. Even though God knows what you want, yet ask. And that intensity of asking is the sort of prayer that Christ recognizes as prayer.

There is something further. Prayer is "the soul's *sincere* desire." It may be a desire for something wrong, but yet it is prayer if it is "the soul's sincere desire."

I often judge of what people think of prayer by the way they ask me to pray for them. People will ask for one's prayers as they will ask for a penny; they will ask you to intercede for them as they might ask a millionaire to write them out a cheque for sixpence. People who would hesitate, perhaps, to trouble me to write a letter, who would hesitate to ask me to give them five pounds, will often ask me to pray for them as though it were a little thing. I do not say that any in this congregation would do so. But have you not shared this experience of mine—that people will ask you for your prayers, as though they were asking for nothing? And yet it is hard to pray sincerely, or even to know what is your sincere desire. [. . .]

You ask, perhaps, for courage. But do you really want to do the things that brave people do? Are you sure that if you saw the whole of the way that courage would make you go—are you absolutely certain that you would really want it? You ask for great gifts. You want to be great. Do you know what it costs to serve the world? If you are, for example, a leader, you will have some day to lead, not only where people do not want to go, but where you do not want to go.

Do you really want it at that price? You ask perhaps for humility. I wonder how many people really want it. You know that cynical and witty saying—that "to do good by stealth, and to have it found out by accident is the supreme joy of life." Have you never felt that? You pray for humility. Do you want the fruits of humility? Does not the truth of that cynical and witty saying penetrate into the very recesses of your heart? Do you really want people not to know how good you are, not to be aware how many good deeds you have to your credit? If you were to realize that to be humble would mean, very likely, that you would succeed in hiding from all the world your good deeds, would you continue to pray for humility? You want all the grace of humility with the advantages of advertisement!

Are you really prepared always to pay the price of the thing you ask God for? Is it your soul's sincere desire? I sometimes think that if we were really honest in our prayers we should be constrained to ask, not that we might be brave, or humble, or chaste, but that we might wish to be so. We should realize that we do not reach the ear and heart of God with our prayers because He knows we are not asking for what we want. We think we are, but He sees into our hearts. That slow, devastating knowledge of oneself that comes when one strives a little to be honest with oneself only reveals what He has known all the time. [. . .]

Do not say you have prayed when you have not sincerely desired. And if you want a test easier to apply than the test of the psychologist or the psychoanalyst, try the test of Jesus Christ. "A certain man heard of a treasure in a field, and with great joy he sold all that he had and bought that field. A certain merchant heard of a pearl of great price, and he sold all the other pearls he had, and bought that pearl" (Matt 13:44–45). If your prayer is the prayer of a sincere desire, you will pay the price for it. If you are not prepared to pay the price for it, then it is not a sincere desire.

It is then no longer rational—is it?—to say to me "What is the use of prayer?" What is the use of prayer? How can you help praying if prayer is the soul's sincere desire? "If God knows already that we want these things, why should we pray for them?" someone asks. How can you prevent yourself praying? If this platitude about "sincere desire" is, in fact, not a platitude, but a searching truth, you cannot help praying. Why should a scientist desire truth? Because he does. Why do you desire spiritual things? Because you do. There is no other reason. And that desire is your prayer. That is praying, though you do not always know it. If you will be quite honest with yourself, you may find, for instance, that you dare not ask God to accept you because you do not know what He will do with you; you dare not ask Him to take your life into His hands because you do not know what He is going to use it for; you dare not ask to be shown the way because you have realized that there are ways that are too hard for you to follow. Instead, then, of going on your knees and glibly asking God to show you the way when you have not the courage to follow it; instead of asking Him to possess your life when you know that He may ask you to do things that you do not really intend to do, be content to ask Him to give you the desire for these things. Do not ask for what you do not really want, and then go about and say that God does not hear your prayers. "Ask, and ye shall receive; seek, and ye shall find; knock, and it shall be opened unto you" (Matt 7:7). That is certain. The hypocrites love to pray standing in the synagogue and at the corners of the streets that they may be seen of men. "Verily I say unto you that they have their reward" (Matt 6:2), says Christ. And so have we all. If we are not prepared to pay the price of the thing we ask for, ours is not really prayer at all. Pray rather that we may be ready to pay the price. Many of us can get as far as that. We think we know what we are praying for; too often we do not; but God does. Behind the clamor of our words, behind the clamor of the prayer with which we besiege the throne of God, behind all the noise and din, God hears the voice of our sincere desire, and that prayer He both hears and answers.

Source

A. Maude Royden, *Prayer as a Force* (New York: Putnam's Sons, 1923), 27–28, 29–30, 31–33, 33–35.

Christ's Law

In this sermon, Royden points out that although we sometimes believe and hope that we can control God through our petitions and prayers—that God, as she says, is "capricious"—none of us really would find such a deity desirable. At least in our better moments, we know that God's unchangeableness is a blessing, because God is love. That love was incarnated in Jesus Christ who, through his life and teachings, supersedes the Ten Commandments, "dead things" that "condemn our failure." The Law of Love endows us with creative and salvific power.

The saints have believed in the trustworthiness of God, "with whom is no variableness, neither shadow cast by turning" (Jas 1:17); the world has never believed it. Only now and then have men caught a glimpse of the great truth that God is changeless and that His changelessness is our peace.

    For the most part we have both believed and hoped that God might be capricious. We know of no man so good that we should wish him never in any particular to change, and, making God in our own image, we hope that, God though He be, we shall persuade Him—as a sincere and eloquent pleader might persuade one of us—to be a little better, to change His mind. We wish He might be at times more merciful, more full of compassion to us when we think we need it more; or more relentless and less pitiful to our enemies, who, we fear, may be besieging His throne of grace with their impious and unwarrantable petitions at the very hour of our own prayers.

    We should, then, find it easy to believe both that God is unchanging and that His unchangingness is not terrible or relentless, but merciful. We should by now be finding it difficult to believe anything else. How could God, who is One, be changeless in a material universe and capricious elsewhere? Why do we still try by prayer to change the mind of God, and, when we fail, speak of "resigning ourselves to His inscrutable will"? Christ taught us not to be "resigned" to the will of God, but actively to carry it out. Even in the Old Testament we are called upon to understand God—"Come now, let us reason together, said the Lord God" (Is 1:18); to stand upon our feet—"Son of man, stand upon thy feet, and I will speak to thee" (Ezek 2:1). How strange that in the twentieth century people should still be found to sing "Thy will be done" as a sort of refrain or chorus to verses containing a list of frightful misfortunes, each of which, it is implied, must be "endured" as coming from the hand of God; when the words used ("Thy will be done") were uttered by our Lord Himself as a promise that where the will of God is done, there the kingdom of God is established, so as to make a heaven on earth.

Christ appeals to His disciples continually to understand His teaching—not to be resigned to His inscrutable will. He told His hearers that those who failed to live by His teaching were foolish—not that they were wicked.

Where is the law written down that we may learn it and obey it? The Ten Commandments? Surely this is not all! They do not satisfy us, neither do they give us that power over life and over ourselves that we so long for and so worship in Christ. These codes of law, lofty though they may be, solve nothing for us. They are dead things. They do not help in their own fulfillment; they only condemn our failure. "All these have I obeyed from my youth up: what lack I yet?" (Matt 19:20).

We lack Christ. The law is nothing to us until it is lived. The Ten Commandments solve no mystery of life, pain, or perplexity for us. Christ superseded them with a law which is love and of which love is the only fulfillment. He lived this law of Love among men, bore suffering as ourselves; and we beheld His glory, the glory as of the only begotten Son of the Father, full of grace and truth.

Laws are not enough for us. We want a life to show them in action and in power. We want to see the One who proclaims the law live in perfect obedience to that law without once seeking to break, evade, or suspend it; and we want to see that, in fact, what He said was true—that such obedience is power, such service perfect freedom.

We must try to enter into Christ's mind. We must seek the meaning behind His words. How could we do this unless we had a life to illustrate the law? How could He trust us to do it if He Himself had written a book? We should have sat down to read the book and get the law by rote! Now we must both read the books His followers wrote and try to understand the spirit of the Man of whom they were written.

Christ, the great Master of life, moved among men as a conqueror. For myself, I believe that He both healed the sick and raised the dead, calmed the storm and rose on Easter Sunday from the grave; but even for those to whom these are mere fairy tales there remains the supreme miracle of the life of Christ—the change He made in the hearts of men. In a short life of from thirty to thirty-three or -four years, this man of lowly birth, without wealth or influence or powerful backing, so changed the history of the world that we date now every event in its history by its distance in time from His Coming. "Before or after Christ"—such is the dating of all our records. Christ cut the history of the world in half.

And this He did by no use of force or of wealth; neither the fear of armies nor of magic entered into His appeal. He achieved all by love. The precepts of conduct which, in cold words, sound either fantastic or unmanly, He made real and glorious by His own life. He gave to all who asked and He lacked nothing. He met hatred with love and unbelief with an authority which owed nothing to astonishing feats of magic. He never defended Himself, and we see in Him the bravest of the brave. He took the sword out of the hand of His friend and went like a lamb to the slaughter, and we cry in admiration, "Behold the Man!" (John 19:5).

It is useless to argue that Christ's laws can never be carried out, for He carried them out Himself; to protest that they are inconsistent with themselves, for the utter consistency of Christ silences the protest on our lips; useless to complain that they are unmanly, for no man ever was so gloriously and perfectly a Man.

It is only when we see how patience and courtesy and "non-resistance" look in Jesus Christ that we realize how empty is the mere commandment—how powerless without the living Example. This only deepens for us our knowledge and belief in Christ's assurance that God is Love. To turn the other cheek! To endure all things, to believe all things—how pitiful it sounds in the ears of the noble, sagacious, and courageous pagan! But when he sees all these in Christ, can he despise them any more? They may seem too high for him—they cannot seem too low for him. They may be set aside as too hard—they can never again be utterly despised.

And so it happens that nearly all men have loved Jesus, though not all worship Him. If God is Love, it is more important to love than to believe, for it is only love which has power to create us in its own image. God is Love.

Here, again, life is based on universal, immutable law. Not Eloi alone, four thousand and four years before Christ, created man in his own image, but Love (which is God) always and everywhere does this. We become, by irresistible compelling, like what we love. This is true of the least as of the greatest. So, loving Christ, we learn to live as He lived and to obey the laws which He obeyed. Law is no longer a dead and empty thing, serving only to condemn us for our failure to keep it: it is a loving power, enabling us to obey.

Thus Christ was the Word of God, creative and creating in God's image according to His words. "And the Word was made flesh, and dwelt among us (and we beheld His glory, the glory as of the only begotten Son of the Father), full of grace and truth" (John 1:14).

Source

A. Maude Royden, "The Trustworthiness of God," in *The World's Great Sermons*, ed. S. E. Frost Jr. (Garden City, NY: Garden City, 1942), 310–12.

Divine Personhood

THERE'S NO GREATER JOY, *asserts Royden, than friendship. This being so, she asks if it's possible to be friends with God. Some people, she concedes, say no. They believe that presuming otherwise reduces God's majestic grandeur to a human level. But her response is that everything which exists comes from the "mind of God," and since personalities exist, God must in some way contain within himself personality. The doctrine of the Trinity gestures at this truth. It is a mistake to think of God's personhood as equivalent to human personhood. There will always be something ineffable about it. But the fact that God in some sense can be thought of in personal terms means that it's entirely possible to enter into a friendship with God—although, again, not identical to friendships between humans.*

To be in the relation of friendship with one who knows all our goodness and all our badness, and, knowing it with a clearness of vision that we can never attain ourselves, yet loves us, gives us a sense of deep security and peace. After all, there is no joy on earth like that joy; nor should we resent the pain that comes of being rebuked, because of the happiness of being wholly understood.

For all of us such friendship is possible. It is the friendship of God. I speak of something which to many of you here seems to put too human an interpretation on the idea of God. God, you think, is something more than personality. He is not personal, he is "immortal, invisible, inaccessible, hid from our eyes."[1] He is the principle of creation; he is the principle behind the universe. To imagine that you can have with him the intimate relationship of a friend is, to some of you, to attribute to him the limitations of human personality, and the conditioned character which we are accustomed to associate with personality. And unless God is in

---

1. "Immortal, Invisible, God Only Wise" (1867), hymn by Walter C. Smith. (KW)

some sense personal, to talk of friendship with him in any real sense is absurd. There is no such relationship as you and I mean by friendship, certainly nothing at all like that which our Lord had with his disciples, between the absolute principle behind the universe, and you and me. Such a relationship is impossible; and, in fact, if you pursue the thought a little further, I believe you will ultimately come to the conclusion that no relationship at all is possible between ourselves and a wholly impersonal God. Even in that lovely Christian hymn we sang just now,[2] how many negatives there are about God—*not* mortal, *not* visible, *not* accessible, *not* resting, *not* hasting, and so on—because when we think of God as Absolute Being, we cannot describe him in anything but negatives. He is not limited, he is not conditioned by any of the things we know, he is not visible, he is not changing; and in the end you will realize, I think, by such a process as that, that he is not anything you can think about at all, and you become in the highest and purest sense of the word an atheist. You are reduced to the thought of absolute negation; and no one can think a negation. God is none of the things we know, and so he passes beyond our thought altogether, although we may still affirm that something is there, that there is a vast creative principle, an absolute God; but since we cannot think of him in any terms whatever, we are not able to think of him at all. The purest form of such a religion is, of course, Buddhism. This is not true of popular Buddhism as practiced and believed by the ordinary average Buddhist, who like the ordinary average Christian, is probably no theologian. But in fact the denial to God of all attributes which the human mind can realize, ends in atheism.

Now it is not possible for there to be anything in creation which does not come from the mind of God. (I have to use such human terms as "the mind of God" because, as Dr. Stanley Mellor says, when we speak of things ineffable, we stammer.)[3] Nothing is here, then, which is not in the mind of God. If you and I are persons, then personality must exist, must be included, in the Godhead. To imagine otherwise is to imagine an impossibility. There cannot be anything which has not come forth from God, and that which comes forth from him must be of his own nature. If you and I are personalities God must include personality, and if we had always spoken of him and thought of him as including personality, and not as being "a person," probably that truth would never have been lost

---

2. "Immortal, Invisible, God Only Wise." (KW)
3. Stanley A. Mellor, English Unitarian pastor and socialist. (KW)

sight of. Christianity has done its best to keep us in mind of that great principle in the doctrine of the Holy Trinity, and this is Trinity Sunday. What does the Trinity mean? It sounds an academic question, and I could give you some very academic replies. But the doctrine of the Trinity is no academic or purely intellectual puzzle, no invention of hair-splitting theologians; it is a doctrine which you will find in the greatest religions of the world. Surely that is because it is not a figment of the intellect but an eternal truth. When humanity arrives at the point of developing a great spiritual religion, it produces a doctrine like the doctrine of the Trinity. What is at the heart of it? God is not "a Person," and whoever says so is heretical. God is absolute; he is infinite; he is something infinitely greater than a person, although he includes personality. The way in which this can be most easily expressed is to say that he is one God, but three Persons; a Trinity like Beauty, Truth, and Goodness, like body, soul, and spirit, like many other fundamental things. Three is a mystic number expressing the infinite and immeasurable. Deity is three Persons in one God. In the Godhead, therefore, there is included that wonderful thing which we call "personality," and it is included in a sense far beyond our imagination. Personality is not less in the Godhead than in us. It is, there, more wonderful, more complex, than we, with our limited little minds, can possibly imagine. All that we can do is to put it in this mystical form and say that God is Three in One, and One in Three, and that his being does indeed include that which is the highest thing we know, although we know it in so imperfect a form—personality.

In our greatest moments we can sometimes, not indeed comprehend, but apprehend the Eternal and the Absolute. Our souls perceive the absolute and eternal God. "No man hath seen God at any time" (John 1:18), but all of us have the instinct of perceiving God sometimes, in perfect love, in perfect beauty. Suddenly there is flashed upon us the sense that there is "a depth beyond the depth and a height beyond the height, our hearing is not hearing, and our seeing is not sight." For a moment we have been with the absolute, the eternal God. These are our highest moments. For the rest—we live in time and space.

There are people who in their anxiety to escape from the irreverence and stupidity of thinking of God as a human being put aside the very idea of friendship with God, and deny themselves the sense of his intimate affection for each of us, thinking, "How is it possible that the absolute God should know or care about anything so small as myself?" Have not all of you felt that sometimes? You have griefs and difficulties which mean everything to you, and perhaps tradition and custom teach you to bring those problems to God; but then there sweeps over you the sense of God's infinite power, and your own microscopically small concerns, and you feel that it is a folly to suppose that your little human affairs can be of any interest to God.

When we try in that way to escape from too human an idea of God, we are really falling into it more deeply than ever. We not only think of God as a man, but as that very odious kind of person, a busy man, a man who is too great and important to see anyone but the heads of departments! He has the universe to look after; how can he look after you and me? He is such a busy person! But is it not the most elementary form of anthropomorphism to think of God in terms of size? If God is absolute and unconditional, the fact that you and your affairs are small, and the universe large has no meaning to him. All things are equally dear and equally present in his mind, and to think otherwise is to attribute to God, not only personality, which you are trying to escape from, but the narrow limitations of human personality. I believe intensely in that personality which God includes, and my religion is the worship of a personal God. The moments that I perceive God as absolute are few indeed compared with those when I think of him as a Friend. But if I were to think of him as a Friend who was sometimes too busy for things so infinitesimally small as myself, I should be thinking of him, not only as a human, but as a most deplorable type of human. Even we who live in time and space rebel against the limitations which make it impossible for us to love all the world, and to make a friend of every person whose friendship we desire. To think of God as though he were so conditioned were anthropomorphism indeed. Even we ourselves hope to transcend such limitations someday.

So I beseech you to think whether it is not possible that in the mind of God greatness and smallness, as we think of them, do not exist, just because, although he includes personality, he is absolute and unconditioned, and time and space to him are nothing. We are small indeed compared with the great world. And the world, how small in the vast universe! What ranks and ranks of existences there are, so great that we cannot see them, so small that we cannot think them! At what point does the infinite God begin to think that things are too big, or too small to be noticed? How big must you be to catch his eye? There is no size in the mind of God, and when you approach God as friend be sure that your affairs are as dear to him as the sustaining of the universe. "Oh, taste and see how gracious the Lord is" (Ps 34:8).

So gracious is he that some have even claimed that they were God's favorites—that God has singled them out for special favor. That idea is repulsive to us; but think what it means. It means that when you take God for your friend you become conscious of a care so exquisite, an understanding so real, that if you are not a very great person you easily fall into the mistake of thinking that God is taking special care of you. It is a childish mistake. It is the mistake of egotism which is the characteristic of a child. But you see how it arises. Look at the experience of the saints, and you will find that they experienced a sense of tenderness and care and understanding; they walked and talked with God as Friend, so that it was almost pardonable that they should think of themselves as more the friends of God than other people. Such a friendship brings such peace that those who know it, even in the least way, desire beyond anything to proclaim it to the world. For the friends of God know his peace which passeth understanding. They are lifted above jealousy, resentment, and anxiety. They suffer—God forbid that any human being should *not* suffer—when human friends have failed them or they have failed their friends, but their suffering is not to the death of the soul, and in the sanctuary of their being is peace.

Source

A. Maude Royden, *The Friendship of God* (New York: Putnam's Sons, 1924), 21–28.

God's Non-Coercive Love

For Royden, moral freedom, our ability to choose, is the "noblest thing about us." One of the defining characteristics of love is that it respects that freedom. Consequently, God—who is Love—will never coerce us to believe in Him, much less to love Him. We may at times desire such coercion because we fear freedom: Make us believe in you, God! Make us love you and our fellows! Tell us what to do! But God refrains, willing to endure what our freedom inflicts on him, out of love. It could so easily have gone the other way, because the continuous temptation of love is to coerce for the beloved's own good. Our frequent misuse of love attests to that. God, however, is eternally patient.

A quality which Christ shows to all human beings and not to his friends only is reverence for a person's reserves, for their freedom, for their personality, which human beings do not always show, even to those they love best. Indeed, perhaps they show it least—unless they are very careful—to the people they love best.

Our Lord never forced people to do what they thought was not right, or to do what they could not see a reason for doing; or even to believe in him. I suppose most of us feel that in that first great scene in his life when he was tempted—what form the temptation took, what lies behind the dramatic narrative, we do not know—that one of the things that he was tempted to do was to use his amazing moral and spiritual power to strike people's imaginations, to do something extraordinary, to use some astonishing power in order to force himself at once on their notice. He was only a carpenter—a person without position and without wealth—and his one advantage was his great spiritual power. No doubt the temptation that came to him was to use that power in order so to strike the imagination of the world as to give him an instant advantage in dealing with it. He put that on one side, and evidently he put it on one side forever. For it is perfectly clear that our Lord dreaded impressing people by some mighty work in such a way as to silence their doubts and to stun their imagination. He saw people beginning to follow him because he did mighty works or miracles. He began to be reluctant to work them. He seemed to withdraw himself. The power which Christians have regarded—and rightly—as one of the proofs of his greatness, he was anxious not to use in that way. He reproached people for being so easily impressed: he was sensitive for their freedom and judgment, for what he wanted was a moral judgment. He was afraid of their regarding a miracle as a kind of conjuring trick and thinking of him as a magician. He was so respectful of their intellectual freedom and their moral judgment that he would not allow them, if he could help it, to be stunned into acquiescence, to have their imaginations so seized that they forgot the deeper things that he was talking about. He did not want to gain their assent or their belief in him by any kind of spectacular advertisement, by any kind of conjuring trick.

This is, however, a very subtle temptation to most of us. We like very often to capture people's imagination or to violate their freedom, to win their judgment by some ways that we hardly realize are a little illegitimate, or not quite fair to the person we are trying to convince. Still we do realize as a principle that people should be free to judge, to judge for themselves, even to make their own mistakes. It was better for Judas to reject Christ than to accept him because he could exercise some magical power. It was better for Peter to fail than for our Lord so to hold him up and coerce his moral judgment that he ceased to be a free person at all.

Parents—especially mothers—know that it is one of the most difficult things to let a child tumble and risk hurting itself. Every moment she wants to run after it and catch it, so that it shall be safe. But she lets it risk hurting itself because it must learn to run. It is not even a risk, it is a certainty. It *will* hurt itself; it *will* fall down. You have to let it fall sometimes. You have to let it make its own mistakes, and the mother who is always catching her child up out of danger is not really the one who is wisest or most loving, any more than are parents who, when their children grow up, will not give them freedom, will not allow them to have a chance to make their own mistakes, who hold them back by the power of their authority, or their purse, or by that still more dread power of their love and gratitude. It is not the most loving parent who will not give his son or his daughter a chance to make their own mistakes.

When you bring children into the world you run a risk, but it is not the people who love children who abstain from having them because they are afraid the children may hurt them, or may hurt themselves, or may do what is wrong when they grow up. I talk of the risk, but again it is not a risk; it is a certainty. You choose it because you love children, because you love them so much that you are prepared to suffer what their freedom may inflict on you. The father who lets the prodigal son take his portion and go away and spend it, would, I suppose, seem to some people very unwise; but he was not. I have known rescue workers tell me sometimes they have to let a girl go.[1] They have done everything in their power to keep her, but the point comes when they must allow her to go, and let her come back of herself if she will. That costs something! But they are surely right. We are learning more and more how reluctant we should be to coerce, but the more we love people the harder it is, for love has a terrible power of coercion.

We can by appealing to love, by appealing to gratitude, by appealing to the rights of a parent or the rights of a friend, make our love a tyranny. Years ago a very witty play called *The Tyranny of Tears* was put on the stage.[2] In it a wife exercised a tyranny over her husband by bursting into tears every time she wanted anything. That is the sort of thing some people do over and over again. They tell you how terribly they are grieving, how much they are hurt. They are not angry, but they are pained, and really the person who is pained is almost impossible! Consequently, you give way, but with such a sense of outrage, such a sense of resentment, because that person has used the most sacred power on earth not to guide you, not to inspire you, not to help you, but to force you, to coerce you; and that is a thing love should never do.

So if we are wise, we try to set our friends and our children free, and we know that that freedom is the mark of nobility in human nature. It is our freedom to give love or to withhold love, to serve or to withhold our services, that makes our help and love worth anything. Otherwise, what is it? It is not possible to force love: but if it were, who would value it? It is because someone gives it to you that it is so lovely. That is why a child's love is so indescribably touching; because a child has no reason whatever

---

1. The "rescue workers" Royden refers to here helped prostitutes find alternate ways of making a living. (KW)

2. C. Haddon Chambers's (1860–1921) comedy *The Tyranny of Tears* premiered in 1899. (KW)

to show love for you except that it really does love. Freedom makes both the happiness and the nobility of human beings.

Yet there is no gift of which Humanity is more afraid than its own freedom. There were slaves who fought against their own enfranchisement in the American Civil War. There were women who refused their political freedom in the fight for the suffrage. Everywhere, where people are enslaved, or oppressed, or subject, there will be among them those who prefer that state of being, to freedom. So, among human beings, there are many who desire that they should be coerced by God. They want to know what they are to do, what they are to think, what they are to be. I remember a clergyman once said to me that I should not complain so much about the jack-in-office attitude of some of the clergy if I knew how hard it was to escape it. He said people come to him and say, "What shall I think about so-and-so?" and he says, "What do you think?" They say, "Oh, I want you to tell me!" And one is tempted to say, "Think this, or that, or the other, only go away!"

The attitude of mind which says, "Please tell me what to think, what to be, what to aim at, what to do," is the slave still lingering in the human heart. It is the slavish desire to escape responsibility, to escape the dangers of freedom, to escape the risk of making mistakes, which asks, "Why does not God prevent war? Why does not God reveal himself so that I can understand? If he is speaking to me, why does he not make me hear? Why does he not make me love him? Force me to understand? If he is comprehensible why has not he given me the power with which to understand?" It sounds very reasonable, and I suppose there is no more universal charge against God than the fact that he does not force us, will not work the miracle which would coerce our judgment, any more than Christ would come down from the cross in order that those who stood around should see and believe.

"Let Christ the King of Israel descend from the cross *that we may see and believe*" (Mark 15:32). Well, if he had come down, would they have believed? Yes, I think they would. What an amazing miracle! Here was a man nailed to the cross, coming down to the ground. Who, indeed, could stop to argue about it? Whose imagination would not be stunned by it? Whose reason would not be suborned? Who would be able to ask himself, "Is this the kind of moral miracle that you expect of God?" Who, in the presence of such a miracle, would not have been silenced? For an hour or two. And then? Then they would have found themselves doubtful. They would have said, "There was some mistake. We were drunk; we were mad. It did not really happen. He was not really nailed to the cross at all. There was some jugglery. The executioners were bribed." And belief would have died. Would the world have believed? There would have been some story perhaps, of an obscure execution in Palestine, of some man who by jugglery or bribery was able to escape death. Do you think you would have believed that this took place, two thousand years ago, or been moved by it if you did believe? It was by dying on the cross that Christ moved the world, because then he appealed to love and with love, as love alone can appeal. Had he descended from the cross, that miracle would have undone all his work. The world would never have been moved by a conjurer. It was because he stayed there that the world has been moved to its very heart by Jesus Christ.

Do you see the difference? The one method would have been a spectacular attack on the intelligence, an attempt to force a judgment, to make us believe. It is as though you should knock a man down and stun him and then appeal to his intellect! If such a miracle had taken place it would have stunned the reason. But the appeal that Christ made was something which could only be prejudiced by such a miracle. The world would have passed by, and rightly, saying, "This has nothing to do with us. It is a trick." But by staying there, hanging on the cross, Christ made that eternal appeal to which the heart responds as it knows how. The thief on the one hand sees the Son of God, and the other thief sees only a more contemptible convict than himself. One soldier cries out, "Verily this was the Son of God" (Matt 27:54), and another, sitting at the foot of the cross, plays dice for his clothes. Half the world sees in this Christ a visionary and a dreamer, and the other half sees in him God. But the appeal to all is the same and must eternally be the same. It is to a moral issue and to your power of judging a moral issue. It is no attempt on the part of God to take your personality and force you, stun you, into acquiescence. It is an appeal to your free judgment, and you respond to it as you choose.

When we have crucified God, we say, "Come down from the cross. Do something astonishing. Force us to believe in you if you want us to believe." Do you not see this is what love can never do? It is not love if it does. So God himself was on the cross when Jesus Christ was crucified two thousand years ago and now is. He is "the Lamb slain from the foundations of the world" (Rev 13:8). He is crucified when one man is shot a few hundred yards from here, or when a negro boy is lynched in Georgia. Wherever human beings suffer, they suffer their own little suffering— hard enough, God knows, to bear. But he is crucified for and in all, and we ask, "Why does he not come down and make us act more reasonably and nobly? Why does he not force us to believe in him?" Why? Do you not know that that moral freedom of yours to choose or reject God is the noblest thing about you? The animals, it has been said, dream of moral responsibility; the plants, a little lower on the slopes of life, are still asleep, safe from suffering and from freedom. But we are called to the high ascent, to higher acts of moral freedom. Is it for us to say to God, "This gift that you gave us we do not desire"? That is the plea of the slave within us! It is the everlasting coward that shrinks from freedom.

We indeed cannot understand the awful patience of God, but that is because we do not love enough, not because he loves too little. There are people who cannot understand the love of a mother which survives every kind of cruelty and ingratitude. It is to them incomprehensible. They say she ought to cast her son off. But she does not—not because she does not love him, but because she does. I sometimes think that a son who is won back by his parents' love and sees in their ravaged faces what his redemption has cost them who brought him into the world and gave him his freedom, must understand a little of what the love of God costs him, who does not destroy us when we starve Russia,[3] who does not destroy us because he loves us with a love that we cannot begin to understand.

We get a glimpse of it in the love of our friends who help us merely by loving us. Thus do they show us the love of God. Have you ever loved anyone? Well, then, what did your love do for them? Has anyone ever loved you? What has their love done for you? It is not that they have made you do this, or that, or the other. It is—what is it? How can one put into words what love does for a human being? Will you not say to your friend, "It is not what you do for me. It is not what you give to me. It is just that you do love me." That is all. One cannot get any further, but we know that such a love is everything and all the world to us, quite apart from anything our friends do. For love itself does everything.

So is it with the love of God. That he does not force you does not mean that he does nothing for you. The fact that he loves you, like the fact that your friend loves you, does everything. Why, if your friend could not do anything to help but love you, would not you say to him, "The fact

---

3. The Russian famine of 1921–22, caused by Lenin's policy of farm collectivization, resulted in the deaths of at least five million. Although England and the United States eventually donated food supplies, especially grain, to the Soviet Union, they were initially reluctant to do anything that would bolster the communist government. This heel-dragging is what Royden refers to here. (KW)

that you love me is everything"? What else God does we cannot know or measure, but the fact that he loves us implies and involves all the rest.

Here is the world. Look at it. Russia is starving, and people say: "Why does not God give food to Russia?" In the *Manchester Guardian* I remember reading a report of a Russian woman who said, on hearing that America was heaped high with corn, "What kind of a god is it that gives corn in America and lets us starve in Russia?" Well, when people are starving they say anything. But English people know that there are millions of bushels of corn on one side of the world and ships lined up for lack of work, while there are starving people in Russia. Then they say to one another, "Why does not God feed Russia?" Why do not *we* feed Russia? Is God to force us by some moral conjuring trick to love and care when we do not love or care? Is he to make us puppets? This is what we are continually asking, with our strange and horrible fear of freedom. I call it horrible, for surely it is a betrayal of the best in us to ask that God should force us to do this and that.

"Let him teach us," some of you say, "to understand him." I tell you that his meaning and his purpose are written right over the universe. They blaze in the stars, they sound in the waves of the sea. He has written so that only the blind cannot see. "If that is so," you say, "then we are blind. God should make us see." We make this world into disorder and say, "Now we cannot see God." We shut our eyes, and then we say we cannot see God.

If you misuse your powers you lose them. If you will not see God, if you do not care to see him, if you let your mind be guided by anything except God, you do lose the power of seeing him, and it would be moral coercion to "make you see" him. You know, I suppose, that almost everyone is born with a fairly correct ear for music, yet if some of you were to go to learn to sing and you sang out of tune, you would say, "I have no ear." But your singing master very likely would say to you, "You cannot sing in tune in the middle register of your voice because you have always sung and sung badly in the middle register. All the popular songs and choruses and hymns are written for the middle notes. You ruin the middle notes of your voice, so that you cannot any longer sing these notes properly; but the notes you did not use—the high and low notes—you can use quite well because you have not spoilt them." So it is not your ear that is at fault, or not at the beginning. It is simply the way in which you have misused your voice and your ear by careless singing. We misuse our power of seeing moral issues also. We confuse our moral judgment. We are indifferent to our spiritual sight, and then our sight gets blurred and we cannot see God. Then comes the time when we say, "If God wants me to understand him, why doesn't He make me understand him? If he is speaking to me, why doesn't he force me to hear him?" He gave you eyes to see him, ears to hear, a spiritual sense to discern him with; but he will never invade the will and *force* you to hear. He will not coerce your judgment and *make* you understand.

> Sure, he that made us with such large discourse,
> Looking before and after, gave us not
> This capability and godlike reason
> To fust in us unused.[4]

I believe that everyone who has heard the voice of God will agree with me in saying that they have a sense that they had been hearing it all the time. If you try to find God and you find him, you will suddenly realize that he was there all the time, and not only that he was there, but that you knew he was. If you were traveling to the sea and suddenly you heard the sound of the sea, you would realize that it had been sounding a long time, and that in some unconscious depths of your being you had heard it. When it breaks in upon your understanding, you know you heard it long ago. So when you suddenly see God, or for a moment hear his voice, it comes with a sense that you had heard it before, but it was in the unconscious depths of your being, and you were so busy with other things, so distracted with other thoughts, that that sounding voice was shut out from your consciousness. It was there all the time. Yes, and you heard it all the time. But it is only when you give yourself to hearing it that you know you hear it. It is that last act—not that God does not speak to you, not that you do not hear, but that you realize you hear—it is that last act of giving which you must do. God himself cannot do it unless he is to destroy your moral judgment altogether. He never ceases to speak to you; you never cease to have ears to hear, nerves to carry the message, a brain to understand; but you can, if you like, shut out that sound. You may become oblivious of the crash of the waves of the sea. And that last act of the will, which is the realization of that eternal sound, that is for you to make, and God himself cannot force you to hear without destroying your moral freedom.

Anything less than the eternal patience of God, and your moral judgment would cease to exist. Your personality would be stunned by

---

4. Shakespeare, *Hamlet*, 4.4. (KW)

the greatness of God. Does not it ever strike you what infinite fineness there must be in the love of God that he does wait for you to "come to yourself"? What eternal, what amazing love, that God can look upon this world and see the use that we have made of our freedom and the way we torture each other and ourselves. Every blow we strike at our brother is a blow at the heart of God, and yet he leaves us free, yet he waits and suffers and we cry out that this eternal patience is the proof of his indifference. "Come down," we say, "from the cross that we may see and believe." I suppose it is really because we cannot understand a love that never varies that the love of God seems to us non-existent. But those who love surely must be able to explain to the world how love uses its power, how it gives us all we have that is worth having, how all human joy and all human nobility depends on the freedom which love allows. We shall understand at last that it is the slave in us which cries out to eternal Love to force us to understand, to compel us to listen. "Come down from the cross that we may see and believe."

Source

A. Maude Royden, *The Friendship of God* (New York: Putnam's Sons, 1924), 86–101.

Two Sides, Same Truth

THERE'S A TENDENCY, NOTICEABLE in both individual Christians and at different historical periods, to emphasize either Christ's power and triumph during his ministry—his healings, his miracles, the positive effect his very presence had on people—or his powerless humiliation, torture, and death on the Cross. The two versions can be labeled the Easter Sunday Christ and the Good Friday Christ. Royden argues here that we ought not to choose one over the other, as if they are conflicting claims, but that we need to see them as "two sides of the same truth." Christ's crucifixion, she argues, is a moment of supreme triumph and glory, a genuine sign by which we know the world of death and sin is conquered.

When one speaks of "the meaning of the Cross today," many are inclined to ask, "Is not the meaning of the Cross always the same? How can it vary from one generation to another?" And, of course, in a sense, it *is* always the same. It is a fundamental and a universal truth. But on the other hand, Christian people have thought about the Crucifixion of Christ, and of the meaning of the Cross to us individually, in very different ways from one age to another. In the early days of the Church, although the Cross itself was always one of the fundamentals of the Christian religion, and Christians used to make the sign of the Cross as a sign of their faith, yet the actual fact of the Crucifixion seems to have held in their minds a different place, or received a different emphasis, from that which it has received in later ages.

In early Christian art there are no representations at all of our Lord upon the Cross. The earliest representations of Christ are of a young man, young and beautiful, and obviously not intended to be realistic at all. They are not portraits of the historical Jesus of Nazareth. They are representations of the Good Shepherd, and are symbolical—not realistic.

Often the symbol of a fish was used or the symbol of the Cross itself. Nowhere do we find in the earliest Christian art any representation of our

Lord on the Cross. This is the more remarkable because in some of those great Christian churches of the early centuries the designers have sought to present to the congregation in a series of pictures the whole story of the salvation of man.

Many of you no doubt know those great churches in Sicily where are some of the earliest and most glorious works of Christian art; where the entire church is, like the church of St. Mark's in Venice, an open Bible, a representation of the Christian faith for those who could not read (for, of course, the vast majority of the worshippers in those churches could not read), and therefore the artist sought to present in the church itself the open Bible of their faith. He begins in the vestibule of the church with some of the earliest scenes from the Old Testament and then as we come into the church, the whole is spread out like a great picture book before us. Along the sides, on the lower part of the wall, are scenes from the Old Testament, foretelling the coming of our Lord; prophets, sybils (pagan prophetesses of our Lord's coming) and historical scenes, which were connected in the people's minds with the coming of Christ. Then along the upper part of the wall of the church are scenes from the New Testament and, at the end of the church, probably the Last Judgment and the Resurrection, and a great figure of our Lord himself, filling the space which in a Gothic church is filled by the east window. In the great mosaic churches the east end is an apse, and the whole curve of the apse is filled with a gigantic representation of our Lord, so full of power and dignity, so awe-inspiring, so glorious that when one goes into the church the entire building seems dominated by that great figure. It dwarfs everything else. It throws everything else into insignificance. It stands as the culminating point of what is called "the scheme of salvation," which began with the pictures at the west end of the church.

That vast picture book of the Christian faith which was, remember, the only book of those who came in, the one book from which they could learn the elements of their Christian faith, has not anywhere, from one end of the church to the other, any representation of the Crucifixion. It is called "the scheme of salvation," and Christ is the central and dominating fact in this history of the salvation of the world. Every incident in the scheme of salvation is there, with this extraordinary exception: there is no picture of our Lord on the Cross.

In later centuries, if there is only one picture in a church, or one carving, it is a picture or a carving of a crucifix. In those old Sicilian churches, modern Roman Catholic art has placed crucifixes, tortured and defeated Christs, hanging upon a cross, horribly realistic, full of pain and the sense of brokenness and defeat. But the original church had no crucified Christ at all.

That is one of the paradoxes that we are trying to solve today. We modern Christians hear a great deal about this risen, triumphant, victorious Christ. Christian Science, and New Thought, and Higher Thought,[1] and all those other schools of thought—many of them deeply imbued with Christian doctrine if not actually Christian in name—all emphasize, as did the early Church, the risen and triumphant Christ. For it is Christ in glory, Christ in triumph, Christ in power, that you find in those early churches. Christ healing the sick, raising the dead, walking on the waters, feeding the multitude, in picture after picture, in early Christian art; and today once more Christianity is presented to us in the same way. We are beginning to escape from the overwhelming sense of the defeat of Christ, from the overwhelming shadow of the Cross, and we are turning back to the risen and glorified Christ who so deeply impressed the first Christians and the early Church—impressed them so deeply that they actually left Christ crucified out of their churches altogether.

Look at the first records of our Christian faith, and you will get very much the same impression. It is not from the Gospels that we get this overwhelming sense of the torture and the failure of Christ on the Cross. If you read with a fresh mind, many of you will be amazed to realize how tremendous is the sense of power conveyed to us by the Gospel record. Sometimes I think that if we could entirely forget the sentimental conception of Christ that modern religious art has given us—dismiss from our minds altogether, and go back to the Gospels—the first impression that would be made upon us would be one of power. Christ was never ill; he was hardly ever tired. Only twice in the four Gospels are we told that he was weary, yet he was always putting forth energy and power. He was so pressed that he had not leisure "so much as to eat" (Mark 6:31) for the people thronging about him. He was ever healing the sick, preaching the gospel, bringing life and health and vitality wherever he went, with such power and authority that we are told nobody "durst ask him any further questions" (Matt 22:46). "When he set his face to go up to Jerusalem, as

---

1. The New Thought movement, generally referred to as Higher Thought in England, originated in the nineteenth century. It was an amalgamation of spiritual teachings from ancient and Eastern religions and philosophies that stressed the presence of the divine Intelligence within each person, the primacy of love, and the ability of the human mind, connected as it is with the divine Mind, to heal physical illness. (KW)

his disciples followed him they were afraid" (Mark 10:32). When he silenced the winds and the waves, men said of him, "What manner of man is this, that even the winds and the waves obey him?" (Matt 8:27). I often think that those to whom the miracles of Christ are (as they are not to me) mere fairy tales, might nevertheless receive the same impression of power; for that kind of fairy tale is a witness to the kind of man of whom it is believed. Men do not say of a person of weak or gloomy character that he healed the sick and called the dead out of the grave and stopped the storm. The very legends, if you must regard them as legends, about our Lord tell us of the tremendous sense of power which he conveyed to those who met him in the flesh.

He promised to us that same power, that same victory over material circumstances. "Be not troubled about the future. Be not anxious" (Matt 6:34). "Seek ye first the kingdom of God and his righteousness, and all these things shall be added unto you" (Matt 6:33). "He that believeth in me, the works that I do shall he do also, and greater workers than these shall he do" (John 14:12).

"Lord, why cannot we cast him out," said the disciples, and the reply is, "Because of your unbelief" (Matt 17:19–20). Not "because you have not got the power" or "because the power is not here for you to use," but simply because you have not got sufficient faith. "He that *believeth* on me, the works that I do shall he do also, and greater works than these shall he do."

That falls in with our conception of what the world ought to be to those who know and obey the laws of God. If this is really God's world, if he did really make it and did really set us here to be in it, then those who understand his laws and obey them ought to have power over material things. It is reasonable, after all, since God put us here and gave us bodies of flesh and blood, to think that if we live as he desires us to, we shall have all the things that are needful to us, and much greater vitality and strength, and power over material things, than most of us have. It seems reasonable "If ye, being evil," human, selfish, limited, "know how to give good gifts to your children, how much more shall your Father which is in heaven give good gifts to them that ask him?" (Matt 7:11).

So when people tell us that Christianity is not a religion of gloom, not a religion of pain, not a religion of weakness, but of joy and health and power, it comes to us, like a flash of light—that is true! That must be true! And when we find Christ able to sustain a life of physical hardship so easily, with such power and vigor and health, that too seems natural and right. "Fear not, little flock. It is your Father's good pleasure to give you the kingdom" (Luke 12:32).

Yet Christ was crucified. There is Good Friday before Easter Sunday. There is that saying of our Lord's, "He that would be my disciple, let him take up his cross and come and follow me" (Matt 16:24). The earliest Christians, with all their sense of miraculous power and energy, suffered persecution. Christ himself, with all that life of joy and power, went through the agony in the garden of Gethsemane, and was crucified on the Cross. It is for us to ask ourselves how are we to reconcile these two tremendous truths, symbolized to us by Good Friday and Easter Sunday. How are we to hold in our minds and in our lives these two apparently conflicting truths, that if we seek first the kingdom of God, all the things we need will be ours—life and success and all the material things of life that we require, clothing and food, and freedom from anxiety, health and vigor and power and love—how are we to reconcile that with the Crucifixion? It is easy for a Christianity that keeps the Cross out of sight to make a perfectly whole and rational scheme of life. It is easy to think only of Christ triumphant; it is equally easy to think only of Christ crucified. But there must be a Christianity which is able to hold both, and to hold them not as two insoluble and conflicting truths but (as all truth really must be) as one; as two sides of the same truth.

I believe that that is possible. Indeed, I believe that Good Friday is the necessary and essential condition for Easter Sunday. I believe that the Cross of Christ is really the cross of all great religions, that at the heart of every great and spiritual faith, but supremely at the heart of Christianity, there is this searching fundamental truth, that if we would be the disciples of Christ we must take up the Cross and follow him.

The solution will be found somewhere here: "In this sign we conquer." That is one of the earliest sayings of the Christian Church. "In this sign we conquer." In this sign and on this Cross Christ was triumphant—not a failure, not broken, not defeated—but here, on the very instrument of his defeat, more full of power, more full of glory, than at any other moment in his life. Good Friday and Easter Sunday are not two truths, but one, and Christ most glorious when he was crucified.

Source

A. Maude Royden, *Christ Triumphant* (New York: Putnam's Sons, 1924), 102–10.

Jesus the Poet

For Royden, Jesus is more than a teacher and moralist: he is a poet and a seer because he's able to use homely, concrete words and images to express deep truths that inspire and enrich us. Philosophers, who specialize in abstractions, are unable to elicit the lived and loving responses of a poet. They can explain in theological terms, for example, the importance of communion with God. But Jesus, in instituting the Eucharist, gets the point across more graphically with simple, everyday bread and wine. When we read the words of Jesus in the Gospels, then, we do well to read them as poetry. It's a grave error to worship the letter rather than the spirit behind it.

A great deal of our difficulty in understanding the Bible—and especially the teaching of our Lord—is based on the fact that we have not understood that He is dealing with eternal things and profound truths, and we treat His words as though He were dealing with superficial facts. [. . .]

Our Lord brings before us those fundamental truths, those eternal principles which can be *suggested* by concrete symbols, but which are not even suggested to most minds by sounding abstract terms. That is why many philosophers are incomprehensible to ordinary people. Philosophers by the very nature, perhaps, of their science, if it be a science, must use great abstract words like One-ness, All-ness, and such barbarisms as these, and when ordinary people try to understand them, they find themselves lost in a mist of incomprehensible expressions.

The mystic who is a poet expresses these same truths in a way quite as profound but more comprehensible to the mind of the ordinary person. That is the supreme greatness of the poet, above the philosopher. For the poet, with all the depth of philosophy, is able to convey the truth in such a form that ordinary people can grasp it.

The common people heard Christ gladly because He put the truths of eternal life in the language of their common, everyday existence. What is All-ness, or One-ness, to an ordinary intelligence? It is an abstraction that we cannot grasp. But the way in which our Lord or any great poet puts a concrete example before us helps us to understand it if we have a spark of poetry in us. [...]

It is precisely because the poet trusts us not to turn a picture, an image, a sudden inspiration, a flash of light, into a hard and fast formula—because he trusts us to have a little imagination—that he dares to use concrete words such as corn and seed and harvest and wine, and all those simple images that are familiar to us in the words of Christ. He is trusting Himself to you to understand, for of course God is not really a shepherd, dressed in sheepskin and carrying a crook in his hand! [...]

A concrete symbol can never express the whole of an eternal principle or truth, such as God, or the love of God. But then nothing can; and a concrete symbol which is something everybody knows in their own life, can at least express *one aspect* of that love. The person who suggests that God is a shepherd or a man with two sons of whom one has gone astray, or a woman looking for a piece of silver in her house, is literalizing and reducing to a misleading fact what Christ put before him as an eternal truth. Christ often uses one figure after another in order to make us realize that we must not stop at one figure and press it to a logical conclusion as though it were part of a syllogism. We are to grasp the point He seeks to bring home, and pass on. Thus when He speaks of the Kingdom of Heaven, Christ uses perhaps eight or nine figures to tell us what it is like. It is like a mustard seed which a man sows in his field. It is like a pearl which a merchant seeks everywhere and, when he finds it, will sell everything to buy it. It is like a treasure hidden in a field to obtain which a man will sell all that he has in order to buy that field. It is like leaven hidden in a measure of meal. Christ passes rapidly from one to another, and from every one of these little pictures you gain some conception of the love of God and of the nature of the Kingdom of God.

If you sit down and think to yourself: "God is like a woman who leavens three measures of meal. What a curious thing! We had no idea that God was a woman!" you see how senseless it is. Yet that is what students of the Bible have done over and over again, and one can therefore readily understand why over and over again the evangelists record that our Lord paused at the close of His parable and cried: "He that hath ears to hear, let him hear!" [...]

What we have to do is to get at the heart of our Lord's teaching, that heart of truth which He gives us in little stories and poems, one after the other; not to treat it as though He supposed that the whole being of Almighty God could be expressed in a woman seeking for a piece of silver—the whole glory of His kingdom into a pearl bought with a price.

I have often thought the imagery of our Lord's Supper is one of the most poetical of any in our religion. Yet how often it has been distorted! Why does our Lord make of eating and drinking an act of worship? Because it is a deep human instinct that when you have given or received hospitality you must not injure or betray. When you have eaten with another, something sacramental has happened. Every meal therefore is in a sense a sacrament, and universal, for all human beings eat and drink. Therefore our Lord takes this common, ordinary, universal act and makes it an act of fellowship and worship. He takes bread and wine—because everyone in the East eats bread and everybody drinks wine. They are the two commonest forms of nourishment; the food that all have, whether rich or poor, the drink that all have, whether rich or poor. Because they are common He takes them. Then observe that these things, though they are common, are not exactly simple. I have often thought that a less profound poetry would have chosen perhaps fruit and water, those two things which come direct from God, which many people would think more "poetic" than bread and wine. But bread and wine owe something to man as well as to God. God gives them, but man has to make them into food. It is the divine love that gives the elements and the human love that makes them and divides them. There is an infinitely deeper poetry in giving as the symbol of God's love something that has been made by human hands than to take even the loveliest of God's gifts that can be had without human help. For in such a sacrament we are united both with God and man. So all the poetry of Christ is deeply and profoundly human and reveals to us the divine if we have ears to hear. But we must always seek the whole of His teaching if we are to understand even one little story. We must have with it the setting of His life and all His teaching. [. . .]

If we lived near enough to Christ to understand Him, we should understand that He is a seer, not merely a teacher; a poet, not a moralist. Does that sound a hard saying? But a seer is greater than a teacher and a poet more profoundly true than a moralist. The moralist can tell you what is the right thing to do, but the poet makes you in love with it. The moralist can set before you a rule of life, but the poet makes you share its spirit. The Seer who cried: "He that hath ears to hear, let him hear," perceived spiritual law and reveals it to us.

He has known, He has seen what God is, and He reveals God to us. That is what we mean by saying Christ was a revelation of God. He showed us what God is like. Can you see it? Can you love it? Well, then, knowledge for you has become salvation.

This is not an easier thing to achieve than that literal interpretation of Christ's sayings which seems at first sight the obvious way to be a Christian. Rather, it is a counsel of despair that makes one give up the effort to get at the heart of Christ and to understand what He meant; for we soon find that literal obedience is impossible. He took care to make it impossible, by those astounding paradoxes which seem like contradictions—so like, that people can take pleasure in hurling texts at one another's heads by the hour!

I often think that is why Christ wrote no gospel of His own. He knew that our idle desire is always to worship the letter, and had He Himself written a gospel, we should have sat down and rationalized and regularized and legalized it until we were as much tied by traditions and conventions as the Pharisees He so often denounced. But He left His teaching and His life in the hands of human beings, who inevitably wrote down those things which most appealed to them, and sometimes, in spite of the inspiration of God, did blur the outline, did tell us things that we cannot reconcile with Christ. He deliberately left us in the hands of other human beings, as He has left all things in our hands to set right.

When we first come up against this difficulty and find that if we literally apply the words of Christ we end by trying to believe things that are self-contradictory, there comes upon us at first a sense of despair. One thinks: "I am not a scholar, a student. How can I know which is right and which is wrong?" What is the upshot? How shall we escape the dilemma? We must get behind the letter to the spirit, and the spirit of Christ shines through the New Testament, so that the impression made by it is one which is constant, which is real, which is vivid. That is because we have been forced to go behind the letter to the spirit, and do the harder, not the easier thing.

I claim that thus to get, by long thought and much love, behind the letter to the spirit is the harder thing. It does not explain away the spirit of Christ. It does not seek to escape from high and difficult demands. It is a valiant effort to get so near to the spirit of Christ, so near His heart, that we can understand what He said, though it be repeated for us by one evangelist after another, translated by one translator after another, expounded or mis-expounded by one theologian after another. To every human being it is still possible to reach the real living Christ, and I believe that nothing short of the difficulties that beset the worship of the letter in the New Testament would have compelled us to get so close to that eternal spirit.

In the future, if the Church is to live and proclaim Christ to the world, it must, I think, take the courage of St. Paul to proclaim love greater than faith, and love as the revelation of God greater than any creed, however "orthodox." If the Church could take courage to do what her Lord did and put love above all, we should get a brighter light upon and a deeper knowledge of all other doctrines.

Christianity would be to us a life and not a creed. "He that doeth the will, shall know the doctrine" (John 7:17) and those eternal truths which our Savior, out of His deep love for human beings, has clothed in such simple human images would be revealed to us in their simplicity, but in their depth and wonder too.

Source

A. Maude Royden, *Beauty in Religion* (London: Putnam's Sons, 1925), 115, 116–17, 117–18, 118–20, 122–23, 126–29.

A Vice of the Mind

THANKS TO THE 1980 *David Lynch film* The Elephant Man, *the story of Joseph Merrick (1862–90) is well-known. Suffering from a genetic disorder known as Proteus syndrome, Merrick's physical deformities made him an object of derision, horror, and mistreatment until Sir Frederick Treves took him under his wing. Royden invokes Merrick's stalwart response to his tragic condition—during his final years he described himself, apparently sincerely, as happy—as an example to those prone to self-pity, which she condemns as a "vice of the mind" and an "ignoble temper." Feeling sorry for oneself because of actual or (more likely) imagined grievances, especially when they're minor in relation to the rest of one's life, is a symptom of the self-centeredness that breeds resentment. We should turn our gaze outward, Royden recommends, and direct our pity to other people.*

A few years ago a great London doctor was walking through one of the mean streets of a poor part of London, when he noticed in a window an announcement of an exhibition where there was to be seen for the price of a shilling an extraordinarily deformed and terrible human being. He was called "the Elephant Man," and Sir Frederick Treves, having a moment's leisure, paid his shilling and went in.

He has told us the story of what he saw and what followed in a book[1] which I for one have not got the courage to read. One's mind sickens at the thought of what life must have meant to that man. But I read, as perhaps many of you did, a review of the book, and the reviewer briefly tells the story. He tells how Sir Frederick Treves went into the shop and was conducted to a room with a curtain hanging across it. The curtain was drawn by the exploiter of this unhappy human curiosity, and Sir Frederick Treves saw behind it a shapeless form, crouching under a kind

---

1. *The Elephant Man and Other Reminiscences* (1923). (KW)

of loose cover. His exploiter ordered him to get up and show himself, and he stood up and dropped his covering. Sir Frederick Treves then saw a man so hideously deformed that the reviewer, having embarked on a descriptive quotation, suddenly breaks off and says, "Let us leave it at that."

Sir Frederick Treves did not know what to do or how to help, but on the impulse of the moment, gave his card to the Elephant Man and left him, telling him if he ever wanted him, to send for him. Then he went away, and, I suppose, for a while forgot about it.

It appears, however, that shortly afterward, the police put a stop to the exhibition, and the exhibitionist took his unhappy prey to Belgium and exhibited him again there; but almost at once the police again stepped in, and he was forbidden to continue the exhibition. Coming to the conclusion that no money was to be made any more out of the Elephant Man, he seems to have put him on board ship for England with a ticket for London. As the reviewer says, one hesitates to imagine what that journey could have been like, but the man somehow got to London. There his courage failed him altogether and he tried to hide himself in the station. He was found by some of the officials, and they discovered Sir Frederick Treves' card still on him and rang him up to ask if he knew anything about the man.

Sir Frederick came down to the station and took that man home to his house, and there he lived for the few years that he had left—I think, if I remember rightly, that he died at the age of twenty-six. During the last two or three years of his life, while he was living in Sir Frederick Treves' house, he had a room to himself; he was never seen by any human being unless he actually desired it; and he had an hour or so in the evening when he could go into the garden under Sir Frederick's absolute promise that no one else would be there. Queen Alexandra[2] (who surely will have an extra star in her crown some day for this!) once—no, not once, but several times—went and sat with him and took his hand. She gave the man her photograph; he put it on the mantelpiece and, as Sir Frederick tells us, he practically worshipped it. And during those last two or three years he said more than once that he was "happy every hour of the day." *Happy!*

He was a man, Sir Frederick tells us, of a sensitive nature, of intelligence above the average. You would not have wondered—indeed, you would almost have expected—that a man's spirit, enclosed in such a

---

2. Alexandra of Denmark (1844–1925), Queen of England and wife of Edward VII. (KW)

prison, would become as deformed as his body; would be poisoned with hatred against a world which had been to him hell. But it was not so. *He was happy every hour of the day.* And he had nothing, absolutely nothing, of the things that make us happy. No work, no gift with which he could serve the world, no sense that he was of value to anyone, no wife, no child, no equality in friendship, no sense that he could give anything to anybody; just an absence of torture. And he was happy—"happy every hour of the day." Is there not something sublime in the human spirit that could remain serene and gentle under so terrible a fate? Go through such a hell of torment unembittered? Be willing to be happy when active torment ceased, and bear—it seems—no angry resentment, no venomous or sullen hate for what was past? I wish he could know—perhaps he does know—that to those who have not even perhaps read the book but have just heard of him, there is a fragrance in the memory of that touching capacity and willingness to be happy, which might almost make him think his life had been worth living.

And some of *us* are sorry for ourselves!

Well, you may say, his suffering does not make it any easier for us to suffer! His was a fate, indeed, beyond imagination for terror and pity, but after all that does not make it any easier for us! Perhaps, in a way, the very sensitiveness that makes us feel for such agony only makes the world seem a more terrible place. That he suffered more than we do ought not to make it easier to suffer: it only makes it the more terrible to live in a world that contains such agony. If we are disappointed, or ill, or out of work, or unsuccessful, or unloved, the fact that this man had worse things to bear does not really make our load any lighter.

No, it does not. I do not want to pretend that it does. I know that, on the contrary, to a sensitive soul, it often makes the world seem more horrible still that such a depth of suffering should be endured in it. But the point I want to make is this. This man had nothing; so far as we can see, absolutely nothing. Only the memory of unspeakable torture. Yet he was happy. If, therefore, he could be happy in such a case, to be sorry for ourselves is not inevitable. It is not due to outward circumstance. It is a vice of the mind. It is an ignoble temper. It is a mean cowardice in the face of pain. It cannot be our circumstances that make us sorry for ourselves, if it is possible for such a being as this man ever to be happy.

If you think of the people who are sorry for themselves—perhaps if you are honest you will see that that class occasionally includes you!—if you think of the people who are sorry for themselves, are they not just as often people who have much to make them happy, as people who have, as this man, everything to make them sad?

I do not know a person who is more sorry for himself when he is a little bit ill than a person who has always been well. Let a person have practically perfect health, and the resentment that he feels when he has a cold or a fit of indigestion would cause you to think that all his life had been one long agony of disease. But that, too, is not invariable. You will sometimes come across the person who is very strong and well as a rule, and who will cheerfully say, when he is ill, "Well, after all I have had an extraordinarily good time hitherto. I have been most fortunate. I have no cause to complain."

"The fault, dear Brutus, is not in our stars, but in ourselves,"[3] that we are thus or thus.

You know people who have some slight disappointment, some little failure, some crumpled rose-leaf. What an uproar they make about it! It blots out the sun for them; it blackens the sky. They have been so accustomed to prosperity that they do not know how to tolerate the injury and the injustice of having occasionally to suffer like other people. [. . .]

It means that you are focusing your thoughts upon yourself. If you were to turn your mind outward you would see people who are gay and gallant in the face of misfortunes which, set down in cold blood, make an apparently overwhelming list; people with such a dauntless spirit that to the end they will be gay; people who have neither health nor influence nor money. There is something they will always have, these gallant spirits who have apparently nothing—no success, no particular talent, no wealth, no health—and yet who will extort from life its joy, and make of life so gallant a thing that they always have friends. For to such a spirit friendship is drawn, while we, when we are sorry for ourselves, repel it. The world may have a rough and ready judgment, but it is not fond of the coward and the skulker. It is not fond of people who have a perpetual sense of their own grievances. And it is right. Fundamentally it is right, for this vice of self-pity is most demoralizing, most disintegrating. Do not indulge, even for a little while, in the pleasant pastime of considering your own grievances and reflecting how odious everybody is to you, for to do so is to waste your strength.

You wake up in the morning, and you think, perhaps, "I won't get up for five minutes." You spend that time in considering what an odious day

---

3. Shakespeare, *Julius Caesar*, 1.2. (KW)

you are going to have. You will find that half an hour has gone like a flash in the consideration of that exquisite subject, yourself and your grievances! Half an hour is gone in a flash, and it does not leave you merely half an hour late: it leaves you demoralized and disintegrated. The psychologist who warns you against daydreams was never more right than when your dreams are of your own grievances. Such dreams result in moral disintegration; they take away your courage; they take away hope and leave you demoralized, anxious, cowardly. The world is too strong for you. Is it? Yet it was not too strong for that deformed, tormented man. The world is cruel to you. Is it a hundredth part as cruel as it was to him? Yet how swiftly his spirit reacted to the first touch of kindness! With how little resentment he brooded on the past! He put it away from him. It was the present in which he lived, because the present was kind to him; as I have known the same kind of spirit live in the future, because the future may be kind.

It is true that that attitude of resentment against the world repels the world. There is nothing the world loves better—and here again it is right—than a gallant spirit, and after all, how can we know what lies behind the face of someone who takes life so gaily? How do you know? Behind any face that you see there may lie—so often there *does* lie—something terribly difficult, not necessarily tragic, though often it is tragic, too. But again and again when I have learned to know someone whose outside life seemed quite smooth, quite prosperous, perhaps even specially so, I have marveled at the precipice edge of difficulty upon which they are, in fact, walking—the nervous strain, the difficulty, the anxiety, perhaps the ill-health, the unknown suffering. You cannot tell of any of those who seem gallant and gay, how difficult their life is, how easily they might pity themselves, if they chose. [. . .]

It is therefore possible to be happy, however cruel the world has been to you. It is possible to turn your gaze outward and, at the first touch of self-pity, to turn and see how others need that pity which you are wasting upon yourself.

Source

A. Maude Royden, *Life's Little Pitfalls* (New York: Putnam's Sons, 1925), 52–57, 59–61, 62.

Pagan Virtues and Christian Graces

Royden's understanding of Christianity was both humane and humanistic. She utterly rejected the doctrine of total depravity embraced by the Reformed tradition, insisting instead that decency is the default position of most persons. In this essay, she argues that "pagan" virtues such as honesty, courage, loyalty, and self-respect—the combination of which Aristotle referred to as "magnanimity"—are necessary requisites for the practice of specifically Christian virtues such as humility, trust, and gentleness. Otherwise, humility may be nothing more than disguised cowardice, trust just a form of unctuousness, and gentleness simply timidity or indifference. Christian virtues, she concludes, can be neither cultivated nor practiced on such a "shoddy foundation."

Not long ago a friend of mine, discussing the ethics of Christ, observed that if we took them too seriously we should become despicable. "A man," he said, "who did not defend himself when attacked, who allowed himself to be insulted and injured without making an effort to vindicate himself, would be despicable; and we all know it." We do all know that point of view and we all realize that there is a great deal in it. And yet, as my friend drew his picture of the insulted, injured, abject victim of ill-usage, I could not help reflecting that the description might, so far as the actual words went, have applied with exactness to Christ before Pilate. Its contrast could be found in Peter, who, desperate and helpless though he was, still drew his sword and struck his blow for the right, and won our everlasting gratitude for doing it (John 18:10).

Which was the greater, Peter or Christ? Lovable, loyal, warm-hearted Peter, who drew his pathetic little sword to defend his Master against a legion of Roman soldiers, or Christ, who took the sword from his hand and, without protest or effort to defend Himself, went to an ignominious trial and a hideous death? We love Saint Peter. No one who has any imagination can fail to love him for his desperate and forlorn attempt to strike one blow in his Master's behalf. We love Saint Peter—but we worship Christ. We do not call ourselves followers of Saint Peter, with his sword. We call ourselves Christians, and, if we cannot follow the example of our Lord, it must at least be with much heart-searching, and with the confession that, if we cannot follow Him, it is because we are not sufficiently like Him.

How is it that Christ was able to behave in a manner which, in an ordinary way, would seem to us despicable, and yet by that very conduct to command the worship of a world of warring men? What is it that He had which we have not—we who call ourselves Christians? What is it that we have not, which makes it in some instances literally impossible for us to do what our Lord did, because we find that in doing so we achieve the exact opposite of what He wished us to achieve? What qualities are lacking in us that we cannot act as He did? Why is it, in what respect is it, that we are not like Him? What is it that He had which we have not?

It is only part of the answer that I want to suggest here. There are certain virtues which are practiced by pagans; our Lord took for granted that every Christian would practice those virtues. "Except," He said, "your righteousness shall exceed the righteousness" of other people (Matt 5:20). We Christians have been very much inclined to emphasize what we may call the Christian virtues; to seek to practice those virtues which made Christ different from other men. We have forgotten that He took for granted the pagan virtues, and built the soaring edifice of Christian holiness upon that splendidly laid foundation.

What are the virtues that pagans admire and seek to practice? I use the word "pagans" to mean non-Christian people; I do not use it in a derogatory sense at all. I mean people who do not call themselves Christians: people perhaps of other faiths, or people of no faith at all. What are the virtues, what are the qualities that they set store by? I suppose courage and honesty and loyalty, and a high spirit; wisdom and justice; what Aristotle called "magnanimity"—a certain greatness of mind, a magnificence of spirit, that takes wide views and is not irked by little things. That is, roughly, the kind of character that the secular man, the non-Christian man or woman, admires: courage, perhaps, first of all, but also a high sense of honor, and loyalty to one's friends, and independence, and wisdom, and so on. These are great virtues. Without them there is no real virtue at all.

If you examine the teaching of Christ you will find that He took these virtues for granted. There is nowhere in His teaching the dreadful doctrine that has been developed by a certain type of Christian, called "the total depravity of man." Christ never suggested that human beings were altogether evil and must be entirely changed if they are to be Christians, but rather assumes that most people are decent people. When He wanted to tell us what God is like, He said that God is like a human father, only greater and better. There are plenty of human fathers who are bad fathers, cruel, unjust, or merely indifferent, but our Lord assumed that most fathers are decent and kind, and said, if they knew how to give good gifts to their children, "how much more shall your Father which is in heaven?" (Matt 7:11). He did not denounce them. He did not speak as though we were all wicked and hopeless creatures. He said, in effect, "You have got a certain distance; you are all, or nearly all, kind to your children. Very well; start with that. Then you will see what God is like to His children." Or again, in the Sermon on the Mount—which is, after all, the high-water mark of Christian teaching, the noblest expression of its ethic—how persistently He assumed that people were, on the whole, decent people. "Ye have heard that it hath been said by them of old time, Thou shalt not forswear thyself, but shalt perform unto the Lord thine oaths" (Matt 5:33). Christ did not go on to say, "I know that you never keep your vows, and therefore I tell you not to swear at all." He said: "You must give up your oaths. Don't you realize that all this casuistry about what constitutes a binding oath and what does not means that your bare word is not enough? In future do not swear at all, by anything, but let your communication be Yea, yea; Nay, nay: for whatsoever is more than these cometh of evil" (Matt 5:37). We Christians ought to be so honest that no one will require us to swear any oaths at all.

"Ye have heard that it hath been said, An eye for an eye, and a tooth for a tooth" (Matt 5:38). That was a very high ideal, and the Jews were by no means always capable of acting on it. As you know, if you have read the Old Testament, they very frequently met an injury by wiping out a whole tribe, putting to the sword all their enemies with their wives and their little ones and their cattle. But the law was that they must not do so; they must not be vindictive; they must be just. If an eye is taken, an eye may be taken; if a tooth is taken, a tooth may be taken—not more. Now our Lord did not speak of the Jews as though they were continually vindictive and unjust. He took them at their highest level. He said: "This is your tradition—that you are not to be revengeful. You are only to be just. Now, I say to you, pass beyond human justice to divine Love."

"Ye have heard that it hath been said, Thou shalt love thy neighbor, and hate thine enemy" (Matt 5:38). Our Lord did not say, "Hateful creatures! You are incapable of loving anybody! You must be completely changed!" He assumed that His hearers really had lived up to that standard, but He said that it was not high enough. They must now learn to love their enemies.

At every step in this great argument, Christ begins with a pagan virtue, and goes on from that to Christianity. Is not some of the disgust that our religious professions and even our religious life have awakened among non-Christian people due to the fact that we seek to practice these amazing virtues, these soaring Christian graces of holiness and sanctity, without having acquired the rudimentary virtues of honesty, courage, loyalty, self-respect?

II

The other day I was among a number of religious people, of whom one spoke rather bitterly of the way in which he had been treated by his fellow theologians. Before I had time to think, I said impulsively, "I hate religious people." Immediately he put his hand across the table and said, "Shake hands! So do I!" Of course I do not really dislike religious people; I love them. A person who is really religious, a person who is truly Christlike, is a person more gracious, more lovely, more adorable, than any pagan character that has ever existed. There is a grace and a loveliness about Saint Francis of Assisi which even a Marcus Aurelius does not share. But what I meant, and what he meant, was that we disliked the kind of person—so terribly common—who seeks to practice the Christian virtues of humility and self-sacrifice and love and peace before he has got courage or honesty or honor.

Our Lord tells us that unless we take up our cross and follow Him we cannot be His disciples. We interpret that—rightly, I think—to mean that we must be ready to sacrifice ourselves even to the death; yet there are people who do this, who sacrifice themselves up to the last limit of sacrifice, and who only succeed in making the people around them intolerably selfish. Why is it? Is it not perhaps because self-sacrifice cannot rightly be practiced by people who have not moral courage? I have sacrificed myself sometimes and have thought I was doing well. When I grew a little older and could look back at what I did from a different experience, I saw plainly enough that, in fact, I had not had the courage to do anything else! To assert myself required, perhaps, courage to face the imputation of selfishness. Perhaps it required that I should seem cruel or self-assertive, and I really "sacrificed myself" not in the least because I was in love with self-sacrifice, but because I had not the courage to do otherwise. How often one sees that kind of self-sacrifice! It becomes merely abject, unless it is made by a person who could assert himself if he chose. It meets with the response of selfishness instead of the response of unselfishness, because, by an invariable spiritual law, we get from the world what we put into it—not immediately, perhaps, but in the end. If the final result of our unselfishness is to make other people selfish, we should surely examine ourselves very closely. Are we sure that we are not indulging in a luxury of unselfishness? Or is it that we have not the courage to be selfish? Do we desire the world's applause and to have it said, "What an unselfish wife!" "What an unselfish daughter!" (The vice of unselfishness is rather more common among women than among men.) If so, only a bad response can be expected, because, at the heart of it, the appeal is bad. Self-sacrifice cannot be rightly practiced except by a person who is perfectly able to assert herself if she chooses.

Christians lay great emphasis, nowadays especially, on such virtues as toleration and courtesy. Is not our toleration also sometimes due to lack of moral courage? When our Lord found a person who ill-treated a child, He did not say, "Let us reflect that this person is probably a badly brought-up person." He said, "It were better for him that a millstone were hanged about his neck, and that he were drowned in the depth of the sea" (Matt 18:6). When He found real spiritual vileness He denounced it in language that terrifies the modern Christian, although it was generally people of power and position who excited that indignation.

Sometimes—for it is safest, perhaps, to speak of one's own experience—I know that I have practiced this "virtue" of Christian courtesy merely because I had not the moral courage to say what I thought. I remember one occasion, when a committee of "religious" people, of which I was a member, was considering how to turn the world upside down. We were considering who should write the literature for this great crusade. Among others, the name was suggested of a man whom no one could deny to be a Christian, but whose political views made him at the time very unpopular. Our chairman said, "I don't think it would be wise to ask him to write for us, because our printing is all going to be done by a certain firm which does religious work, and it naturally would not like to risk offending its subscribers." I remember my feeling of indignation, and also of despair. How on earth were we going to have any effect on the world at all if we began by considering the subscribers to a certain firm? But I looked at our chairman and thought, "After all, he is a very good old man, doubtless a great deal better than I am, and it would be very rude and rough of me to say what I think." So I did not say it; but I did not say it because I was afraid to say it, not at all because I had any real consideration for his feelings. It is easy for us to persuade ourselves that we have to practice the Christian virtues of gentleness and grace, when our real trouble is that we have not the pagan virtue of courage to begin with!

Over and over again, in a genuine effort to achieve something good, something worth doing, as a member perhaps of some great society whose ends we approve and to which we are proud to belong, something is proposed that we feel to be wrong, and we decide that "it would not be Christian to judge." "Judge not, that ye be not judged" (Matt 7:1). We refrain from "judging"; we refrain from protesting. It would be so awkward if we did protest! Everybody would be set by the ears, and the work which is at stake would be imperiled. Have we not all laid that flattering unction to our souls many times? But Christ did not care about any of these things, and we try in vain to imitate Him before we have laid the foundations of character. One of the most dishonest things in public life is the dreadful plea that to say or to do the audacious thing—which at a given moment may be the right thing—will do harm to the work or to the society that we belong to.

A little while ago I heard of a woman who had done most valuable work for her society, and who broke down—largely, of course, from overwork. She was dismissed, and those who were responsible for the dismissal told her that she should in future, for her maintenance and her support, "put her trust in God." To disregard the claims of common loyalty to people who have worked for you and served you, and then tell them to put their trust in God, is unctuous, repulsive. If you cannot afford to look after your servants when they break down, at least face the fact as to what you are doing, and do not pretend that it is because you have such trust in God that you can sack anybody and everybody and put them on the street, and if they starve it is their fault, because *they* had not sufficient trust in God! I have found honesty, common honesty, to be the rarest of the virtues practiced by religious people. We want the common, decent, pagan virtue of loyalty to other human beings before we begin to talk about trust in God.

Take the question of pacifism. A conscientious objector to war who is afraid of fighting has no right to his objection. He must be braver than the soldier before he has the right to be a pacifist. "Except your righteousness shall *exceed* the righteousness of the scribes and Pharisees!" (Matt 5:20). Even in the height of war, even in the poisoned atmosphere of hate which war engenders, there were, I think, few people who in their hearts despised men like Stephen Hobhouse and Clifford Allen.[1] They might think them mad, but they could not think them despicable, for it was obvious that their position required a courage at least as great as, perhaps greater—indeed, in my heart I think certainly greater—than that required of the soldier. To suppose that their objection to war was based on cowardice would be a senseless denial of the facts. But as our righteousness must exceed the righteousness of the scribes and Pharisees, so must the courage of those of us who call ourselves pacifists exceed the courage of the soldier. When I heard of conscientious objectors who, in the hour of danger, desired to be rescued, it seemed to me that there was something wrong with that kind of pacifism. Why, there were many soldiers who had none of the Christian graces, whose lives as private citizens had been marred by many faults, who yet would have scorned to ask to be brought back out of the trenches or sent home to what was called a "cushy job." The pacifism of the future must exceed the courage of Saint Peter. Without this courage we cannot really win the world for Christ.

There is something that disgusts in Christian grace on a shoddy foundation. It is like a poor and cheap building which we cover with elaborate ornament. It is like a mean melody supported with interesting harmonies. It is like an ill-cut dress overloaded with embroidery and lace. It is like anything that is false. And the average decent pagan is revolted by its dishonesty.

I often think that the farcical exaggeration which Dickens has given us in Uriah Heep is—like all Dickens's conceptions—true at heart. Humility is loathsome if it is not founded on self-respect. it disgusts. We

---

1. Stephen Henry Hobhouse (1881–1961), English Quaker, pacifist, and prison reformer, who was jailed as a conscientious objector during World War I. Reginald Clifford Allen (1889–1939), Independent Labor Party politician and socialist, also imprisoned during World War I. Hobhouse suffered psychological trauma from his prison experience that plagued him for the rest of his life. Allen contracted tuberculosis while behind bars, eventually dying of it. (KW)

must have the pagan virtue of self-respect before we dare to have the Christian virtue of humility.

III

Had not Christ just those pagan virtues that so many of us Christians lack? With all His love and gentleness and mercy, how utterly courageous was His denunciation of all that was false and cowardly and bad! The tenderness with which He speaks of the outcast and the sinner is matched by His fierce denunciation of spiritual pride in high places, in places of power and dignity and influence. Those to whom He spoke with such pitiful compassion could not doubt His power to judge sternly if He chose. That was why His tenderness counted for so much. Had He done as we are so fond of doing with people we love—sometimes too with people whom we do not love—pretending that all is right when it is not, shutting our eyes to things that we know are wrong because we love to praise, refusing to see what is blameworthy because it seems cruel to see it, His praise would have been worth as little as ours so often is; His love would have effected nothing. But because men knew that His mercy was justice, because they realized that He was able to see through and through them and love them all the same, because His love rose up on the great foundation of truth and justice and clear-sightedness, it moved the world as nothing else has moved it.

Christ had strength of character, courage of mind and body, great physical courage as well as great moral courage. He had high-mindedness, magnanimity, or "magnificence," as our English poet Spenser calls it.[2] If He trusted His disciples, it was not because He did not see how they might fail Him. If He kept Judas with Him, it was not because He did not know that Judas was quite ready to betray Him. His very self-sacrifice was accompanied by a self-assertion which sometimes horrifies those by whom it is not understood. His gift of Himself to us is accompanied by a demand upon us in return which is relentless. In Him every Christian grace was founded upon the rock of honor and loyalty, courage and justice, a piercing vision, a great strength. It is only the strong who can really be gentle. The gentleness of the feeble has in it something that repels; but

---

2. In Edmund Spenser's (1552–99) unfinished epic *The Faerie Queene*, the character of Prince Arthur represents the virtue of magnificence or magnanimity, the perfection of all the virtues. (KW)

the gentleness of strength, whether strength of body or strength of spirit, or both together, as with Christ, is adorable.

When Christ stood before Pilate with no sword in His hand and no protest on His lips, Pilate was afraid of Him. One can see that at every step. Christ was the judge—not Pilate. And the world has been in love with Him and afraid of Him ever since. We Christians have to begin at the beginning, and must not expect any more that the world will be moved, or attracted, or anything but repelled, by grace and beauty sought without strength, by a Christian grace of character which has not common honesty and courage at the heart of it. We have to realize that we Christians often repel the world as much as our Lord attracted it, because at the heart of our mercy there is weakness, at the heart of our self-sacrifice, fear.

Source

A. Maude Royden, "Pagan Virtues and Christian Graces," *The Atlantic* 137:6 (June 1926) 746–51.

Part 6.

"From the Beginning There Were Three of Us"

Selections from Royden's memoir

Selections from *A Threefold Cord*

ROYDEN'S OUTPUT AS AN *author peaked in the 1920s. During the final twenty years of her life, she published much less, producing only two books:* The Problem of Palestine *(1939) and* A Threefold Cord *(1947). The latter was a personal record of her decades-long love of the Rev. Hudson Shaw, an Anglican priest she met at the beginning of the twentieth century. With the knowledge, approval, and friendship of his invalid wife Effie, Royden and Shaw were open with their love for one another. It was only after Effie's death in 1944 that Royden married Shaw. He died two months later at the age of eighty-five, and* A Threefold Cord *is Royden's loving memoir about the relationship the three shared. Its title is taken from Ecclesiastes 4:12: "A threefold cord is not quickly broken."*

Hudson Shaw and I met for the first time in Oxford in 1903. We loved each other at sight.

We did not realize this at first. He was in Oxford for the University Extension Summer School at which he was a great and beloved personality, lecturing brilliantly and wanted everywhere by everyone. I had only gone down from Lady Margaret Hall a year or two before, and I attended partly as a student, but chiefly because a friend of mine was Assistant Secretary to the Delegacy; and anyhow I always wanted an excuse to be in Oxford.[1]

---

1. Oxford University began offering "extension" courses to non-traditional students in 1878. The courses were held at different locations throughout England. Participants like Hudson Shaw were traveling tutors. A decade later, the program began offering intensive summer courses in Oxford, considered the highlights of the entire year of instruction at various locales. The "Delegacy" was the administrative body responsible for the program. Royden's friend who served as the Delegacy's assistant secretary was Evelyn Gunter, whom Royden met when she was a student of history at Lady Margaret Hall. The two remained friends for life. (KW)

Hudson was lecturing on Ruskin, whom he idolized. I detested Ruskin for his conceited attitude toward women, and had never recovered from an early disgust created by *Sesame and Lilies*.[2] But Hudson's lectures were magnificent and, though not permanently converted to his view of Ruskin, I was carried away by the lecturer.

I was at that time in much perplexity about my religion. The Roman Catholic Church attracted me and I could not find rest for my soul. Hudson was a parson, and as he was willing to talk the matter over with me I went to see him. I arrived at his lodgings in Merton Street a little early: he was out. I sat, feeling nervous, and looked out of the window onto that enchanting street. Is it enchanting still? Yes, I think so. I never drive through Oxford without going there to sit and remember.

Very soon Hudson came in. I heard his footsteps coming up the stairs. I hear them still. Is it Maeterlinck[3] who says one should always listen to approaching footsteps with awe and expectation for one knows not who is coming into one's life?

We talked of many things and parted with regret. But before leaving Oxford we had one more meeting, this time on the river. We spent a long afternoon together and, as we came back to the landing-place at Magdalen Bridge, I looked up at the great tower. When I brought my eyes back into the boat I saw that Hudson was watching me. "It's that sort of thing that knocks you over, isn't it?" he asked.

Many years after, when I was asked to broadcast in a series "Why I believe in God," and began "I believe in God because of Beauty," I remembered that day. Some of my hearers were shocked and wrote to tell me so. However, it remains true. It is because of Beauty that, at the worst, I have never disbelieved in God, and it has been the care for beauty in the Roman Catholic Church that has sometimes made me homesick for it.

It is a pest to be lame,[4] and one result of the certainty that I was lame and would be so always has its importance in this story. It made me believe that I should never marry.

I have been told that my lameness only made those who loved me love me more, and I now know that that can be true. Men can be very

2. See "A Soft Theological Revolution," above, note 3. (KW)
3. Maurice Maeterlinck (1869–1942), Belgian poet and playwright. (KW)
4. See the introduction.

chivalrous. One man even assured me with admirable gravity that, if I ever had a daughter and wanted her to marry, I had nothing to do but ill-treat her at home and men would hurry to the rescue of the poor little thing! I have an adopted daughter, but have never been able to adopt this no doubt excellent expedient, partly because I could not be perfectly convinced of its invariable success and partly because she married too early for me to make the experiment. But that a lover can love the beloved all the more for pity I do know. How often has Hudson said to me—"I want you to be cured of your lameness—I would give anything for you to be cured—but, for myself, I should miss it." I don't think anything more sweet and consoling to the heart than this can ever be said by one human being to another. Only those who suffer from some such physical defect as mine can understand how sweet. It is our secret and our balm. Nevertheless, I did not believe it for a long time. I knew what a nuisance lameness was and I could not believe that, whatever a man might feel about it at first, he would not feel it to be a nuisance in the end. And so I remained sure that I should not marry and that my life must be lived some other way.

In 1902, Shaw invited Royden to join him at his East Midlands parish of South Luffenham, ostensibly to help out with Effie as well as lend a hand with parish work. The deeper motive was the love they felt for one another. South Luffenham, a rural village of around three hundred people, was something of a shock to the city-bred Royden. But she immediately took to Effie.

It was my first meeting with her. Every memory of it is engraved on my heart.

Dear, strange, enchanting Effie! How shall I convey to strangers the kind of spirit she was whose spirit was so unlike any of us? I think Shelley might have described her, for she, if like anyone, was like him. If not a poet she was a musician, an artist, and a wit. She had an unearthly grace and charm and other-worldliness. But I heap words on words and none find her.

For with all her gifts, there was a strange spell on her—a shyness almost frantic sometimes, a fear of life which lay on her like frost upon a flower.

That night she stood looking at Hudson and me and I did not guess at the shyness that held her. I fell in love with her, too, at first sight. This was the real beginning of the love that changed all our three lives. If she had not loved me and I her, what happened afterward would have been impossible.

Almost immediately after Royden arrived at South Luffenham, Shaw departed for a months-long lecture tour in America, leaving the two women alone.

It was understood that Effie was an invalid and must not be expected to work. That was really why I was needed: I understood that. What I did not understand was Effie herself. I adored her, but I hardly knew her. I had no idea of the almost frenzied shyness that often made her speechless. I was perplexed and, no doubt, stupid. She could not understand why I babbled like a brook when Hudson was there and fell into unaccountable silences when he was not. The idea that conversation cannot be a monologue was one she never got hold of. It was, she held, easy for me to talk and difficult for her. Why then did I not talk, whether Hudson was there or not? It could only be that I thought her not worth talking to! While I sweated and toiled to find subjects of conversation with one whom I loved to desperation, but hardly knew at all, she sat in an island of silence and dropped every ball I sent across. The result was much misunderstanding and even tears. I re-read now letters that I wrote to her when I happened to be away for a night or two, and which she kept, and I am filled with amusement and amazement. They are hysterical in their devotion and despair. I loved her and could not bear to fail her while Hudson was away. I loved him and felt he had entrusted to me her happiness and well-being, and I was failing him too.

I am sure Effie never knew what I suffered, and only a very immature young woman could have suffered in just this way. I am amazed at myself. But those months set a mark on me that I have never lost, and I was older by much more than four months when Hudson came back from America.

I didn't know that my adored Effie, with all her strange and lovely charm, was mentally unstable and possessed by an overwhelming fear of life. I didn't know that Hudson was to her strength and security and that, without him, no one, however loved, could save her from that strange terror of which she once said to me that "if she only knew what she was afraid of she wouldn't be afraid."

Effie *never* felt safe when Hudson was not there.

He came back [from America] and we rejoiced. Conversation flowed. Effie listened and was most content to listen. She used to laugh at us or perhaps it would be more true to say that she and I together laughed at Hudson and she and he together laughed at me.

It is a commonplace to say that people who love each other find themselves laughing at the same things, but it is not always true. Hudson and I rarely laughed at the same things: Effie and I always did. Hudson was transported with glee at things that left us cold. He used to say we had no sense of humor, but he only meant that we hadn't his sense of humor. It never strikes me as really funny when someone sits on his hat or plays a practical joke which almost always hurts someone else's feelings. I loathe practical jokes. So did Effie. Hudson adored them, and it was only after several painful explosions on my part that he realized my sad lack of humor and stopped playing them on me. He turned the garden hose on me in my best pale *grey crêpe de Chine* frock, and that was the end of that.

Effie and I thought him funny in quite a different way and we laughed ourselves to exhaustion at him, but he only regarded us with indulgent pity and said, "Silly women!" [. . .]

I don't think anyone who lived with Hudson would help laughing at him. He was often so enchantingly absurd! He was always convinced that everyone wanted what he wanted and generally we did. When we didn't it did not make the slightest difference: he did it all the same. No one was more earnest in asking advice and none disregarded it more completely. [Once] he took it into his head that the church needed a new organ. As was always the case with him when a new interest seized him, nothing else was spoken of or thought about for months. It was a wonder that so small an object could arouse such ardor. So small was it that we could not decide whether it should have four stops or six. Round this difficult point discussion raged. We had it for breakfast, for lunch, tea, and dinner. At last while interest and argument were still at their height, Hudson remarked casually that we needn't worry ourselves as he had already given the order for six.

Effie was delighted at my fury. He always behaved like that, she said—and he always did. He was quite sure we should find that he was right. If we didn't—but then he didn't notice that, and we were obliged to give up noticing it too. [. . .]

Life with him was always interesting, often infuriating, sometimes, in fits of depression, almost tragic; but never dull.

Our love for each other grew. We went on thinking of it as fatherly on his side and hero-worship on mine. Then suddenly, as a crystal is formed by a shake of the glass, our awareness crystallized.

The shake was given by a friend who was staying at the rectory for a long visit. She was older than I and far more a woman of the world. She saw what was happening to us and, very kindly, gave me a word of advice. I—like an idiot—was amazed and enraged. Her friendly warning seemed to me an attempt to poison an innocent and happy relationship which was my dearest possession. Like the bull in a china shop which all my life I have too closely resembled, I rushed straight to Hudson and poured out my indignation and disgust. "She thinks I'm in love with you," I roared. And he roared too, for Hudson also a little resembled the china shop bull. We mingled our indignation and our plaints. I blush now to think of our injustice to our mutual friend. We didn't even trouble to assure each other that we were not in love: the idea still seemed preposterous. We didn't think of it. It could not be. That was enough.

It was not enough. Effie knew what was happening. She saw that, unconsciously, we were already living under a great strain. I, at least, had reached a point at which the smallest disagreement, the slightest difference, between Hudson and myself was unbearable. I became irritable and quarrelsome, never with her but often with him. [. . .]

If Hudson and I knew our minds, Effie knew our hearts. Whether she too received a friendly warning from our friend, I do not know, but I think it may have been so. Her reaction to it was as surprising as mine. She believed that I could never have all I needed as long as Hudson gave to me, and I to him, no more than affection, no more than friendship. She was aware that we sometimes, in spite of friendship, got on each other's nerves. Hudson, at least, got on mine. He was very rarely angry with me, partly because he had not set me up on a pedestal as I had set him, and so was not appalled at finding flaws in my character partly because he had an intellectual outlet denied to me. But I was often angry with him and we were both living under strains that we did not recognize or understand.

Effie understood. After one of our flare-ups, which were becoming painfully frequent, I found her in tears. This was a rare thing and I was horror-stricken. What was the matter? I had behaved badly to the Man,[5] but surely not to her? What was troubling her so deeply?

How well I remember her answer! "You are spoiling one of the loveliest things in the world."

One of the loveliest things in the world! What did she mean? What was I spoiling? "The Man's and your love for each other." [. . .]

Effie was utterly without possessiveness. This was true of her in every way. She had no lust for possessions, she had no care for money, it was the most difficult thing in the world to find for her a Christmas or a birthday present. And now? She had no other thought, no other desire, than that the people she loved should have as far as possible what would make them happiest.

I try to make this clear. Effie was repelled by passion. It frightened her. She shrank instinctively from demands on her which she knew she could not meet without in some obscure way endangering that delicate mental balance which was in her always precarious. Hudson knew this. He told me that he had often tried to make her face life and had been exasperated and angry when she put up a defense against such attempts. People had blamed him for not being "more firm" with her, and he had sometimes blamed himself. But he had come to the conclusion that Effie knew herself better than anyone else did. She knew instinctively how much—or rather how little—she could bear of life without danger. And she fled from it. Sometimes (but this was before I knew her) she would literally flee—lock herself into her room, refuse to come down if there were strangers in the house, and stay till they went away.

She knew herself. She had never (for instance) meant to have a child. She had one and she loved him greatly, but the months of his coming were hell to her and she was out of her mind for two years afterward. To her, life itself and love that asked too much, were alike terrifying.

There are, nevertheless, few women or men who can face the thought of another giving to the one they love even what they themselves cannot give and do not want. This is where Effie Shaw was apart from the rest of us. She did not wish her husband and her friend to transgress their moral standards or hers: she did want us to have all that was possible for us—not love only, but passionate love.

---

5. "The Man" was the affectionately mocking name Effie and Royden gave Shaw. (KW)

I marvel as I write it. Will anyone believe that she was never jealous of our love? Perhaps not: yet it is true. She never was. I am certain that she never had to fight against jealousy and never felt it. She was glad that Hudson should have something at least of what he needed: she was glad that I should. She understood our deepest need and met it without effort, with the perfection that only comes from perfect love.

I say that what she gave us met our deepest need. It did so. It did so in spite of all that was denied us. [. . .]

From the beginning there were three of us. That made possible everything that was impossible. Hudson and I knew that we must always think of life as including all three. We must never think of any other relationship than this. This was to be our life: Hudson, Effie, and I.

Love is always life and love costs and love is human and divine—for us all.

Hudson never thought of himself as a "rare and gifted soul": he only claimed for himself, as I for myself, that our lives had been worth living because of our love.

How often have I been reminded, when with him, of those most true words of Studdert Kennedy's, *"When we are with someone who loves us and whom we love, we no longer ask why we were born or what life is for. We know it is for this."*[6]

Sometimes we tried to imagine what our lives would have been if we had never met or never loved; or, living, parted as once we tried to do. We never could imagine it. We could as well imagine how we could have lived if we had not lived. At the heart of all we were and did was this passion. No blows of fortune, failures, or disappointments could touch that and we could suffer no mortal wound nor be tired of living.

Now that I grow tired and old, and he is gone, I marvel at the immense energy and zest that filled us for so many years. In the post-war stage we were more fortunate than ever in working together. We devoted ourselves to the cause of world peace, believed in the League of Nations, and were sure it could only succeed if it accepted the ideals if not the name of Christianity.

---

6. Geoffrey Anketell Studdert Kennedy (1883–1929), Anglican priest, poet, author and decorated (Military Cross) World War I frontline chaplain who became an outspoken pacifist after the war. See my *After War, Is Faith Possible? The Life and Message of Geoffrey 'Woodbine Willie' Studdert Kennedy* (Eugene, OR: Cascade, 2008). (KW)

Time passed. Between our first meeting and Hudson's death was forty-three years. And all that time we loved each other and all that time we loved each other more and more. I do not pretend that we were never for a moment alienated, and I see, looking back, that this was the fault of both of us but more mine than his. The jars that sometimes hurt us arose not from any difference about our relationship but from a divergence in our way of handling it. It was my plan to throw myself into other interests and even other human relationships with energy. I was fortunate in that this didn't really demand a plan: the people I loved and the work I did were so dear to me that in any case, and even had Hudson and I been married, they would have been very near to my heart. And it seemed to me that to give all I could to them was, besides being natural to me, both right and wise for us two. I own that I sometimes gave Hudson grounds for feeling that I gave to others what he felt belonged to him. I thought he should have understood and agreed. He didn't—at least not always. I realized that, partly at the time, but after our marriage more clearly.

Hudson, of course, did the same in many ways and most of the time; but it was his inclination, when we were together, to dwell much on what might have been. He did this without rebellion or resentment but he did it, and I often found the strain unbearable. I wanted to put such thoughts, however dear, out of mind and to concentrate our minds (for it is dangerous to leave them unconcentrated) on our work. For many years we had a standing engagement to read theology together on Saturday mornings. [. . .] I was always more than content to be in the same room with Hudson, he with his work, I with mine: but in certain moods this exasperated him. Why are we wasting our time? he would ask. What is the sense of our sitting in the same room in silence? Well, we both had work to do and we *needed* to work; but this did not content him.

I thought I was right then not to dwell overmuch on other things. To do so, I thought, made life needlessly hard for us. Now I wonder if I was mistaken—if it was a desire to escape pain—a piece of cowardice of which Hudson would not be guilty. One must not try to escape the pain of life. What do we suffer for if we lose the knowledge it gives by trying to evade it?

I shall never know. I chronicle what we did, and sometimes this difference in our way of meeting life made a rift between us and he was jealous and I gave him cause. I was impatient when he thought I was doing too much. It irked me when he complained that I had other friends more dear to me than his to him. Perhaps he had cause—how can I judge? Was I ungenerous? Was he exacting? I do not know. Only I know that his faithfulness was something that one might dream of but hardly hope to know, and that it continued with utter steadfastness till he died.

The time came at last when Hudson had to give up his work. He was growing old and the terrific energy with which he had poured himself out when young and in middle life was now telling on him. He was subject, as ever, to devastating periods of depression, but now he could not fight against them. More and more frequently he was absent from London. All his life he had dreamed of possessing a cottage somewhere in the country to which he could go for a rest sometimes, and for his old age when it came.

There are perhaps few people who realize the dreams they dream for their old age. By a blessed miracle, Hudson did. He found a cottage, not too far from London, which fulfilled them all. It is fourteenth century and almost wholly unspoiled. It is, in fact, almost incredible. Hudson's constant cry was—"What have we done to deserve this?"—and the answer could only be "Nothing!" Who could deserve it? [. . .]

It was impossible not to realize, however, that Hudson's life was not a good one from a medical point of view. Equally impossible to expect him to go slowly or contemplate resignation as long as he had long intervals during which he felt magnificently well. This he did, though, of course, there were intervals, not so long, when he fell into depression and felt unspeakably weary. [. . .]

There is something heart-rending about the gradual loss of physical strength in one we love, especially one who had been superbly strong. Hudson never cared for games but, in spite of his short stature, he had been a great runner and the winner of many trophies. It was anguish to him to realize that he had no longer strength enough to lift me off my feet or even, at last, to see me across our two small gardens in the evening. He persisted in doing this long after his failing strength made it an anxiety to all of us. We used to devise means of watching him as he went along the rough little path and three or four stone steps, never knowing whether it was better to endure the anxiety ourselves or inflict on him the exasperation of knowing that we were trying to take care of him. At last he accepted his fate and would stand at his door and watch me till I was safely up the steps: but he minded so much—so much. We both hated it, I for his sake, he for mine.

Still, his mind retained its extraordinary grip and he not only read, but planned to write. Realizing that almost nothing of all he had thought and taught had been printed, he and I used to go over the lectures and sermons he judged his best and plan a book of them to be published "after the war." Still more he hoped to write a book on the Gospel according to St. Luke, and I hoped it, too. Though I recognized many of his lectures as masterpieces of scholarship and style—Hudson wrote noble English—I doubted whether their subjects were not too isolated and diverse to make a book: that his studies of the Gospels, and above all St. Luke, would have made a great one was and is my unshakable conviction.

Almost to the last we were planning it. Hudson produced summaries, syllabi, notes, and lists of books; together we discussed the shape and scope of the work. I believed that he would write quickly and easily when once he had started. Alas! He could not start. He had written too little and spoken too much to be at ease with a pen in his hand. The faculty had gone. I don't think there ever came a moment in which he knew for certain that it was too late, though sometimes he said it was. For my part I fought against the conviction. I could not accept the verdict. It seemed to me an intolerable thing that all that thought, that fresh vision of new things, that matchless power of imparting knowledge should leave no lasting record behind. I have even thought of trying to write his book myself, now he is gone. It is beyond me. Only Hudson could have done it. I don't know when I realized that the book would not be written. It was not more than a few months—even weeks—before his death. I doubt whether he realized it ever.

Then Effie died.[7] In the last years of her life she had been happier than, during my knowledge of her, she had ever been before. No demands were made on her and she had neither to try to do things nor to resist the feeling that others thought she ought to try. And for the years after Hudson's resignation, she had him constantly with her. Effie gradually ceased (I believe) to be much afraid of life. I never knew whether she ceased to be afraid of death, but at least she no longer seemed to be afraid of anything. [. . .]

---

7. February 1944. (KW)

Hudson had known how ill she was—really he knew that she was dying: but we had believed for many years that, frail as she was, she would outlive him with his greater age and dangerous heart, and when she went it was a shock that I thought would kill him. He seemed unable to believe it and kept shivering and looking so ghastly that I was in terror for him. I had to arrange everything, of course, and knew that he could not possibly go to her funeral; but when the day came he wouldn't let me go either and looked so stricken that I stayed with him.

Is it foolish to mind these things, I wonder? I don't know. But I went downstairs just for a moment while the coffin was being carried out and I felt a pang of anguish at seeing it. There were some friends there who loved her, but I could not imagine Effie going anywhere without *either* Hudson or me; and now she was setting out alone on that unknown way and we could not help her or save her from fear. [. . .]

It was characteristic of our ingrained habit of thinking of life always as lived by three that it didn't occur to either of us at first that there was now nothing to prevent our marriage. After a little while, however, I realized it with a sense of shock. It seemed unbelievable. I thought it *was* unbelievable and hoped Hudson wouldn't think of it. However astonishing his powers of resilience were, he was now an old man and his heart might fail at any time. For years I (and he) had known that whenever we parted it might be forever. I might come home and find him gone. Then suddenly one day, he said to me, "Do you realize that there is now no legal obstacle to our being married?" I said I had. "When?" "Oh, a day or two ago."

We said no more at the time, but soon he began to press me. We couldn't be married at once, of course, but how soon. He reminded me of that old promise Effie had asked of him many years ago that if she died first he should, as soon as possible, marry me. I hesitated very much and spoke of it to a few very close friends. Some were opposed to it, others vehemently in favor. It seemed unnecessary to risk hurting anyone's feelings since (we said to one another) nothing could add to our love and nothing change it. Why not go on as we were? What difference could it make?

We both hesitated. On his part was the dread he had of making me "nurse to an old invalid" and also the fear that people who loved me—my known and unknown friends—might disapprove and perhaps be shocked at our marriage. It was the first consideration that weighted most heavily with him. Hudson had a horror of the miseries of physical illness. He hated my being burdened by his. One day I went into his room and found him in great misery. When he saw me he cried out that his heart was broken "because it is too late—it is too late." I accepted this and thought it true. "It has always been hard," I said, "let it be hard to the end." And for a time he also accepted it.

After a while Hudson's health improved. With this we began once more to think of marriage, and soon I found he was thinking of it as a fixed thing. He told his friends when they came to visit him that it was so, and it was partly their generous and lovely reception of this surely rather astonishing news that made me, too, begin to think it possible. While I still hesitated he asked in a burst of indignation "whether I was ashamed of him?" No one who has read this story will wonder that I could not answer other than I did. As he said with great content "Why should we care what anyone says or thinks?" [. . .]

We were married on October 2nd, 1944. [. . .]

Hudson had gone through the [marriage] ceremony better than I dared to hope, in spite of the emotional strain. We had both wished to be married in church. Our beloved Bishop had made everything easy for us and the ceremony was short. Our dread was, of course, lest Hudson should have a heart attack and be unable to go through with it, and we were both nervous about him when the time came. But the familiar words of the service—which he had pronounced so often in marrying others—and I, too, sometimes, for I had been minister at the marriages of some of my Guildhouse congregation—came to us with benediction. His hand was in mine as the Bishop read the great chapter from the Epistle to the Corinthians and, as sentence followed sentence, I could feel the relaxation of nervous tension and the benediction of their familiar beauty.

We went from the church and to his home rejoicing. He was well—he had had no attack—we were married. It seemed as if those who had prophesied that happiness would give him a new lease of life were right. How happy we were!

Then suddenly that evening, came an attack so exhausting that I thought he could not live. He had gone upstairs and I was out of the room at the moment. I was called and found him—as it seemed—dying. Dying! At that moment! I could not bear it. Once I could tell him, once I had told him, not to struggle—not to fight death for my sake—but now! I cried out to him not to go, not to leave me, and even at that hour my voice reached him. He heard me and he turned and came back from the shadow of death.

With his almost miraculous power of recovery he fought through a few days of exhaustion and began to live again. On the day after our wedding he said to me, "How long have we been married?" I looked at my watch. It was five minutes to twelve. "In five minutes," I said, "we shall have been married exactly twenty-four hours." Again and again he put that question to me half jestingly—"How long have we been married? How long have you been my wife?" Three days—a week—a month—two months.

Two months—two months of joy and grief. In that short time Hudson recovered, gathered strength again and again, got up and dressed, came down into his beloved garden, planned its future, laughed at me when I reported that someone had lived to be over ninety and promised that he would try to do the same.

He said to me in tones of infinite content: "I shall never be jealous again, of your friends or your work or *anything*; for, after all, you did marry me." [...]

But again and again came attacks which sapped even his strength and at last forced me to realize that he was losing ground.

There are times when joy is so complete that one ceases to ask, "Have we deserved this?" or "Can it last?" Times when we ask nothing, when there is nothing to ask, when time is timeless. So it was with us. What pain would we not have endured for such a heaven? What does it matter that our time was short? Is infinity short?

One consolation I had which is not given to all: it was that with all his love of life Hudson was never afraid of death. He wanted to live. With all the hated disabilities of increasing weakness he still wanted life. When I counted up the nonagenarians in the columns of *The Times* he laughed at me, but he himself would sometimes say with longing, as the days shortened and winter drew on, "If I could have *one* more spring, *one* more summer!" We told each other that the war would be over and we could go for drives again and see the loveliness of the countryside. It was a beautiful dream. But we knew it might be only a dream and Hudson would speak of death without anxiety or fear, only once more promising me to live as long as he could that I "might not have long to wait." How I pity those whose beloved are fearful and must not be told they are dying! How dreadful to have to be playing a part when time is so short!

I don't know when I knew that Hudson was leaving me. He knew it before I did, I think. The knowledge came near me when he ceased to want to get up and dress. He had always hated staying in bed and disobeyed his doctor's orders when told to do so. Now his doctor urged him to get up and he no longer cared to. He would try, to please me, for I knew how ill a sign this languor was, but gradually he ceased to try. He was too tired. More than once when our eyes met, he gently shook his head. I wanted to say, "What is it? Why do you shake your head?" But my courage failed me. I did not want to hear him say he was leaving me.

Gradually he did leave me. The day came when Hudson's doctor told me he would not live more than twenty-four hours. I sat beside him, counting the moments, but now I didn't try to call him back. He wanted to live, but the struggle was too great. That mortal fatigue which had possessed him often when in the height of his powers was no longer to be denied. I could not wish him to endure it longer.

He fell into unconsciousness and in his sleep he died. He had no pain and I was with him, his hand in mine.

We had had forty-three years of work and love and we had been married eight weeks and three days. For all this I thank God.

Looking back on my own life I say with conviction, "I regret little, I would change still less."[8] In our threefold life each of us gave and each took. And all of us were the richer for the giving. Hudson and I by Effie's giving as well as Effie by ours.

Source

A. Maude Royden (Mrs. Hudson Shaw), *A Threefold Cord* (New York: Macmillan, 1948), 9–10, 13–14, 14–15, 17–19, 22, 23, 24, 25–27, 28, 74–75, 78–79, 81, 91, 92–93, 95, 97, 99–100, 105, 106, 111–12, 113–14, 104.

8. Robert Browning, "Andrea del Sarto" (1855). (KW)

For Further Reading

Books and Pamphlets by Maude Royden

The Great Adventure: The Way to Peace. London: Headley Brothers, 1915.
Women and the Church of England. London: George Allen & Unwin, 1916.
Women and the Sovereign State. London: Headley Bros., 1917.
The Hour and the Church: An Appeal to the Church of England. London: Allen & Unwin, 1918.
Blessed Joan of Arc. London: Sidgwick and Jackson, 1918.
National Endowment of Motherhood. London: Hodgson & Son, 1919.
"Women and Theology." Pamphlet in the *Women and Church* series. London: League of the Church Militant, Anglican, 1920.
Political Christianity. New York: Putnam's Sons, 1922.
Sex and Common-Sense. 8th ed. New York: Putnam's Sons, 1928.
Women at the World's Crossroads. New York: Womans, 1922.
Prayer as a Force. New York: Putnam's Sons, 1923.
The Church and Woman. New York: Doran, 1924.
Christ Triumphant. New York: Putnam's Sons, 1924.
The Friendship of God. New York: Putnam's Sons, 1924.
Beauty in Religion. London: Putnam's Sons, 1925.
Life's Little Pitfalls. New York: Putnam's Sons, 1925.
I Believe in God. New York: Harper & Brothers, 1927.
Here—and Hereafter. London: Putnam, 1933.
The Problem of Palestine. London: Hutchinson & Co., 1939.
Women's Partnership in the New World. London: Allen & Unwin, 1941.
A Threefold Cord. New York: Macmillan, 1947.

Selected Secondary Sources

Baker, William King. *Penn the Statesman and Gulielma: A Quaker Idyll.* Edinburgh: Oliphants, 1926.
Baylen, J. O. "A Remarkable Life: Maude Royden." *English Literature in Transition, 1880–1920* 34 (1991) 111–16.

Begbie, Harold. "Miss Maude Royden." In *Painted Windows: Studies in Religious Personality*, 103–20. London: Putnam's Sons, 1922.
Ceadel, Martin. *Pacifism in Britain, 1914–45: The Defining of a Faith*. Oxford: Clarendon, 1980.
Dixon, Joy. "Maude Royden and the 'Sacrament of Love.'" *Modern Believing* 64 (2023) 406–12.
Downing, Arthur. "Political Christianity in Action: The Crusades of Agnes Maude Royden." *Journal of the Rutgers University Libraries* 46 (1984) 28–38.
Falby, Alison. "Maude Royden's Guildhouse: A Nexus of Religious Change in Britain Between the Wars." *Historical Papers: Canadian Society of Church History* (2004) 165–75.
Fletcher, Sheila. *Maude Royden: A Life*. Oxford: Basil Blackwell, 1989.
Frost, S. E., Jr., ed. *The World's Great Sermons*. Garden City, NY: Garden City Publishing, 1942.
Gardiner, A. G. *Certain People of Importance*. London: Dent & Sons, 1929.
Gollancz, Victor, ed. *The Making of Women: Oxford Essays in Feminism*. London: Allen & Unwin, 1917.
Harrison, Brian. *Separate Spheres: The Opposition to Women's Suffrage in Britain*. New York: Holmes & Meier, 1978.
Heeney, Brian. *The Women's Movement in the Church of England, 1850–1930*. London: Oxford University Press, 1988.
Kennedy, G. A. Studdert. *The Wicket Gate, or Plain Bread*. London: Doubleday, Doran & Co., 1923.
Keyes, Frances Parkinson. "Torchbearers to Humanity." *Good Housekeeping* 86 (1928) 30–31, 90, 95–96.
Methuen, Charlotte. "Maude Royden: Preacher of Peace in Conflict and War." *Kirchliche Zeitgeschichte* 31 (2008) 58–80.
Morgan, Sue. "A 'Feminist Conspiracy': Maude Royden, Women's Ministry, and the British Press, 1916–1921." *Women's History Review* 22 (2013) 777–800.
———. "'Sex and Common-Sense': Maude Royden, Religion, and Modern Sexuality." *Journal of British Studies* 52 (2013) 153–78.
Murry, Middleton. *The Life of Jesus*. London: Butler & Tanner, 1926.
Newton, Joseph Fort. "Maude Royden: The Story of a Great Woman's Great Opportunity." *Century Magazine* (1928) 562–68.
Oxford (Asquith), Margot, ed. *Myself When Young*. London: Muller, 1938.
Rademaker, Laura. "Religion for the Modern Girl: Maude Royden in Australia, 1928." *Australian Feminist Studies* 31.89 (2016) 336–54.
Ruskin, John. *Sesame and Lilies*. Boston: Silver, Burdett & Co., 1900.
Schreiner, Olive. "Women and War." In *Woman and Labor*, 157–86. New York: Stokes, 1911.
Wiltsher, Anne. *Most Dangerous Women: Feminist Peace Campaigners of the Great War*. London: Pandora, 1985.

Index

Abraham, 153
agony, 46, 70, 186, 194, 196, 203, 247, 255–56
Allen, Reginald Clifford, 264
All-ness, 201, 203, 248–49
American Baptist Church, 17
American Civil War, 46, 237
angels, 76–77, 178, 181
Anglican Prayer-Book, 130
Anselm, 153
anti-feminism, ecclesial, 108, 113, 117.
    See also: women, subordination of; women and ministry
apostolic succession, 121, 123, 137
architecture, beauty, 5, 21, 165
art in worship, 164
art as sacramental, 161–62, 164

Baker, Josephine, 116
Baker, William King, 55, 57, 59, 285
baptism, 25, 31, 145, 165, 182
    administered by layperson, 130
    and children, 163
    as sacrament, 164
beauty, 5–6, 21, 56, 84, 96, 163–65, 185, 190, 195, 266, 281
    conjugal, 93
    divine, 150, 184, 196, 231
    in love, 34
    natural, 30, 162, 169, 179
    and truth, 57
beauty and conversion, 138
beauty and Roman Catholicism, 270
Becket, Thomas, Saint, 153
Belgium, 38, 46–49, 54, 65–66, 254

belief, 49, 53, 64–66, 110, 129, 148, 161–62, 166, 180–81, 185, 188, 202–4, 206, 217, 219, 227, 235, 238
belief in morality of war, 51
Bell, Florence Eveleen, Lady, 84
Bible, 122, 155, 184, 190, 201, 215, 248–49
    and unity of truth, 184
biblical criticism, 105, 174, 209
Blackwell, Basil, 2, 286
bodies, 95–96, 126, 132, 158, 161–62, 167, 202, 205, 246, 266
Boer War, 12
Bright, William, 197
British colonialism, 12, 26
Browning, Robert, 148, 283
Buddhism, 126, 160, 203
Butler, Josephine, 116, 157

Catherine of Siena, Saint, 113, 116, 210
ceremonies
    magic, 149
    marriage, 88
    religious, 88
    ritualism, 219
child labor, 23, 82, 154, 156–57
Christ, 38, 100, 183, 245
    death of, 196
    healings of, 127, 141, 144, 227, 245–46
    love of, 216
Christian art, 162, 243–44. *See Also:* art in worship

INDEX

Christian churches and liturgical
  regulations, 109, 129
  and militarism, 49
  and the exploited, 157
  and uniformity, 135
  and women, 100
Christianity, 19, 70, 101, 155, 160, 162, 185, 246–47, 258
  as religion of escape, 161
  and fear, 183
  and feminism, 33
  and joy, 246
  and personality, 202
  and sin, 42
  and truth, 247
  and war, 51
  and women, 100
  as social religion, 126
  as way of life, 252
Christians, modern, 201, 203, 245, 262
Christian Science, 96, 245
Christian union, 127
Christian virtues, 258–59, 261, 263, 265
  See also: moral issues
Christlike behavior, 38, 186, 219, 261
church, 6, 11–12, 16–17, 20, 24, 32, 34, 101–4, 106–11, 113–14, 116, 121–25, 128–30, 132–37, 140–41, 143, 145–46, 153, 155, 158–60, 165, 207, 215, 244–45
  early, 144, 156
  infallibility of, 114, 132
  and women, 15, 26, 105, 33
  and women's ordination, 115, 210
  and women's rights, 2
Church League for Women's Suffrage, 11, 15, 20
Church of England, 2, 16–17, 20, 27–28, 31–33, 101, 108, 116, 122–23, 131–34, 143–44, 286
church unity, 128
City Temple, 17–22, 28–29, 31, 33–34
Code Napoleon, 11, 64
Coltman, Constance, 116
commandments, 177, 192, 225–27
communion, sacramental, 131
communion in prayer, 221
  of saints, 165
  of sin, 42
compassion, 14, 59, 113, 194, 225
Congregational Union, 116
conscience, 1, 44, 65, 143, 155
conscientious objectors, 127, 264
Contagious Diseases Acts, 156, 158
Cotton Factories Regulation Act, 156
Courtney, Kathleen, 5, 12
Cross of Christ, 42, 46, 51, 104, 106, 152, 186, 192–94, 237–38, 242–45, 247, 261
cruelty, 49, 51, 62, 149, 185–86, 239

Dante, 219
Darwin, Charles, 91
Dearmer, Percy, 21, 24
death, finality of, 192
  See also: postmortem survival
devil, 136, 162, 174, 205
devotion, 56, 83, 86–87, 90, 117, 138, 141, 143, 191, 272
Dickens, Charles, 83, 264
differences, men and women, 77, 80, 111
discipleship, 33, 39–40, 42–43, 52, 70, 106, 113, 124, 126, 141, 143, 145, 161, 183, 218–19, 226, 230, 246–47, 261, 265
divine grace, 139, 169
Dobson, Daisy, 2, 25, 27, 31
doctrines
  Atonement, 33, 189, 193, 196, 209
  Baptism, 163
  Eucharist, 131, 163, 167, 169, 250
  love, 217
  ordination, 114
  Resurrection, 121–22, 125, 244
  theological, 196–97
  total depravity, 162, 260
  Trinity, 176, 229, 231
Drummond, Eric, 69

E. B. (poet), 196
Elephant Man. *See* Merrick, Joseph
Emergency Peace Campaign, 28–29
English Hymnal, The, 21
evil, 38, 40–42, 46–47, 54, 194, 204, 222
  and disloyalty, 53
  God's patience with, 194

social institutions, 154
evolution, 177, 179, 202–3, 216
    and human survival, 191
    and revelation, 185
    of spirit, 176

Fawcett, Millicent Garrett, 10
feminism, 10, 12, 33, 60–61, 63, 65–67
feminism and militarism, 75, 2, 62, 64, 66–67
forgiveness, 3, 131, 158–59, 182–83, 186, 190–91, 197–200, 222, 254
France, 11, 14, 22, 29, 38, 46, 52, 54, 64, 136
Francis de Sales, Saint, 113
Francis of Assisi, Saint, 261
Frankby Hall, 1, 3–6, 32
Free Churchman, 138, 140, 165
freedom, fighting for, 49
freedom and love, 242
free will, 193, 204
friendship, 167, 229–33, 255–56, 269, 274
fundamental truths, 77, 154, 191, 243, 252

Gandhi, Mohandas, 26, 68, 70–71
Gardiner, A. G., 1, 286
gender subordination, 2, 109
gentleness, 258, 263, 265–66
George, David Lloyd, 50, 65, 86
Germany, 14, 29, 45, 48–51, 64
Glasgow University, 28
Gloucestershire Cheltenham Ladies College, 4
Glover, T. R., 137
God
    absolute, 230–31
    anthropomorphism, 232
    crucified, 238
    eternal, 231
    friend, 232
    Immanent, 201–2
    impersonal, 230
    infinite, 232
    as Love, 183–84, 186, 196, 242
    and suffering, 193–94
    as truth, 204

Gollancz, Victor, 80, 99, 286
Gollock, M.C., 102
government, 9, 11, 62, 64–65, 67, 125
grace, 115, 140–41, 143–44, 166, 168, 197, 200, 225–26, 228, 261, 263, 266, 271
Gray, Herbert, 27, 68–69
Great Commandment, 177
greatness, 136, 248
Great War, The, 29, 55, 60, 135, 207
Guild Fellowship, 21–25, 27–28, 33–34
Guildhouse, 22–24, 28–29, 31, 154, 215
    congregation, 281
    prayer, 221
Gunter, Evelyn, 5, 7, 269
Gunter, Kathleen, 6

Haig, Douglas, Sir, 75
Haldane, Richard Burdon, Lord, 50
Harrison, Agatha, 68
Harrison, Brian, 15, 286
Harrison, Jane Ellen, 147
hatred, 39, 42, 46, 51, 58–59, 183–86, 195, 218, 227, 255, 261, 264
heaven, 34, 41, 43, 47, 101, 137, 139, 144, 163, 165, 178–82, 184, 192, 199, 201, 203, 217, 226, 246, 282
heresies, 49–51, 138, 179, 194, 207
heroism, 14, 45, 49, 51, 55–56, 141
Hobbes, John Oliver, 115
Hobhouse, Stephen Henry, 264
Holy Communion, 123, 131, 134, 163–68. *See also:* doctrines, Eucharist
Holy Orders, 16, 20, 28, 108, 114–15, 130, 207. *See also:* women, ordination of
Home, Daniel Dunglass, 148
Hopkins, Ellice, 116
Hudson, Effie, 11, 276. *See also:* Royden, Maude
Hudson, Shaw, 8, 30–31, 270–83. *See also:* Royden, Maude
humanity, 10, 19, 42, 47, 52, 54, 56, 65–66, 91, 111–12, 125, 140, 150–51, 173, 176–77, 179, 181, 184, 187, 191, 196, 198–99, 216, 231, 237

human life, 132, 194, 202, 204
human mind, 66, 150, 173, 194, 230, 245
human nature, 85, 90–91, 125, 130, 236
human personality, 41, 229
human race, 178, 185, 187, 189, 191, 193, 198–99, 203
human relationships, 67, 277
humility, 135, 141, 174, 199, 221–22, 258, 261, 264–65

ideals, 43, 53–55, 110, 276
imagination, 55, 194, 209, 231, 234–35, 237, 249, 255, 259
intellect, 208, 231

Japanese Manchurian War, 27
Jesus, 37, 39, 45, 68, 160, 175–77, 180–81, 219, 248–49. *See also:* Christ
  character of, 135, 137
  disciples of, 43
  divinity of, 178
  humanity, 181
  and love, 189, 200
  political message, 23
Jesus and gender equality, 106
Jesus and nonviolence, 13
Jesus as poet, 251
Jews, 43, 101, 104, 123, 127, 149, 153, 155–56, 177, 184–85, 191, 260
joy, 141, 145, 149, 161, 165, 216–17, 219, 222–23, 229, 247
Judas Iscariot, 56, 145, 195, 198, 235, 265
judgment, 76, 90–91, 153, 159, 192, 195, 207, 209, 222, 235, 237–38, 241, 256, 263, 265–66
justice, 23, 57, 109, 177, 190, 207, 211, 259, 265

Keats, John, 57–58
Kelvin, William Thomson, 138–39
Keyes, Frances Parkinson, 1, 32, 286
Kingdom of God, 11, 38, 40, 52, 64, 126–27, 141, 144, 182–83, 195, 209, 226, 246–47, 249–50
knowledge, 93, 96–97, 174, 194, 203, 252, 283
  of self, 223

Lady Margaret Hall, 4–5, 269
Lambeth Conference, 19–20, 25–27, 109–10
Lane, Homer, 211
Lanfranc, 153
Langton, Stephen, 153
League of Nations, 19, 24, 27, 69, 276
Little Company of Christ, 24–25
Liverpool, 1, 3, 5, 20, 28
Liverpool Victoria Women's settlement house, 6
logic, 58, 63, 66, 109
London Blitz, 29
Lord Shaftesbury (Anthony Ashley-Cooper), 157
love, 11, 33, 39–41, 52, 54, 58–59, 90–94, 96, 117, 140, 146–47, 173–74, 177–78, 183, 185–93, 195, 198, 202, 207, 215, 217, 226, 228, 232, 235–40, 247, 250–52, 259, 265–66, 270–71, 273–75, 278, 282–83
  divine, 176, 183, 216, 250, 261
  kingdom of, 141, 145
  law of, 206, 226
  non-coercive, 235, 237, 239, 241
  passionate, 113, 275
  sacrament of, 94, 286
lovers, 59, 89, 95, 98, 116, 174, 178, 200, 219, 271
loyalty, 38, 53, 57, 61–62, 130, 258–59, 261, 263–65
  to Christ, 42
  to fellow humans, 52

magic, 147–50, 162, 164, 227
magnanimity, 258–59, 265
Maisons Tolerées, 11
Marcus Aurelius, 261
marriage, 3, 8, 25, 30, 88–99, 270–71, 277, 280–82
  and freedom, 98
  as sacrament of unity, 97
material world, 161–62, 165–66, 169, 187, 204, 246–47
matter, sacredness of, 166, 187
Meredith, George, 93
Merrick, Joseph, 253–54

INDEX

Middle Ages, 152, 178, 210, 219
militarism, 2, 12, 45, 49–51, 60–67
militarism and feminism, 2, 62, 64, 66–67
miracles, 227, 235, 237–38, 243, 246
modern lovers, 96, 98
moral freedom, 234, 239, 241
moral issues, 1, 23, 156, 204, 238, 240. *See also:* Christian virtues
morality, 13, 18, 88–91, 213
moral judgment, 235
moral uncertainty, 34
motherhood, 75, 79–80, 85–86, 111
    spiritual, 111

National Endowment of Motherhood, 80–83, 85–87, 285
National Mission of Repentance and Hope, 16, 143
Neil, Judge, 86
Newman, John Henry, Saint, 6, 153
Newton, Joseph Fort, 11, 17–18, 21, 33, 286
New York, 1–2, 6, 10, 33–34, 60, 63, 67, 91, 224, 283, 285–86
nonviolence, 13, 29, 45
nonviolent resistance. *See:* resistance, nonviolence

Old Testament, 52, 149, 156, 185, 226, 244, 260
orthodoxy, 33, 127, 173–75
Oxford, 2, 4–6, 8, 12, 138, 269–70, 286
Oxford Students' Debating Society, 5
Oxford University, 4, 269
Oxford University Extension program, 7–8, 10, 18

pacifism, 1–2, 12, 15, 18–19, 26, 29, 31, 40, 45, 49–51, 53, 55–56, 68, 70, 264, 286
pacifism and Quakerism, 56
pacifists, 1, 13, 24, 27–29, 56, 61, 68–70, 116, 264, 276
pagans, 227
pagan virtues, 258–59, 261, 263–66
Paradise Lost (Milton), 96
Parson's Handbook, The (Dearmer), 21

patience, divine, 241
Paul, Saint, 105, 108–9, 113, 156, 209, 252
Peace Army, 13, 27, 47, 68–69
Peace Pledge Union, 29
Pearl Harbor, 30
Penn, William, 55–57, 59, 285
personhood, divine, 229, 231, 233
politics and Christianity, 154–58
Pontius Pilate, 193, 258, 266
poor laws, 83–84
postmortem survival, 101, 123–24, 145, 178, 189–91, 201–3, 205–6, 209, 230–32, 236. *See also:* death, finality of
prayer, 15, 144, 165, 167, 180, 196–97, 200, 215, 217–18, 222–25, 285
    meaning of, 135, 137
    Quaker, 22
    as request, 221
    sacramental, 164
    as union, 221
Prayer Mission, 104
praying, 218, 223–24
priesthood, 32, 111, 113–16, 125
prophets, 23, 42, 57–58, 108, 112–14, 116–17, 125, 133, 151–52, 155–56, 177, 182, 184, 196, 244
prostitution, 9–10, 41, 90
purgatory, 219

Quakers, 56, 59, 70, 126, 128, 165–66
Queen Mab (Shelley), 183

redemption, 121, 161, 169, 185, 187, 196, 239
religion, 33, 38, 96, 100, 104–5, 126, 144, 147, 150, 160, 164, 184–85, 205, 212, 217–19, 230, 232, 247, 286
    primitive, 149, 166
    sacramental, 160
    and magic, 147
    and temperament, 143
    as "personal matter," 127, 140
    of Christ, 96, 101
religious people, 143, 155–56, 218, 261–63

resistance, nonviolent, 27, 32, 37, 70
responsibility, moral, 201, 204–5, 239
revelation, 53, 150, 161–62, 173, 179, 181, 184–85, 209–10, 251–52
Richards, Pearl Mary Teresa, 115
Roman Catholic Church, 6, 117, 123, 125–26, 134
Roman Catholic theology, 138–39, 174
Roman Catholic tradition, 140
Roman Catholics, 126, 158, 165
Royden, Maude
    adopts war orphans, 21
    and City Temple, 19
    and Effie Hudson, 272
    and Effie Shaw, 7, 272, 275
    and Fellowship Guild, 22
    and Hudson Shaw, 19, 30–31, 267
    and pacifism, 11–12, 29
    and Peace Army, 27
    and Peace Pledge Union, 29
    and suffragism, 9
    and women's ordination, 26
    attraction to Roman Catholicism, 6
    birth, 3
    childhood, 4
    death, 2
    early religious belief, 5
    education, 4
    friendships, 5
    Guildhouse preaching, 23, 33
    legacy, 2
    lifelong Anglican, 33
    meets Hudson Shaw, 7
    memorial plaque, 1
    Nazism, 29
    opposition to war, 1, 12, 29
    Peace Pledge Union, 29
    physical infirmities, 3, 31
    preaching, 18
    relationships, 8, 18, 21, 31, 274, 276–77
    religious crisis, 6
    religious development, 5
    responses to her marriage, 280
    retirement years, 30
    speaking tour, 10
    struggles with Church of England, 15
    struggle with Church of England, 17
    suffragism, 9, 16
    world tour, 25, 27
    See also: Shaw, Effie; Shaw, Hudson
    pacifist, 17, 19
    peace mission, 14
Ruskin, John, 210, 270, 286
Russell, Bertrand, 68, 92

sacraments, 96–97, 121, 123–25, 131, 134, 136, 139, 160–69, 250
salvation, 116, 127, 140, 251
Salvation Army, 116, 130
Satyagraha, 70
Schreiner, Olive, 60, 286
Schweitzer, Albert, 24
science, 66, 174, 179, 185, 202–3, 207, 210, 248
science and truth, 223
Selbie, William Boothby, 138
self-sacrifice, 191, 261–62, 265–66
Sermon on the Mount, 177, 260
sermons, 19–20, 24, 43, 155
sexual freedom, 92, 98
sexual love, 92–97, 99
sex workers, 10
Shakespeare, William, 41, 58, 65, 241, 256
Shaw, Anna Howard, 79
Shaw, Effie, 7–8, 14–15, 19, 30–31, 34, 269, 271–75, 279–80, 283
Shaw, Hudson, 6–8, 13–15, 19–20, 22, 24, 28, 30–31, 34, 88, 210, 269, 271–72, 275, 283
Shaw, Martin, 22
Shelley, Percy Bysshe, 58, 183, 190, 271
Sheppard, H.R.L. (Dick), 13, 27, 29, 47, 68, 69
Sherman, William Tecumseh, 46
sins, 41–43, 48, 53, 96, 98, 131, 134–35, 138, 190–92, 194, 196–200, 243
    and propitiation, 189
    and redemption, 169
    and repentance, 130
    and stupidity, 190

slavery, 23, 38, 41, 101, 154, 157–58, 237, 239, 242
    morality of, 156
Society of Friends, 55–57, 125–26, 134, 164, 218
soldiers, 11, 50, 59, 61, 69, 83, 136, 143, 195, 264
    and conscientious objectors, 127
    and heroism, 56
    and militarism, 49
    and peace, 70
    and prostitution, 156
    and war, 46
souls, 38, 53, 59, 91, 96, 101, 114, 158, 161, 167, 174, 202–3, 205–6, 221–23, 231, 233, 270
South Luffenham, 8, 271–72
Spenser, Edmund, 96, 265
spiritual gifts, 129–30, 136
spiritual things, 112, 117, 149, 161, 165–66, 206, 223
Studdert Kennedy, Geoffrey "Woodbine Willie," 276
Student Christian Movement (SCM), 20, 69
suffragism, 1, 7, 9, 10, 15, 19, 63–64, 79, 116, 157, 202

Temple, William, 11, 101
Tennyson, Alfred, Lord, 22, 161, 198
theology, 162, 179, 207–8, 210–11
Theresa of Spain (Avila), Saint, 116, 210
toleration, religious, 134, 153, 262
Tractarian Movement, 6
Treitschke, Heinrich von, 63
Treves, Frederick, 253–54. *See also:* Joseph Merrick
trust, 88, 146, 264
    as Christian virtue, 258
    in knowledge of God, 173
    in prayer, 167
    Jesus' for us, 249
truth, 23, 34, 39, 41, 53–54, 56–59, 91, 136, 146, 148, 173–74, 178–79, 182, 199, 219, 228–29, 231, 245, 248
    eternal, 110, 231, 249
    and sexual love, 96
    as virtue, 90
    truth in Bible, 184

unbelief, 180–81, 186, 227, 246
union, 96–97, 145
United States, 10, 19, 22, 24–25, 28–30, 239
unity, 132, 164, 180
    and uniformity, 134
unity of spirit, 181
universalism, 203

vicarious punishment, 189, 193. *See also:* doctrines, Atonement
vicarious suffering, 193, 196
virocentric world, 79

war, 2, 9, 13–14, 30–32, 38, 42, 45–46, 48–52, 55–56, 61–62, 65–67, 75–77, 80–81, 136–37, 286
    denunciation of, 12
    and courage, 47
    and God, 237
    and love, 42, 47, 51, 57
    self-defense, 38
war effort, 12, 14, 29, 75
warfare, modern, 68–69
wartime, 30, 58, 75
Wesley, John, 113, 137
Wilberforce, William, 156–57
Winnington-Ingram, Arthur Foley, Bishop, 13
Women, ordination of, 1, 15, 20, 25–27, 31–33, 103, 108, 112–15, 123
    rights of, 2, 9, 11–12, 32–33, 73
    St. Paul's view on, 108
    subordination of, 92, 109, 111. *See also:* anti-feminism, ecclesial
women and ministry, 17, 19, 108, 112, 116, 208, 210. *See also:* anti-feminism, ecclesial
women and missions, 102
Women and the Church of England, 16, 100, 107, 285
women and war, 60, 82, 85, 103, 286
Women's International League for Peace and Freedom, 12

Women's Movement, 60, 62–67, 76–77, 80, 102, 286
Women's Social and Political Union (WSPU), 9
Women's Suffrage Societies, 10
women theologians, 207, 210
Wordsworth, William, 58
workers, 84, 124, 236, 246
  women, 101, 129
World War I, 1, 8, 13, 45, 50, 102, 143, 264
World War II, 68

www.ingramcontent.com/pod-product-compliance
Lightning Source LLC
Chambersburg PA
CBHW070235230426
43664CB00014B/2309